ROUTLEDGE LIBRARY EDITIONS:
HISTORY OF MONEY, BANKING AND FINANCE

Volume 13

A SHORT FISCAL AND FINANCIAL HISTORY OF ENGLAND 1815–1918

A SHORT FISCAL AND FINANCIAL HISTORY OF ENGLAND 1815–1918

J.F. REES

Routledge
Taylor & Francis Group
LONDON AND NEW YORK

First published in 1921 by Methuen & Co. Ltd.

This edition first published in 2018
by Routledge
2 Park Square, Milton Park, Abingdon, Oxon OX14 4RN

and by Routledge
711 Third Avenue, New York, NY 10017

Routledge is an imprint of the Taylor & Francis Group, an informa business

British Library Cataloguing in Publication Data
A catalogue record for this book is available from the British Library

ISBN: 978-1-138-70169-4 (Set)
ISBN: 978-1-315-10595-6 (Set) (ebk)
ISBN: 978-1-138-05744-9 (Volume 13) (hbk)
ISBN: 978-1-315-16486-1 (Volume 13) (ebk)

Publisher's Note
The publisher has gone to great lengths to ensure the quality of this reprint but points out that some imperfections in the original copies may be apparent.

Disclaimer
The publisher has made every effort to trace copyright holders and would welcome correspondence from those they have been unable to trace.

A SHORT FISCAL AND FINANCIAL HISTORY OF ENGLAND 1815-1918

BY

J. F. REES, M.A.

METHUEN & CO. LTD.
36 ESSEX STREET W.C.
LONDON

First Published in 1921

PREFACE

THE present widespread interest in the social and industrial history of the nineteenth century has encouraged me to believe that an introduction to the fiscal and financial history of the period would be welcomed. This belief has been strengthened by my experience that many who would like to understand the financial questions of to-day feel that they want to know how they arose. For, in this, as in other social and economic inquiries, historical perspective is essential. I am conscious of many imperfections in my attempt to supply it. The task of considering the claims of different issues and of allotting to each a due amount of space has been difficult. It is easier to write a long book than a short one and to address the specialist than the general reader. Perhaps the present circumstances—the cost of book production, on the one hand, and the importance of diffusing knowledge of the subject, on the other—will serve as a justification for my endeavour to grapple with the more difficult task. I have prefaced my chapters with statistical summaries which are some general indication of the results of the years with which they deal. In the appendixes will be found some guidance to further reading and some additional figures. The mention of a book there should also be taken as an acknowledgment of my indebtedness to its author.

The book has been read in manuscript by Mr. Arthur Birnie, M.A., Lecturer on Economic History in the University of Aberdeen. He offered many valuable suggestions for which I have shown my gratitude by acting upon them in practically every instance.

J. F. R.

Edinburgh,
St. David's Day, 1921.

CONTENTS

A SHORT FISCAL & FINANCIAL HISTORY OF ENGLAND, 1815-1918

CHAPTER I

INTRODUCTORY

THE details of the annual Exchequer receipts and issues[1] may be approached either analytically or historically:[2] they may be examined in their present implications or expounded by reference to their origin and development. If the latter method be adopted the items and amounts suggest contrasts which serve to indicate the main changes in the history of public finance. The historian would probably first apply to the figures the distinction between tax and non-tax revenue, and he would discover the fact that the former now enormously exceeds the latter. He would recall that in the Middle Ages the maxim that " the king should live of his own " was constantly appealed to as a guarantee against taxation in normal times. The theory was that the king had non-tax sources of revenue, consisting chiefly of the rents of Crown lands, the feudal dues, and the profits of justice, which supplied him with sufficient income to discharge the ordinary functions of government. Taxation was regarded

[1] A summary of the Exchequer Receipts and Issues for 1913-4 will be found in Appendix " B."

[2] An excellent analysis for the general reader is given in Henry Higgs, " A Primer of National Finance."

as exceptional; a device only to be resorted to when special circumstances, such as the expenses of a war, demanded it. This distinction between revenue strictly so-called (which was a non-tax annual income) and taxation (which was an extraordinary charge imposed by Parliament at irregular intervals) survived until the seventeenth century. But it was already becoming a little blurred during the Tudor period, for a variety of causes contributed to make the non-tax revenue inadequate. While the expenses of government were growing progressively heavier the yield of the various sources of revenue was shrinking. For instance, the grants of Crown lands to individuals, in order to reward their services or to secure their support, tended to outrun the rate at which land reverted to the Crown by forfeiture or escheat. Consequently, the annual rental was not maintained. Fines and fees were usually fixed in amount and with the rise in prices in the sixteenth century they depreciated in value. The inevitable result was a more frequent use of taxation. Financial embarrassment was at the root of most of the difficulties experienced by James I and Charles I, and the attempts of the latter to discover new sources of income were largely responsible for the friction between him and Parliament which led to the Civil War. In that struggle the traditional system was destroyed. Crown lands were extensively sold during the interregnum and the feudal dues were abolished at the Restoration. Meanwhile new experiments had been made. In 1643 John Pym introduced the excise, a form of tax well known on the Continent but regarded with great disfavour in England. Accepted as a war tax, it gained for itself a permanent place, and provided a revenue which compensated for the loss of the feudal dues.

The adoption of the excise suggests a second feature of the modern Exchequer receipts, namely, the proportion of direct to indirect taxation. At present a larger proportion of revenue is raised by direct than by indirect taxation. This is a complete departure from the method employed when the deficiency of the non-tax revenue had to be supplied by the imposition of new taxes in the seventeenth century. Practically all of them were indirect taxes. It is true that attempts were made to devise a satisfactory direct tax, but they all ended in failure. So, while the Government under William III depended, like that of modern times, on an annual tax revenue, the basis of taxation was different. The objections to indirect taxation have been so often urged in our own days that it is a little difficult to understand the complacency with which it was regarded in the seventeenth and eighteenth centuries. There were, of course, practical administrative advantages in levying taxes by means of customs and excise on the consumption of certain commodities. It did not involve any assessment of means or income. Collection was comparatively easy for the tax would normally be paid by merchants who would recover it from their customers by making an addition to the price of the commodity. The Government thus secured the money with the minimum of effort and the consumer paid whenever he made a purchase. Writers on taxation, however, were not content to adduce these practical considerations: they advanced much higher claims in favour of indirect taxes. Taxation on expenditure, they held, enabled everyone to tax himself by regulating his consumption of the taxed commodities in accordance with his ability to pay. Some went further and argued that indirect taxation was in reality optional because an individual might refrain from consuming any of the commodities on which a duty was charged. These two propositions could not both be true. If a tax can be evaded at will it cannot also be distributively just. As a matter of fact expenditure is not a fair criterion of ability to pay: it is absurd, for instance, to suppose that a wealthy man will pay the same proportion of his income as a poor man if taxation falls on necessaries. With his superior resources he may also find evasion, by consuming some alternative commodities, much more easy than the poor man does. The supposed optional nature of indirect taxation is so often insisted on by contemporaries that it deserves notice. Against this view it may be urged that there is no peculiar sense in which indirect, as distinguished from direct, taxes are optional. All taxes are optional because the individual can avoid the condition which makes him chargeable; for instance, the income tax may be evaded by refusing to take an income above the exemption level, and the inhabited house duty may similarly be evaded by living in a house below a certain rental. To this the eighteenth century writers would probably reply that they considered that indirect taxes ought properly to fall on luxuries and therefore they could be evaded if wished. This plea, however, cannot be admitted. Whatever the theory may have been, indirect taxes were by no means confined to luxuries, for the sufficient reason that the Exchequer found that necessaries gave a larger and an expanding return. Further, the distinction between luxuries and necessaries is always difficult to draw. Throughout the eighteenth century the idea that tea was a luxury was fanatically held by some in spite of the fact that its use was becoming almost universal. Pitt taxed newspapers because he regarded them as essentially luxuries, and he thought houses ought to be exempted because they were necessaries; a position which now seems to be reversed.

By the end of the seventeenth century annual taxation (largely indirect) supplied the main source of revenue. But it in turn was proving insufficient to meet the charges of government. During William III's war with France, taxes failed to yield the necessary supplies. The third point which would strike the historian in examining the modern Exchequer issues is the presence and amount of the charge for "National Debt Services." It would remind him that at the end of the seventeenth century the funding system was introduced, the principle, that is, by which the Government borrowed money in anticipation of the yield of certain taxes specially imposed to pay the interest on it. It is true that borrowing on the security of the taxes had long been practised in an informal and ruinously expensive way. Montagu, William III's financial minister, placed it on a regular and permanent basis. The pressure of urgent necessity had forced him to resort to every possible expedient for raising money. After all inducements in the way of heavy commissions, premiums and appeals to the gambling instinct had failed to attract the public lender, he resolved to adopt a scheme which had been strongly advocated by William Paterson,[1] namely, that a public bank should be founded on the basis of a loan to the Government. The suggestion was that £1,200,000 should be raised by subscription and lent to the Government in return for a guaranteed annual payment of £100,000 to meet the charge of interest and management. The subscribers were to be incorporated as "the Governor and Company of the Bank of England" and were to enjoy certain privileges enumerated in the charter. Among these the most important was the right to issue bank-notes to the extent of the total capital, that is, up to an initial maximum of £1,200,000. The appeal for subscriptions met with an immediate response and the Bank of England was duly incorporated on July 27th, 1694. The consequences of this experiment, so largely political in its inception, were far-reaching. It gave a central institution to the growing London money market and exercised a profound influence on its development. Provision was made in the Bank's charter for the possible repayment of the Government loan before a fixed date. But new Government necessities precluded this possibility. From time to time the charter was renewed; further loans were made to the Government and the Bank's privileges extended until it enjoyed a highly favoured position in the banking world. Through the Bank the Government did its business, of which the National Debt Services constituted the most important item in the eighteenth century. Every war in a century of wars added a larger sum to the total of public indebtedness than its predecessor. Considerable alarm was felt about the increase of this burden and opinion was prepared for any plan which promised some relief. The problem, like others of a statistical nature, attracted the attention of Dr. Richard Price, the well-known

---

[1] William Paterson (1658–1719) was a native of Dumfriesshire. He travelled extensively and took a particular interest in questions of trade and finance. His project of a trading settlement at Darien ended in failure and had important consequences in Scotland.

Nonconformist minister and publicist.[1] He put forward a series of proposals for dealing with what he called "the monstrous accumulation of artificial debt." It is probable that Lord Shelburne, who was impressed by Price's arguments, would have adopted some of his suggestions had he succeeded in establishing a strong Ministry in 1782. His failure, however, postponed the question for four years.

To recapitulate—the returns of Exchequer receipts and issues suggest three main historical generalisations. First, that the tax revenue has now taken the predominant place in the receipts; second, that a greater amount of revenue is now raised by direct than by indirect taxation; third, that by means of loans the State has contracted immense liabilities which are a heavy charge on its annual income. A more detailed commentary on the development of the modern financial system need not be pressed back beyond Pitt's tenure of the Chancellorship of the Exchequer.

William Pitt entered the House of Commons in January, 1781. He was not yet twenty-two, and bore a name which seemed to justify the highest hopes, and therefore courted the keenest disappointment. Fortunately for the young man his maiden speech was judged to be a brilliant success, and he soon gained the respect which was due to his own merits. The occasion he chose is significant. It was the second reading of Edmund Burke's bill to effect certain reforms in the expenditure on the Civil List, which raised the vexed question of what was then called "economical reform," and in particular the large sums spent on sinecures. Pitt declared himself in favour of the bill because

[1] Richard Price (1723–1791) was born at Llangeinor in Glamorganshire. He spent most of his life in London. Apart from his writings on political and moral questions he conducted several inquiries on the mathematical theory of probabilities. This led him to deal with questions of the expectation of life, the problems of population and the possible redemption of the National Debt. He is now remembered as the preacher of the discourse on "Love of our Country," in which he acclaimed the French Revolution and provoked Burke to write his "Reflections."

he thought economy was " essentially necessary to national salvation," and he ridiculed the view, which had been expressed in the course of the debate, that the saving effected would be negligible, for, he declared, it was absurd to hold that, having spent millions, thousands were beneath consideration.[1] It is difficult to say whether his own aptitude for finance or the circumstances of the time determined the course of Pitt's parliamentary career. There can be no question that the country had drifted into such a position that bankruptcy seemed imminent. The war against the American Colonies had brought with it one disaster after another. The chief European powers had ranged themselves in open hostility. Mismanagement and corruption had thrown the public finances into hopeless confusion. Pitt's opportunity came at the end of the year which witnessed the return of peace. In December, 1783, George III sent for him and entrusted him with the offices of First Lord of the Treasury and Chancellor of the Exchequer. He had had nearly three years' experience of public life and had already filled the office of Chancellor of the Exchequer in the short-lived Shelburne Administration. His accession to power, however, proved a new departure; it marked the end of the recent instability of Governments. Pitt was destined to remain in office continuously for seventeen years.

The outlook in December, 1783, was sufficiently depressing to challenge the optimism of youth. The Government 3 per cent. stock stood at 56; the National Debt, when account was taken of the wealth of the country and the yield of the taxes, seemed an almost insupportable burden; a huge floating debt demanded immediate attention. In the face of these problems the remedies proposed by Pitt do not now seem by any means heroic. But they impressed contemporaries and restored confidence. He decided that it was impossible to balance income and expenditure in the first year and proposed to raise a loan of £6,000,000 to meet outstanding accounts. In the

---

[1] " The Speeches of William Pitt " (1806 edition), Vol. I, pp. 3 and 6.

existing state of the market this was an expensive operation. In addition, he had to deal with an unfunded debt of £14,000,000 for which Parliament had made no provision. To fund the whole of this he considered to be out of the question, but he provided for £6,600,000 by issuing 5 per cent. stock at 93. To the modern mind his handling of the instrument of taxation appears far from courageous. In his first Budget the most striking feature was the reduction of the duty on tea from 119 to 12½ per cent., for the possible loss on which he sought compensation by additions to the window tax. The excessively high duty had been a premium on smuggling, the Exchequer gaining little or nothing from the growing habit of tea drinking. The new taxes were in keeping with eighteenth-century practice. Instead of attempting to construct a tax which would yield a substantial return the greatest ingenuity was exercised in trying to find a variety of objects of taxation which, it was supposed, spread the burden so broadly that it would not weigh heavily at any point. Pitt accordingly taxed horses kept for pleasure, hats and bricks ; he increased the taxes on candles, paper, printed linen and calico ; he introduced a sporting licence and also a licence on the dealers in excisable articles. The plea that it was inadvisable to make any important new departures may well excuse this side of the Budget for 1784 ; but the fact remains that Pitt did not improve on this performance during the years of peace. The explanation is that the taxational practice of the eighteenth century had hardened into a doctrine from which it was very difficult to break away.

The presumption in favour of indirect taxes has already been noticed. It rested partly on the conviction that direct taxes involved methods of assessment which were highly objectionable. Adam Smith voiced this opinion, declaring that it was very difficult to impose a tax on stock or money without very arbitrary proceedings. These proceedings, he considered, would amount to " an inquisition more intolerable than any tax." Anything in the nature of an income tax was therefore ruled out. The only important direct tax was the Land Tax, which had been originally designed under William III to cover real and personal property. The latter, however, had soon evaded the charge, and the tax on the former continued to be paid on the old basis of assessment. In the course of time it came to fall unequally on different parts of the country and was generally recognised to be unsatisfactory from the point of view of the Exchequer. But all objections were overruled by the single merit to the minds of contemporaries that it did not necessitate any new assessment.[1] This attitude towards direct taxes precluded the possibility of finding any very lucrative single tax. It threw the Chancellor back on the principle of diffusion, that is, on a complicated system of indirect taxes and licences of various kinds. Here again opinion prescribed certain limits. He was expected to avoid taxes on necessaries. This rule was based on two theories which were really contradictory: some held that the poor could not be taxed, others that they ought not to be taxed. The first contention depended on the assumption that the poor lived at a bare subsistence level, and, consequently, if a tax added anything to the price of a necessary, it merely meant a rise of wages to that extent. In other words, the tax was shifted on to the employer. Higher wages tended to cripple the country in its competition with other countries. A tax on necessaries was therefore mischievous in its operation. Expression was constantly given, however, to the view that the poor ought not to be taxed on the consumption of necessaries on compassionate grounds, the assumption being that they could pay but would suffer hardship in doing so. "Our taxes, for the far greater portion," Burke boasted,[2] "fly over the heads of the lowest classes." Pitt frequently noticed this objection to taxes on necessaries, apologising when he had to resort to

---

[1] Pitt ultimately recognised that it had become a mere rent-charge by converting it into a redeemable rent-charge in 1798. For the future it was to fall on land at the old rates in perpetuity, unless it was bought out for a capital amount. A certain proportion has been redeemed, but the Land Tax still figures in the Exchequer receipts, yielding about £700,000 a year.

[2] "Letters on a Regicide Peace," III. He adds: "They escape too, who, with better ability, voluntarily subject themselves to the harsh discipline of a rigid necessity."

such a tax as that on candles and pleading that the need of a productive tax forced him to do so. The Chancellor, since the objections to a direct assessment seemed insuperable and necessaries were considered improper objects of taxation, was left with the positive principle that he should raise the revenue by taxing luxuries. No assessment was necessary. The poor were exempt and even the well-to-do were under no compulsion to make themselves liable to pay. " Every man's contribution," wrote Adam Smith, " is altogether voluntary, it being in his power either to consume or not to consume the commodity taxed." A general exercise of the option not to consume would obviously deprive the Chancellor of any revenue from the one taxational method which was universally approved.

Pressure of circumstances ultimately compelled Pitt to break through these limitations. The eighteenth century principles were openly contravened and consequently lost their authority. Until the outbreak of the war with France, however, Pitt observed the spirit, if not the letter, of this body of doctrine. He made many experiments in taxes on non-necessaries with such little success that he had himself to abandon some of the taxes because of their disappointing yield. These comparative failures must not be allowed to obscure his notable achievements in reforming the existing administration. Two examples will suffice. In 1785 he grouped together a number of taxes which had in common the character that they fell on the luxurious expenditure of the wealthy, for instance, on carriages, menservants, racehorses, etc. They had been under the management of three different sets of commissioners working independently of one another, with the result that irregularities were not easily detected. They were now entrusted to one board and came to be known as the Assessed Taxes. Two years later he grappled with the entanglement of custom rates. Many articles paid a series of charges which had been imposed at different times. These were now consolidated into one rate on each article.[1]

---

[1] Adam Smith pointed out a number of defects in the Customs and recommended several reforms. He advocated an extension of

At the same time he simplified the system of public accounts. Separate items of expenditure had been charged

---

warehousing in order to replace the complicated system of drawbacks. In his opinion, " A revenue, at least equal to the present net revenue of the customs. might be drawn from duties upon the importation of only a few sorts of goods of the most general use and consumption "—" Wealth of Nations," Book V, Chap. II. Such simplification, however, was not undertaken until long after Pitt's time. He seems to have been influenced less by Adam Smith than by the Committee of Public Accounts, which in 1785 drew attention " to the intricacy and perplexity that involve the collection and accounts of this part of the revenue."—" Customs Tariffs of the United Kingdom " (1897 ; c. 8706), p. 15. Following their advice he repealed all compound duties in favour of a single rate for each article. Altogether 2,615 resolutions had to be submitted to the House of Commons. The tariff still remained formidable, for it contained 1,414 articles or subdivisions of articles. That Pitt entertained liberal ideas on the question of trade is proved by his efforts to arrange reciprocity between the United Kingdom and Ireland. Although the commercial restrictions which had hampered Irish development were removed in 1779 and 1780, the tariffs between the countries were unfavourable to Ireland. Pitt's suggestions for moderating them were accepted by the Irish Parliament, but they aroused such an outcry among manufacturers in Great Britain that he had to revise them. His second set of proposals was not acceptable in Ireland. Consequently his efforts proved fruitless.—Murray, " Commercial Relations between England and Ireland," Chap. XII ; and O'Brien, " Economic History of Ireland in the 18th Century," Chap. XXI. There is no doubt that Pitt put this plan before that of a commercial treaty with France. The 18th Article of the Treaty of Versailles formed a basis for an understanding with France. Vergennes had pressed for a commercial agreement, and Shelburne was well disposed towards the idea. Pitt did little to bring matters to a conclusion until he sent William Eden (afterwards Lord Auckland) to take up the threads of negotiations in March, 1786. The upshot was a very important commercial treaty by which each country gave complete freedom of navigation and trading rates in their European possessions to the other. The tariffs were mutually lowered, some to 10 per cent., and none remained above 30 per cent. It was to last for twelve years in the first instance. The trade between the two countries made considerable progress under this arrangement, but, of course, the war of 1793 put an end to its benefits. Gladstone, in recommending the French Commercial Treaty of 1860 to the House, called Pitt's Treaty " one of the best and one of the wisest measures ever adopted by Parliament," and declared that it contributed " at least as much as any other passage of his brilliant career to the fame of the great statesman who introduced it." (For a further note on Pitt's supposed indebtedness to Adam Smith *see* p. 225 *infra.*)

against particular taxes, involving a complicated system of book-keeping. Pitt adopted the principle of one fund—the Consolidated Fund—into which all the revenue should flow (unless other provision was made in particular cases) and out of which all payments should come.

The new taxes and the administrative reforms would result, it was hoped, in an annual surplus which could be devoted to the reduction of the National Debt. In 1786 it stood at nearly £245,500,000, representing an annual charge of £9,600,000. Pitt was acquainted with the suggestions put forward by Dr. Price and entered into direct communication with him in January of that year. But the precise degree of his indebtedness has never been ascertained. On March 29th Pitt placed his proposals before the House of Commons. He anticipated a surplus of £900,000, which he recommended should be increased to £1,000,000 by imposing additional taxes for the purpose. This surplus was to constitute a Sinking Fund to operate on the general principles advocated by Price. To prevent the Government from raiding the fund when in difficulties—as Walpole had done in a former experiment—the £1,000,000 was to be paid over to independent Commissioners charged with the responsibility of expending it quarterly on the purchase of Government stock. But, again in accordance with Price's advice, the stock was not to be cancelled. The Commissioners were to draw the interest on the stock they had purchased and employ it to augment their annual £1,000,000. In this way they would have a larger sum in each successive year, the increase (apart from the annual £1,000,000) being in the nature of compound interest. It was estimated that by 1812 they would have an annual income of £4,000,000, after which Parliament was to be free to dispose of it. Price's contention was that the Sinking Fund would increase while the debt would decrease and ultimately be extinguished. This is sound enough provided the Government refrains from borrowing during the process. At this point it is sufficient to notice that Pitt's £1,000,000 was a true surplus, representing an excess of income over expenditure. His enthusiasm for the scheme is indicated by his rhetorical peroration. "This plan," he declared, " has long been the wish and the hope of all men ; and I am proud to flatter myself that my name may be inscribed on that firm column now about to be raised to national faith and national prosperity."[1]

In 1792 Pitt thought that he was in a position to review the results of the reforms of the previous eight years. The yield of the taxes had increased by about £5,000,000 and provision had been made for the steady reduction of the National Debt. The results of the improvements in agriculture and the application of new inventions to industry were reflected in the growing national prosperity. Public confidence had been completely restored ; the funds stood at 97. It seemed, therefore, desirable to effect a balance between income and expenditure, employing the figures of the previous four years in order to arrive at what might be regarded as the estimated permanent income and expenditure. Pitt calculated that the probable future income would be £16,212,000 and the expenditure £15,811,000. In the current year he anticipated a surplus, which would involve an adjustment. He consequently proposed to repeal taxes to the extent of £200,000 and to add £400,000 to the Sinking Fund. A Chancellor of the Exchequer probably reveals his point of view more clearly in remitting than in imposing taxation. It gives him an opportunity of indicating the particular taxes which seem to him most open to objection. Fortunately, Pitt not only mentioned the taxes he proposed to repeal but also gave his reasons for his choice. " In making this selection," he said, " there are two objects which I wish principally to keep in view. The first, to which it is very material to attend, is, that the actual relief felt by the public should be proportioned to the amount of revenue which is relinquished. Under these descriptions those taxes seem most clearly to be included, which are raised by the mode of assessment, because as they are paid directly out of the pocket of the individual, and do not pass through circuitous channels like taxes upon the articles of consumption, where the tax is often blended with the price of the

[1] " Pitt's Speeches," Vol. I, p. 317

commodity, there can be little doubt that the relief intended to be given will in these instances be effectual to its fullest extent. The other object which I naturally have in view, is, that the relief intended should apply peculiarly to that class, to whom, on every account, it ought first to be extended—I mean the most necessitous, and the most industrious part of the community."[1] The taxes which were considered to fall within these canons were :—(1) The tax on female servants, which was direct and fell on the relatively poorer families; (2) the tax on carts and wagons, which was largely paid by the yeomanry and smaller tenant farmers; (3) the tax of three shillings on houses of less than seven windows; (4) the last additional halfpenny a pound on candles. The specific proposals illustrate the preference for indirect taxes, and the objection felt to the taxation of the poor.

The proposal to add £400,000 to the Sinking Fund led Pitt to make a declaration which has often been quoted as an example of the short-sightedness of statesmen. He was pointing out that if £400,000 were handed over annually to the Commissioners for the National Debt their income would reach the limit of four millions earlier than was contemplated when the Sinking Fund was instituted. It would roughly be a matter of fifteen years. Digressing for a moment he warned his hearers that the present prosperity could not with certainty be counted upon to continue for that period, but added "unquestionably there never was a time in the history of this country, when, from the situation of Europe, we might more reasonably expect fifteen years of peace, than at the present moment."[2] Within twelve months Great Britain was launched upon the war with France which was destined to make an incomparably greater call on her resources than any previous war. So far Pitt's financial policy has been stated—as in common justice it ought to be—without reference to the intolerable strain to which it was subjected after 1793. It may be granted that the war would have exposed the

---

[1] "Pitt's Speeches," Vol. II, pp. 38–9.
[2] "Pitt's Speeches," Vol. II, p. 36.

weakness of any conceivable system; but the particular weaknesses it revealed in Pitt's schemes are of considerable interest.

Pitt's financial policy during the first six years of the war has often been severely censured. It is perfectly obvious when the war period (1793–1815) is regarded as a whole that initial mistakes were made from the consequences of which it was impossible to recover. This is to be wise after the event. In 1793 Pitt contemplated a short war; he clung to the conviction that France was on the verge of collapse in spite of all evidence to the contrary. His belief was based on the supposed inability of France to endure the financial strain, a question on which he considered himself to be a good judge. The war finance of the first phase of the war must be regarded therefore as governed by the desire to bring matters to a conclusion without departing from the principles which had hitherto been followed. To Pitt's mind the problem was how to hasten the inevitable downfall of the enemy with the slightest damage to the resources of his country.

First, he did not at the outset impose any considerable additions to the taxes.

Second, he raised an undue proportion of the necessary supplies by means of loans.

Third, he retained the Sinking Fund in full operation in spite of the fact that expenditure now greatly exceeded income.

In the first year Pitt proposed to increase the yield of the taxes by an additional 10 per cent on the Assessed Taxes and an additional one-sixth on spirits. The total increase he estimated at £287,000 and this he intended to employ as the interest on a loan of £4,500,000. During the following years he steadily added to the taxes, but the annual deficit grew at an alarming rate; it was one and a half millions in 1793, ten millions in 1794, and twenty in 1795. The principle of diffusion was exploited to the full, taxes being imposed on every variety of luxury and necessary. In the critical year 1797, however, Pitt was forced to recognise that an attempt had to be made to discover a tax which would yield a considerable sum. Within the limits of eighteenth century doctrine that was impossible.

The failure to secure supplies by taxation meant that resort had to be made to loans every financial year. And it was not only that excessively large sums were raised in this way, but they involved a future charge which was out of proportion to the present benefit. For the most part, the loans were in 3 per cents. issued at a considerable discount, that is, there was a great difference between the amount actually raised by the loan and the obligation assumed by the State when it was funded.[1] Pitt must be held responsible for the undue reliance on loans, but he probably had no option as to the terms. For his first loan he found only one set of subscribers who were willing to tender; they preferred 3 per cents. issued at 72 to 5 per cents. at or nearer par. Personally the Chancellor of the Exchequer would have liked 5 per cents. because they would probably offer an opportunity for conversion at a fairly early date. The subscribers regarded the lower rate as a virtual guarantee against future conversion and they were, and continued to be, in a position to dictate their terms.

Pitt announced in his first war Budget speech that he intended to keep the Sinking Fund intact despite the change of circumstances, his reason being that the situation at the moment ought not to be allowed to damage the permanent interests of the community. He did not wish the outbreak of war to interrupt the beneficent work of paying off the National Debt. But the only possible justification of such a decision was the anticipation of a purely temporary dislocation which would not involve any

[1] For example, from 1793 to 1798, inclusive, £138,372,000 was actually raised by loans; the amount funded was £205,900,000. The whole question of Pitt's loans during the period 1793–1801 is discussed by W. Newmarch in his essay, "On the Loans Raised by Mr. Pitt," published in 1855. Newmarch defends Pitt's policy partly by alleging that he had no alternative and partly by arguing that no ultimate loss accrued from raising loans at a considerable discount.

great expense. A war which created a rapidly growing deficit, however, changed the whole basis of the Sinking Fund. There was obviously no longer a surplus. So the sum handed over to the Commissioners had to be borrowed, frequently on more unfavourable terms than the previous loans, which it was intended to extinguish, had been. In other words, the Government was borrowing money at a high rate of interest in order to cancel stock standing at a low rate. To maintain a Sinking Fund alongside of an increasing debt is indefensible. If the money can be borrowed on the same terms as those on which the debt is redeemed it is merely marking time; if the money is borrowed at a higher rate it means that the debt is being increased. This is what actually happened. At the end of the war the National Debt was some millions larger than it would have been had the Sinking Fund been suspended at the outset. The only plea advanced in defence of Pitt is that the continued operation of the Sinking Fund strengthened public confidence, for the underlying fallacy was not detected.[1]

The maintenance of financial stability was recognised to be an important factor in the struggle with France. It involved much wider questions than those of taxation and borrowing. For public finance necessarily functions within a more or less highly developed money market, that is, within a system which provides the requisite currency, facilitates payment and supplies credit. In the course of the eighteenth century a relatively complex mechanism had evolved in England. At the centre was the Bank of England, which in the terms of its charter as confirmed by the Act of 1742, enjoyed a monopoly of note-issue, or rather a guarantee against the erection of a bank which could in

---

[1] It was exposed in 1813 by Robert Hamilton in his "Inquiry Concerning the Rise and Progress, the Redemption and Present State and Management of the National Debt." Hamilton estimated the loss occasioned by the Sinking Fund at £10,861,688 up to February, 1812. In the second edition (1814) he brought it up to February, 1813, and put it at £12,585,580, and in the third edition, to February, 1817, when it amounted to £16,450,661. *See* third edition (1818), p. 198, and Note xxviii.

any sense be a rival. No partnership exceeding six persons was allowed to issue notes payable on demand. Content with its position in London, the Bank made no special effort to extend its business in the provinces. The industrial development of the north and west was therefore accompanied by the rise of a great number of country banks after the middle of the century. In order to enjoy the right of note-issue these banks had to be limited to six partners and consequently were fairly small businesses. They advanced credit in their own notes. Against these they naturally did not hold sufficient gold to meet an unusual demand, for their profits largely depended on remitting as much as they could to their agents in London. The agents in turn kept their balances at the Bank of England. A "run" on a country bank meant, therefore, that gold had to be secured from London, that is, the reversal of the normal procedure. The agents had to withdraw their balances or realise securities. Even if the country bank was perfectly solvent (which was by no means always the case) it might well fail to mobilise its resources in time to ward off disaster, the difficulty of communications with London considerably complicating the position. If one bank had to refuse to cash its notes a panic might ensue which would involve other banks in the same fate. The mortality of country banks was exceedingly high and their instability on more than one occasion proved to be the weak point in the credit system. When a crisis arose the official policy of the Bank of England tended to accentuate it. Instead of expanding its issues and thereby assisting all sound concerns to meet their liabilities—for Bank of England notes were generally accepted—it contracted them as soon as there was any sign of an unusual outflow of gold from the reserve. The outbreak of war in 1793, for instance, was followed by a crisis which threatened the failure of the country banks; there was an acute shortage of specie and a general desire to secure coin or notes which could be regarded with confidence. But the Bank of England strictly limited its discounts, refusing to make advances on good securities. To prevent a general collapse the Government undertook to issue £5,000,000 of Exchequer bills in sums of £100, £50, and £20. As soon as it became known that these were available the panic was allayed and it was not necessary to issue bills for more than £2,202,000.

The credit economy was therefore already characterised by one central reserve, that of the Bank of England, though that institution had not yet fallen upon the best method of meeting a crisis.[1] Its history during the war is necessarily closely bound up with its relations with the Government. In spite of a clause in the original charter of the Bank the practice had arisen of the Bank making temporary advances to the Government without the express sanction of Parliament, the amount being limited by a mutual understanding. A Bill was introduced in 1793 to cover these past irregularities, but it was so drawn that advances to an unlimited extent were allowed in the future. Pitt used this power extensively. In the opinion of the directors of the Bank his requests for accommodation were excessive; they lodged their protests, but they had no protection apart from the extreme step of refusing to honour his bills. Since Pitt was sending large sums to the Continent as subsidies to the Allies, notably the loan of £1,200,000 to Austria in July, 1796, his opponents sought to connect this policy with the embarrassments which confronted the Bank at the beginning of 1797. It was no doubt an element in the situation, but other and wider influences were also operating. The crisis of 1797 was characterised in the words of the Royal Message to the House of Commons by "the unusual demand of specie lately made from different parts of the country on the metropolis." What were the causes of this demand? In the first place, it is certain that the country banks had not recovered from the shock of 1793 and their note circulation was probably not half of what it had been. Secondly, the rise in prices and the general increase in the number of

[1] Namely, by making advances against good securities at a high discount rate; otherwise, the securities would have to be sold at a heavy loss. It must be remembered, however, that at the time the Usury Laws prevented the Bank from freely manipulating its discount rate.

payments which had to be made created a demand for a larger currency. Thirdly, the uncertainty of public affairs was reflected in a desire to hold money in the form of coins of the realm. The internal demand was probably more acute because France was re-establishing her currency on a specie basis and consequently exercising an attraction on bullion.[1] Whatever the causes may have been, the demand for coin was inevitably reflected in the depletion of the reserve of the Bank of England. On February 25th, 1797, it had fallen to £1,272,000. The desperate efforts of the Bank to restrict had only increased the stringency. The country banks were already finding it necessary to suspend payment when the news of the landing of a French force on the coast of Pembrokeshire produced a scare.[2] On Sunday morning, February 26th, an emergency meeting of the Privy Council was summoned, and it was resolved "that it is indispensably necessary for the public service that the Directors of the Bank of England should forbear issuing any cash in payment until the sense of Parliament can be taken on that subject and the proper measures adopted thereupon for the maintaining the means of circulation and supporting the public and commercial credit of the kingdom." This decision was confirmed by Parliament in the Bank Restriction Act, which suspended cash payment by the Bank of England, or, in other words made its notes inconvertible. Pitt explained that the measure was to be a purely temporary one, the restriction being limited in the first instance to June 24th. As a matter of fact complete resumption of cash payments was not effected until 1821.

The crisis of February, 1797, made a profound impression on Pitt. He was well aware of the dangers which beset inconvertible paper money. The hopes which he had

---

[1] This factor is examined by R. G. Hawtrey in the *Economic Journal*, Vol. XXVIII, pp. 52–65. The article is incorporated in his "Currency and Credit," Chap. XVI.

[2] The landing occurred on Wednesday, February 22nd, at Carreg Wasted, near Fishguard. A group of country banks in the North of England had decided to suspend cash payments on the 18th.—Bisschop, "Rise of the London Money Market," p. 182.

entertained of the collapse of France depended on the depreciation of the *assignats*. He was not likely therefore to drift into the easy finance of an undue expansion of inconvertible paper. But to avoid it he saw that it was necessary to strain every effort to raise a greater proportion of the annual supply by means of taxation. This was the leading note in his Budget Speech of November 24th, 1797. After noticing that the normal way of securing the amount he wished would be by means of loan, he went on to argue that it was necessary "to reduce the advantages which the funding system is calculated to afford within due limits, and to prevent the depreciation of our national securities."[1] It was therefore necessary to find a single tax which would yield a substantial amount. Pitt still felt that the accepted limits of eighteenth century doctrine had to be observed and proposed a tax—the Triple Assessment—which, superficially at any rate, seemed to fall within its canons.[2] Previous payments to the Assessed Taxes were to be taken as an indication of a person's ability to pay, that is, the criterion was to be expenditure on articles and services generally considered to be luxuries. The Assessed Taxes covered a variety of charges which ensured sufficient diffusion of the burden, they did not involve any direct assessment of means, and they were not paid by the poor. There could not be a better test of expenditure, Pitt declared, than the way in which the Assessed Taxes were combined. In a subsequent debate he admitted that if the amount of every man's property could be ascertained it would be a most desirable thing to make people contribute in proportion to their wealth. But he had to confess that there existed no means of ascertaining the property of individuals, excepting such as were of a nature that could not be resorted to.[3] Since a tax on property was impossible he adopted a tax on expenditure. It was admittedly an attempt to raise a greater revenue

[1] "Pitt's Speeches," Vol. III, p. 180.

[2] Pitt gained little by his attempt to meet popular prejudices. The tax was violently denounced in the House of Commons, and he was mobbed in the streets of London.

[3] "Pitt's Speeches," Vol. III, p. 231.

"without the necessity of such investigation of property as the customs, the manners, the pursuits of the people would render odious and vexatious."

The Triple Assessment was an unwieldy tax and proved a complete disappointment, its yield not coming up to half the estimate. Pitt had to admit that the criterion of expenditure was imperfect and that the tax had been shamefully evaded. On these grounds he proposed in the following year that the presumption based on the Assessed Taxes should be laid aside and a general tax imposed on all the leading branches of income. He recognised that this was a step only to be excused by the plea of emergency. The objections to an income tax had lost none of their force; circumstances required that they should be temporarily overruled. It has, indeed, often been urged that Pitt ought to have imposed an income tax on the outbreak of the war. But this is to misread the situation. Every expedient was exhausted before Pitt thought he was justified in bringing forward such a novel proposal, and then he did not pretend that it was a better tax than any other. It was indeed highly exceptional. Since it was an emergency tax no serious attempt was made to perfect it. Pitt resisted the suggestion that incomes should be differentiated. Argument turned rather on the old questions of the greater merits of indirect taxes and the evils of assessment. On the former, Pitt maintained with justice that no increase in the already heavy indirect taxes would produce the amount needed. The latter point he had himself often noticed, but the evasions which had ruined the Triple Assessment had evidently led him to realise the necessity of a degree of compulsion.

The income tax came into operation in April, 1799. It was levied at two shillings in the pound on all incomes above £200; incomes under £60 were exempt, and those between £60 and £200 were charged at various rates. In the next three years the tax produced on the average £6,000,000 a year. This was a final demonstration of its superiority over the tax on expenditure. The opposition, however, remained very bitter. On the conclusion of the Peace of Amiens (1802), Addington, who had succeeded

Pitt at the Exchequer in the previous year, was forced to forgo the tax because opinion would not tolerate it in peace time. The resumption of hostilities in 1803 was followed by its reimposition at a shilling in the pound, coupled with the assurance that it would cease six months after the return of peace. The assessment of the tax was also improved by the adoption of the principle of stoppage at the source.[1] In 1805 the great national emergency recalled Pitt to office and he prepared his nineteenth and last Budget. The income tax was raised to one and threepence and a general increase made in produce of the customs. His successor, Lord Henry Petty,[2] advanced it to two shillings in the next year and at that point it stood until the end of the war, for Petty declared that to be its "natural limit." Although its yield greatly increased, the charges of the war necessitated constant additions to the indirect taxes.

---

1 This change is of great importance. Previously the taxpayer was assessed directly on his total income. Under the Act of 1803 the income was divided into schedules and, wherever possible, the tax was made payable at the source, that is, deducted from the sums which went to make up the income of the individual, e.g., the tax on the owner of a house was charged against the tenant who deducted it from his rent. There were five schedules referring: (*a*) to owners of land and houses, (*b*) to tenant farmers, (*c*) to dividends and annuities, (*d*) to property or business abroad and income from professions, trades and employments at home, and (*e*) to public offices or employments of profit. *See* Seligman: "The Income Tax," pp. 90–101.

2 Lord Henry Petty (1780–1863) became second Marquis of Lansdowne in 1809, see p. 60, *infra*.

A FISCAL & FINANCIAL HISTORY OF ENGLAND

APPENDIX TO CHAPTER I

Since figures are given at the beginning of all the subsequent chapters it may be useful to append to this introductory statement a statistical summary which is, in a general way, comparable with them. The charge of Pitt's Sinking Fund is also added. In this period the Exchequers of Great Britain and Ireland were separate.

(NOTE.—Figures are given to the nearest thousand, and 000's are omitted.)

Year (ending) October 10th.*		Net Public Income.	Total Public Expenditure.	Surplus (+) or Deficiency (−).	Total Debt Charge.	Sinking Fund.
		£	£	£	£	£
1782	G.B.	13,765	29,234	− 15,469	7,364	—
	Ireland	*764*	*838*	− *74*	*101*	
1783	G.B.	12,677	23,510	− 10,833	8,054	—
	Ireland	*1,107*	*1,314*	− *207*	121	—
1784	G.B.	13,214	24,245	− 11,031	8,678	—
	Ireland	*1,014*	*1,142*	− *128*	*127*	
1785	G.B.	15,257	25,832	− 10,305	9,229	—
	Ireland	*881*	*1,009*	− *128*	*130*	
1786	G.B.	15,246	16,978	− 1,732	9,481	250
	Ireland	*1,128*	*1,179*	− *51*	*144*	
1787	G.B.	16,453	15,484	+ 969	9,292	1,059
	Ireland	*1,228*	*1,178*	+ *50*	*140*	
1788	G.B.	16,779	16,338	+ 441	9,407	1,113
	Ireland	*1,260*	*1,350*	− *90*	*148*	
1789	G.B.	16,669	16,018	+ 651	9,425	1,187
	Ireland	*1,233*	*1,235*	− *2*	*143*	
1790	G.B.	17,014	16,798	+ 216	9,370	1,207
	Ireland	*1,381*	*1,296*	+ *85*	*141*	
1791	G.B.	18,506	17,996	+ 510	9,430	1,256
	Ireland	*1,313*	*1,384*	− *71*	*129*	
1792	G.B.	18,607	16,953	+ 1,654	9,310	1,730
	Ireland	*1,368*	*1,396*	− *28*	*133*	

* Until 1800 the Irish Financial Year ended on March 25th; thereafter it coincided with that of Great Britain. The Irish figures up to and including 1799 are therefore six months in advance of those for Great Britain. All amounts are expressed in British currency.

Year (ending October 10th.)*	Net Public Income.		Total Public Expenditure.	Surplus (+) or Deficiency (-).	Total Debt Charge.	Sinking Fund.
		£	£	£	£	£
1793	G.B.	18,131	19,623	— 1,492	9,149	1,622
	Ireland	*1,364*	*1,363*	+ *1*	*133*	
1794	G.B.	18,732	28,706	— 9,974	9,797	1,610
	Ireland	*1,179*	*1,581*	— *402*	*147*	
1975	G.B.	19,053	38,996	— 19,943	10,470	2,069
	Ireland	*1,475*	*2,509*	— *1,034*	*214*	
1796	G.B.	19,391	42,372	— 22,981	11,602	2,462
	Ireland	*1,552*	*2,803*	— *1,251*	*245*	
1797	G.B.	21,380	57,649	— 36,269	13,594	3,184
	Ireland	*1,703*	*3,102*	— *1,399*	*408*	
1798	G.B.	26,945	47,422	— 20,477	16,029	3,844
	Ireland	*2,084*	*4,678*	— *2,594*	*561*	
1799	G.B.	31,783	47,419	— 15,636	16,856	4,260
	Ireland	*2,146*	*5,373*	— *3,227*	*628*	
(Ending Jan. 5th.)	Gross Public Income.		Gross Public Expenditure.	Surplus (+) or Deficiency (—).	Total Debt Charge.	Sinking Fund.
[1] 1801	G.B.	41,260	63,374	— 22,114	20,136	5,837
	Ireland	*5,222*	*11,242*	— *6,020*	*1,909*	
1802	G.B.	35,890	58,641	— 22,751	18,481	5,118
	Ireland	*3,204*	*7,198*	— *3,994*	*1,583*	
1803	G.B.	37,403	48,644	— 11,241	18,981	5,688
	Ireland	*3,804*	*6,174*	— *2,370*	*1,447*	
1804	G.B.	39,130	46,957	— 7,827	19 200	5,968
	Ireland	*3,361*	*6,117*	— *2,756*	*1,518*	
1805	G.B.	46,544	55,655	— 9,111	18,919	6,521
	Ireland	*3,714*	*7,257*	— *3,543*	*1,818*	
1806	G.B.	51,150	64,454	— 13,304	20,350	7,181
	Ireland	*3,904*	*7,029*	— *3,125*	*1,979*	
1807	G.B.	55,707	65,728	— 10,021	21,103	7,830
	Ireland	*4,515*	*7,214*	— *2,699*	*2,173*	
1808	G.B.	59,791	65,835	— 6,044	21,585	8,909
	Ireland	*5,072*	*7,530*	— *2,458*	*2,240*	

[1] It should be noticed that there is a change in the financial year in 1799 which makes the "year" ending January 5th, 1801, fifteen months long in the case of Great Britain and twenty-one months long in the case of Ireland. From January, 1801, the figures give *gross* Income and Expenditure.

Year (ending January 5th.)	Gross Public Income.		Gross Public Expenditure.	Surplus (+) or Deficiency (-).	Total Debt Charge.	Sinking Fnnd.
		£	£	£	£	£
1809	G.B.	62,921	69,981	– 7,060	20,744	9,556
	Ireland	*5,283*	*8,085*	– *2,802*	*2,306*	
1810	G.B.	64,102	73,410	– 9,308	21,662	[1]10,158
	Ireland	*5,116*	*8,280*	– *3,164*	*2,539*	
1811	G.B.	69,559	73,743	– 4,184	21,822	10,813
	Ireland	*4,714*	*9,204*	– *4,490*	*2,614*	
1812	G.B.	67,498	78,866	– 11,368	21,732	11,544
	Ireland	*5,042*	*9,910*	– *4,868*	*2,847*	
1813	G.B.	64,672	86,628	– 21,956	23,510	12,440
	Ireland	*5,731*	*9,953*	– *4,222*	*2,964*	
1814	G.B.	72,808	102,614	– 29,806	24,044	14,181
	Ireland	*5,879*	*11,250*	– *5,371*	*3,311*	
1815	G.B.	74,289	104,089	– 29,800	26,409	12,748
	Ireland	*6,429*	*11,349*	– *4,920*[2]	*3,592*	

(These figures are extracted from "Accounts and Papers," 366, of 1868–9.)

[1] Certain deductions were made from the Sinking Fund in and after 1810, and applied to the payment of life annuities.

[2] The comparative inelasticity of the Irish public income, the increasingly heavy deficits and consequent enormous Debt Charge should be noticed. The income tax was not extended to Ireland.

(Note.—Figures are given to the nearest thousand, and 000's are omitted).

Year (ending January 5th).	Exchequer Receipts.	Exchequer Issues.	Surplus (+) or Deficiency (−).	Debt Charge.
1816	72,111	92,135 20,242	−40,266	32,281
1817	62,265	64,846 514	− 3,095	32,924
1818	52,056	53,454 1,827	− 3,225	31,486
1819	53,748	51,724 1,625	+ 399	31,169
1820	52,649	52,215 3,163	− 2,729	31,355
1821	54,283	52,402 1,918	− 37	31,105
1822	55,834	53,007 4,104	− 1,277	29,723

These figures are taken from the " Fourth Report from the Select Committee on Public Income and Expenditure, 1828," except those for the Debt Charge, which are from the " Return of the Whole Amount of the National Debt, 1691–1857," (Vol. XXXIII of 1857–8). It should be noticed that the figures here given are for *net* amounts and therefore are on a different basis from those given for 1801–1815 on pp. 25–26, *supra*. The Exchequers of Great Britain and Ireland were amalgamated from January 5th, 1817. The Irish figures, however, are included in the above table for 1816 and 1817. It is extremely difficult to give a summary statement of the financial operations of these years. Large sums were devoted annually to the discharge of debt, but they were mostly considerably outbalanced by the amount of new debt contracted. Under Exchequer Issues I have added as a second sum the net result of these operations in each year. It will be noticed that only in 1819 was there a margin on the right side.

CHAPTER II

THE AFTERMATH OF WAR—1815–1822

THE peculiar interest which now attaches to the period immediately after a great European war would seem to justify the devotion of a somewhat disproportionate amount of space to the seven years which followed the overthrow of Napoleon. Then the consequences of the long contest were so acutely felt and the social and industrial problems appeared so complex that the Government adopted repressive measures to prevent what it conceived to be the impending dissolution of society. This was the inevitable result of the lack of any kind of a constructive policy. Lord Liverpool's ministry had been formed in 1812, and it remained in power until 1827 largely owing to the pliability of the Prime Minister. His chief asset was his skill in securing the co-operation of men who differed from one another on personal and public grounds. On more than one occasion he professed liberal sympathies; but he could be depended on not to press any question which a group within the Cabinet did not wish to be raised. Eldon, the Lord Chancellor, has become the typical example of the opponent to all change. Addington, now Lord Sidmouth, was Home Secretary, a mediocrity whose weakness and readiness to give credence to the wildest rumours ill-fitted him for the responsibility of dealing with the widespread unrest. At the Exchequer was Nicholas Vansittart, the son of a former Governor of Bengal. A financier of average ability, he was quite incapable of coping with a situation of unprecedented difficulty. The Foreign Secretary, Lord Castlereagh, was the most striking personality in the Ministry, but, whatever his merits were as a diplomatist, he was extremely unpopular at home.

The return to peace conditions was gradual. Napoleon, bowing to the inevitable, abdicated and retired to Elba in April, 1814. His conquerors then began to confer on the future of Europe at Vienna; but a glance at Vansittart's Budget of June of that year will show that it was a war Budget, differing in no important respect from that of 1813. Part of the explanation is that the war with America continued to the end of the year. By that time, however, questions began to be asked about the effects of peace, particularly with regard to lightening the burden of taxation. When Parliament reassembled in November, the Government gave no indication of its intentions, contenting itself with pointing out that the yield of the taxes was well maintained and that the long war had entailed heavy arrears for which provision had to be made. This reticence was suspected by some to mean that the income tax was to be retained after the expiry of six months from the date of peace. The City of London prepared a petition on the subject in December, an example which was followed by other towns. On the reopening of Parliament in February, 1815, Vansittart announced that the Government intended to drop the tax. At the same time he promised to submit to the House a new financial scheme. The speech in which he did so is notable for the stress he laid on the benefits which the country had derived from the income tax. He claimed that it should be considered as "a great and powerful resource which, in times of public emergency, might and ought to be resorted to."[1] The objection to it was still that it was inquisitorial. Vansittart argued that it was perfect as applied to funded property, for there could neither be evasion nor overcharge; it approached perfection with respect to landed property; but it was imperfect with regard to trade, for here the Commissioners had to be given extensive powers to secure regular returns. He confessed that he had contemplated

[1] Smart: "Economic Annals," Vol. I, p. 422, quoting Hansard, xxix, 853.

the continuation of the tax to cover the winding-up charges of the war, a step which he held could be justified, but, owing to the fluctuations in prices, which would render it "peculiarly vexatious and disagreeable," he had decided not to renew it.

The abandonment of the income tax would mean a loss to the Exchequer of over £14,000,000. There was no prospect of an immediate reduction in expenditure to anything like that extent. Consequently it would be necessary to continue all the other war taxes, to impose new taxes which would produce £5,000,000, and also to raise a loan. Vansittart followed precedents in proposing to find the additional revenue by increasing the Assessed Taxes, Customs and Excise, and Stamp Duties. While the promised repeal of the income tax was received with enthusiasm the suggested means of getting some compensation met with considerable opposition. Attempts were made to prove that the Chancellor of the Exchequer was providing for the peace establishment at an extravagant rate and greater economy was demanded. George Rose, however, drew the true moral, and his long association with Pitt lent weight to his opinion.[1] He contended that in the circumstances the income tax in some modified form ought to be retained. It was obviously the only way to avoid fiscal confusion. Vansittart's own tribute to its efficacy in the past seems to indicate that he had allowed public clamour and the prejudice against the tax to override his own opinion on the subject.

Vansittart was also challenged on the question of the resumption of cash payments by the Bank of England. The Restriction Act was supposed to lapse six months after the signing of a definitive treaty of peace. In July of the previous year it had been stated that the Bank would be required to resume payment on March 25th. The Chancellor now indicated that he intended to propose a further postponement. This intimation elicited the

---

[1] George Rose (1744–1818) sat in Parliament from 1786 to his death. His ability in finance was not supported by other personal qualities, and he never occupied a high position.

strongest protests, but the Government held that an extension of the period was absolutely necessary.

These discussions in February, 1815, are often overlooked because the escape of Napoleon from Elba later in that month and his amazing success in gathering an army around him completely upset the calculations on which they were based. Still, it will be seen that they have an important bearing on what happened in the next year. But even at the time financial questions were overshadowed by the agricultural crisis which was declared to be a matter of special urgency. It was indeed the one direction in which Parliament had some appreciation of the probable consequences of the return to peace conditions. During the war high prices had naturally encouraged farmers to extend the area under cultivation. In the absence of any kind of guarantee against a sudden fall in prices this was highly speculative. Enclosure and cultivation of waste lands, however, commended itself to the governing classes, and it seemed wise to promote it by endeavouring to secure and maintain a high level of prices. With this object in view the Corn Laws were adjusted in 1804; when home wheat fell below 63s. a quarter a high duty was imposed on imported wheat, but when the price rose to 66s. the import duty became nominal; if home wheat fell below 48s. a duty of 5s. was to be paid on exportation, but when it was above 54s. exportation was prohibited. As a matter of fact this law remained inoperative during the war because the home price was above 66s., that is, wheat came in on paying a nominal duty and export was prohibited. At the time it seemed a sufficient safeguard against a sudden and disastrous fall of prices. But a decade of high prices stimulated agriculture to such an extent that much capital was invested and resort had to inferior soils. The competition for land had driven up rents and the general standard of living among tenant farmers had been considerably raised. Until 1813 the agricultural interest accepted the prosperity which indifferent harvests and the restrictions imposed on international trade by the war afforded it. Then a Select Committee of the House of Commons was obtained by Sir

Henry Parnell to inquire into the corn trade of the United Kingdom.[1] Parnell was himself an Irish landlord and it is clear that the original purpose was to draw attention to a specifically Irish grievance. The cultivation of wheat in Ireland was, owing to the dietary of the peasantry, primarily for export. It had greatly extended during the war period, and the Corn Law of 1804 was actually operating as a restriction; the prohibition on export meant that the surplus could not be sent to foreign countries, where there was a good demand, for, as long as the high prices ruled, Great Britain was the only market, and there it had to compete with foreign supplies admitted on payment of a nominal duty. The Irish landlords, therefore, wished the embargo on export to be removed and also to secure a stronger position for themselves in the British market. The inquiry revealed the fact that considerable quantities were imported into Great Britain from the Continent every year. This was represented as a source of weakness and the suggestion was made that advantage should be taken of the investment of new capital in agriculture so to increase home supplies as to be independent of foreign imports. Sir John Sinclair expressed the opinion that the country's financial difficulties were due to the fact that enormous sums of money were sent abroad to pay for wheat.[2] This was to overlook the important fact that the industrial developments in England had led to a great

[1] Sir Henry Parnell (1776–1842) had been a member of the Irish Parliament. He was elected to the Parliament of the United Kingdom in 1807. His reputation as an authority on financial matters grew steadily. He was a member of the Bullion Committee and Chairman of the Finance Committee of 1828. On economy he had strong views, and he came to favour Free Trade. He is best known on account of his "Financial Reform," which was published in 1830.

[2] Sir John Sinclair (1754–1835) was an agricultural enthusiast and the first president of the unofficial Board of Agriculture of which Arthur Young was secretary. It is interesting to notice that Napoleon agreed with the above theory. He encouraged the export of corn to England in the hope that it would so drain the country of gold that bankruptcy would ensue. Had he forbidden export, particularly during the year 1810–11, when the English harvest was bad, the position would have become critical. *See* Holland Rose, "Life of Napoleon," II, 221.

increase in the export of manufactured goods. The opposing interests of landlords and manufacturers, however, were not yet clearly revealed.

The discussion was carried a stage further in 1814. The previous year's harvest had been abundant and prices had consequently fallen considerably, but not quite so low as to bring the provisions of the Act of 1804 into operation. The disastrous effects of a good harvest, however, enabled Parnell to appeal to the landed class in favour of a higher import duty to save agriculture from a complete collapse. He secured a Bill to remove the prohibition on export and a new Select Committee was appointed to consider proposed changes in the duty on importation. It is significant that this Committee received petitions against an increased duty from most of the industrial centres. But the members of it were chiefly impressed by the rapid progress of agriculture during the war—the application of new capital, the conversion of pasture into arable and the reclamation of waste—and they came to the conclusion that all this would be undone unless the farmer could count on a minimum price of 80s. a quarter.

A second good harvest brought matters to an issue. The House of Commons had before it the findings of two Select Committees and in the last two years the whole question had been fully discussed. The distress in agriculture was acute. Resolutions of special urgency were introduced on February 17th, 1815. It was proposed that no wheat should be imported until the home price rose to 80s. a quarter, the prohibition to apply to other kinds of grains at the accepted proportionate rates. The objections of the manufacturing interest were clearly stated by George Philips, who argued in favour of cheap corn. He criticised the policy of encouraging the cultivation of inferior soils by means of protection and asserted that a manufacturing country had nothing to fear from the importation of corn, for it would be balanced by the export of goods. It merely encouraged foreign countries to establish and protect new industries. In spite of the renewal of protests, on a much more extensive scale than in the previous year, the resolutions were carried and a Bill introduced accordingly.[1] The second reading was the occasion of rioting at Westminster. In the Houses of Parliament, however, the strength of the landed interest ensured its safe passage.

To sum up:—When the Government considered its post-war policy in February, 1815, it decided (1) that the income tax should be repealed; (2) that it was necessary to continue the Bank Restriction Act, and (3) that high protection was required to prevent the collapse of agriculture.

The hope of returning to Vansittart's peace establishment was completely dissipated by Napoleon's escape from Elba and the welcome he received in France. The Allies declared him a public enemy and made preparations to bring him to justice. Large sums were at once voted by the House of Commons for the equipment of the fighting forces. Vansittart announced that the continuation of the income tax was necessary and he accordingly did not propose to go on with the Bill which authorised the increases in the Assessed Taxes. Protests, in the circumstances, were futile. The suggestion that the tax should be extended to Ireland and the plea that special relief should be given to farmers were both met by the argument that any extension or modification was not worth considering in view of the fact that it would only be levied for one year. The tax was therefore reimposed without change. The Budget, which was introduced on June 14th —four days before the battle of Waterloo—was the heaviest of the whole series of war Budgets. In addition £39,000,000

---

[1] The opinion of Robert Owen represents that of the manufacturers. "The direct effect of the Corn Bill lately passed will be to hasten this decline, and prematurely to destroy that trade (*i.e., the export trade*). In this view it is deeply to be regretted that the bill passed into law; and I am persuaded its promoters will ere long discover the absolute necessity for its repeal, to prevent the misery which must ensue to the great mass of the people."—"Observations on the Effect of the Manufacturing System," by Robert Owen, of New Lanark (published 1815).

was raised by loans, the interest on which more than exhausted the yield of such new taxes as seemed feasible.[1]

When Parliament assembled in February, 1816, Vansittart had again to forecast a peace establishment. The position was in every way worse than it had been a year ago. Agricultural distress had been deepened and to it was added widespread industrial dislocation. Napoleon's reappearance had involved heavy expenses and additions to the National Debt. In the opinion of the Government it was necessary to maintain large military forces to ensure the settlement of Europe. The Chancellor intimated that he wished to reduce the burden of taxation and to strengthen public credit. Under the former head he proposed the reduction of the income tax by half to 5 per cent. and the repeal of the war tax on malt, together with other minor modifications in customs duties. He estimated that these changes would relieve agriculture to the extent of £4,000,000. To effect the stabilising of public credit he hoped to avoid resort to borrowing and at the same time pay off £14,000,000, through the Sinking Fund. The attempt to represent the continuation of the

[1] The total yield of the taxes was £67,266,000, distributed in the following manner:

Direct Taxes:	(a) Land Tax ..	1,196,000	
	(b) Assessed Taxes .	6,500,000	Total
	(c) Income Tax ..	14,600,000	£25,438,000
	(d) Succession Tax .	1,297,000	
	(e) Miscellaneous ..	1,845,000	
Indirect Taxes:	(a) Food: Salt, Sugar, Currants, etc. ..	5,068,000	
	(b) Drinks:		
	Hops, Malt and Beer	9,596,000	
	Wine and Spirits	8,600,000	
	Tea and Coffee	3,868,000	Total
	(c) Tobacco ..	2,025,000	£39,085,000
	(d) Coal and Raw Materials ...	6,062,000	
	(e) Manufactures ..	3,866,000	
Stamp Duties:	Bills, Notes, Receipts, etc.	2,743,000	Total £2,743,000

This does not include the separate Irish revenue, *see* pp. 24 and 25 *supra*. Dowell: "Taxation and Taxes," Vol. II, pp. 239–251.

income tax at half rates as a concession was somewhat disingenuous. Vansittart had apparently been influenced by arguments in favour of the tax and the wisdom of his continuing it would hardly now be questioned. But he was singularly lacking in insight if he supposed that the proposition would seem either just or reasonable to a majority in the House of Commons. The old objections were restated with greater violence than ever; the tax was characterised as "detestable," "shameful," "mischievous," and "immoral." Lord John Russell asserted that "there could be no more dreadful calamity for this country than its continuance." It was said to be largely responsible for the general distress in the country. Petitions poured in from all parts. No doubt the opposition was reinforced by the conviction that the Government was proposing to maintain excessively large military forces at home and abroad. Castlereagh was accused of having imbibed Continental ideas, and, forgetting that Britain was an island, of attempting to make her one of the great military powers. He further irritated feeling by his contemptuous attitude towards the clamour. The Government indeed underestimated the strength of the opposition and seemed to count on its majority in the House to carry its proposal. Vansittart was himself conciliatory; he declared that he did not contemplate a permanent tax but merely the continuation of a war tax for two or three years, and he was willing to give some relief to farmers. After prolonged discussion of the question the Chancellor at last, on March 18th, moved a resolution in favour of the retention of the tax. Henry Brougham,[1] who had been the soul of the opposition, immediately before the division read the preamble to the Act of 1815—"this Act shall continue in force during the present war and until April 6th next and after the definite signing of a treaty of peace, and no longer." Feeling ran high; 201 voted for the resolution, 238 against. Brougham followed up his success by carrying a motion that all the records of the tax should be destroyed.

[1] Henry Peter Brougham (1778–1868) became Lord Chancellor in 1830.

This defeat, unexpected but decisive, was accepted by Vansittart. It upset all his calculations and presented to him a problem which would have challenged the ingenuity of a much abler financier. His project of avoiding a loan had to be abandoned. But he decided to carry out his original intention of remitting the malt tax and the other duties. As he had to resort to the money market he held that it was of little consequence if he borrowed £2,000,000 more than was represented by the loss of the income tax. This complacent view—with which Castlereagh agreed—has often been quoted as an example of Vansittart's incompetence. He was no doubt led to this decision by the fact that the repeal of the malt duty was a direct concession to the agricultural interest. His resolve to cling to this part of his scheme, even at the cost of raising a proportionately larger loan, can be defended: his acceptance of his defeat on the income tax resolution was the origin of all his later troubles. A Chancellor who is deprived of the means which he thinks necessary to meet the national charges, should resign. Vansittart did not do so. His attempts to make the necessary adjustments did not secure the gratitude of his contemporaries nor have they gained him the sympathy of posterity.

The results of the adoption of the income tax, 1798–1815, are dealt with in a well-known passage by Gladstone in his Budget speech of 1853. He reminded his hearers how Pitt, finding that the resources of taxation were failing under him, fell back on the income tax. He went on to compare three phases in the financing of the war. From 1793 to 1798 there was no income tax; from 1799 to 1802 it was in operation but not yet perfected; from 1806 to 1815 it was in full force. Then he made the striking assertion that if the tax had been imposed earlier the National Debt would not then (1853) have existed. Taking the charge of government, war and pre-war debt (but omitting that of debt contracted during the war), he demonstrated that it amounted to £15,404,000 a year in excess of the revenue from 1793 to 1798. Then Pitt introduced the income tax, and in spite of increases in the annual expenditure, the excess over revenue from 1799 to

1802 was reduced to £13,689,000. In the last period—1806 to 1815—it was only £2,004,000 a year. Deducting the charge for the pre-war debt, Gladstone reached the conclusion that during the last and most trying period of the war taxes exceeded the charges of government and war by as much as £7,000,000 a year. "This, then, is the purpose which the income tax has served," he concluded, "that, in a time of mortal struggle, it enabled you to raise the income of the country above its expenditure (at the time) of war and civil government."[1]

The immediate effect of the loss of the income tax is to be seen in the 1816 Budget. At 5 per cent. it would have produced rather more than £7,000,000. The adverse vote had deprived Vansittart of this amount; he chose to adhere, it has been noticed, to his intention to repeal the war malt duty, which meant a further loss of £2,790,000 and the other remissions came to over £1,000,000. Consequently he had to borrow, and he announced that the Bank of England had, in return for permission to increase its capital and other concessions, agreed to advance £9,000,000 to the State. He had to find money to pay interest on the necessary loans and for that purpose he raised the excise on soap and imposed duties on butter and cheese. To the first, as falling on a necessary, Pitt had felt the objections were so strong that he had avoided making any increase during the war. Brougham now revived the old argument that it would inevitably involve a rise in wages. The Chancellor's excuse was that the increase was a small one—from 2½d. to 3d. a pound—while it would give him about £150,000 and also encourage the whale fisheries. The duties on butter and cheese were primarily protective; an attempt to give to the dairy farmer something corresponding to the benefit conferred

[1] W. E. Gladstone: "Financial Statements of 1853, 1860–1863," pp. 14–18. Vansittart himself pointed out on February 20th, 1814, that the Income Tax had produced since the Peace of Amiens (roughly Gladstone's third phase) £126,000,000, which meant that the addition of £180,000,000 to the Debt, involving an annual charge of nearly £9,000,000, had been avoided. Smart: "Economic Annals," Vol. I, p. 422 ("Hansard," XXIX, 853).

on the agriculturist by the Corn Law. They were expected to bring in about £100,000. The total tax revenue for the year proved to be £56,214,000, of which over £34,000,000 came from the Customs and Excise. In the same financial year the National Debt charges amounted to £32,894,000, that is, to about 57 per cent. of the whole tax revenue. As the Sinking Fund was still in operation a further sum of £11,000,000 had to be handed over to the Commissioners for the Redemption of the National Debt. The total receipts of the Exchequer—tax and non-tax—were quite inadequate to meet the expenses of government in addition to these charges.

The problem of how to escape from this burden of national indebtedness seemed to defy solution. Year after year loans had to be raised to supply the deficit. The difficulties of the Chancellor become clearer if the possible ways of balancing income and expenditure are explored. (1) Why not impose taxes which would reduce, if not eliminate the adverse balance? The answer is simple. Without the income tax this was not possible. Already the resources of indirect taxes were drained to the full. In 1819, for instance, Vansittart did attempt to raise an additional three millions by increasing the duties on malt, spirits, tobacco, coffee, tea, etc., but the taxes proved a failure. Except in the year 1818, when there was a temporary improvement in trade, the existing taxes had shown no increase; in some cases the yield had shrunk. The general view of contemporaries was that taxation had reached its maximum. Subsequent events were to demonstrate that the total produce of the taxes was more likely to be increased by reductions than by additions, or, in other words, the high rates were seriously restricting consumption. (2) If a larger revenue could not be raised by taxation, was it not possible to reduce the difference between income and expenditure by effecting economies in the latter? The Opposition naturally pressed this claim for economy. It was held that the fighting forces were much too large and that there was much waste in other directions. Economy was no doubt possible and desirable, but the sphere of its operation was relatively limited. J. R. M'Culloch, who strongly advocated it, recognised this fact. "Assuming that the Government," he wrote in 1816[1] "is justly compelled to be much more economical, both in the military and the civil departments, and supposing that the expenditure is thereby lessened twelve or fifteen millions, the effect of this would be to allow the half of the property (i.e. income) tax proposed to be continued to be taken off, and about seven or ten millions of other taxes. We must not deceive ourselves by thinking that this great reduction, greater we are afraid than will be speedily realised, would be anything like adequate relief to our distresses. We must reflect, that our peace establishment would still be fourteen or seventeen millions, besides being oppressed with the interest of the national debt, amounting to about thirty-four millions and with ten or eleven millions more, raised to be expended in the worse than quixotic attempt of paying it off. The taxes would still be excessive; and such a reduction would neither enable the manufacturer to stand a competition with foreigners, now that peace has restored a free intercourse among nations, nor would it enable the landholder to enjoy the comforts and necessaries of life." Economies, it will be noticed, were in M'Culloch's opinion to result in remission of taxes, a form of relief essential to the prosperity of commerce and agriculture. But the extent of the relief would remain inadequate so long as money had to be found for the interest on the National Debt, the maintenance of the Sinking Fund and the lowest conceivable peace establishment. The Debt charge and the Sinking Fund not only made remission of taxes practically impossible, they also made the annual deficits inevitable. (3) Were there no means of reducing the Debt charge and amending the expensive Sinking Fund?

Take, first, the Sinking Fund; every year the Chancellor had to hand over an appreciable proportion of his income

[1] "An Essay on a Reduction of the Interest on the National Debt," by J. R. M'Culloch (1816), pp. 38–9. M'Culloch (1789–1864) abandoned law for journalism. For two years he was editor of the *Scotsman*, and from 1828–32 Professor of Political Economy in University College, London.

to the Commissioners for the Redemption of the National Debt. It will be recalled that Pitt retained his Sinking Fund on the outbreak of war. In principle it was still in operation, though it had been modified in several particulars. The first important change was made by Addington in 1802. He removed the limitation of four millions, that is, the Fund was to go on accumulating after the income of the Commissioners (made up of the annual million and the interest on the stock they had purchased) exceeded that sum. At the same time the special Sinking Funds of one per cent. of each loan raised after the beginning of the war were amalgamated with the main Sinking Fund to form a single whole. As the purchases of the Commissioners did not relieve the Debt charge—for they continued to draw the interest—the revised Sinking Fund involved an increasingly heavy burden on the Exchequer year after year. Addington's computation was that this system would redeem the whole National Debt in forty-five years. But by 1813 it became clear that the country could not bear the annual charge. Vansittart therefore introduced an amendment of the 1802 plan. He returned to the original suggestion that when the stock in the hands of the Commissioners was equivalent to the debt at the inception of the Sinking Fund in 1786 it should be cancelled. This point had been reached in 1813.[1] The cancellation meant such a relief in the payment of interest that no new taxes would be necessary for four years. But new loans, with their special arrangements for redemption and the continuation of the payments from the Consolidated Fund to the Commissioners, soon raised the annual charge again to such figures that further relief became necessary. By 1819 the annual charge for Sinking Fund had reached £15,500,000. Apart from this, income exceeded expenditure by £2,000,000; consequently the Fund made it necessary to borrow £13,500,000. The criticisms of the policy of borrowing in order to pay off debt were now beginning to carry weight. One member described the

[1] The Debt at the inception of Pitt's Sinking Fund in 1786 stood at £245,000,000.

operation as "creating a new debt for no other purpose than to extinguish an old one; selling new stock cheap in order to buy old stock dear; buying at a very high rate of interest to pay off a debt contracted at a very low one."[1] At first Vansittart repeated the old argument that the regular purchases by the Commissioners caused a steadiness in prices and maintained a feeling of security in the money market. Later, however, he himself introduced a series of resolutions, which included a proposal to take from the Sinking Fund £12,000,000 for the services of the year. This course was followed in 1820 and 1821. Although the Commissioners still received their quarterly payments they were not devoted to the buying of stock but lent to the Government for other purposes. It was a complicated arrangement by which the charge of the Sinking Fund was really evaded; the money nominally set aside for the redemption of the debt was actually spent to meet current expenses. Ricardo expressed the common-sense point of view when he said in the House, "Let us have no Sinking Fund; let the money remain in the pockets of the people. When Ministers want supplies . . . let them come down to the House and ask for them, without having any such fund to resort to."

Secondly, the debt charge might be reduced by effecting a conversion, that is, by lowering the rate of interest. This was the solution advocated by J. R. M'Culloch in the pamphlet already noticed. He argued that the weight of taxation was the real cause of distress in commerce and agriculture and that an all-round fall in prices was essential to the renewal of prosperity. On this ground he condemned the policy of the 1815 Corn Law. Just as the artificial maintenance of the high price of corn tended to prevent a fall in other prices, so the high interest on stock precluded an adjustment. The general level of prices had been raised by the undue expansion of the paper currency. The subscribers to the loans had lent in this depreciated paper money. Had they any right to demand the same nominal rate of interest if the old standard of value were

[1] Smart: "Economic Annals," Vol. I, p. 683.

restored? He quoted the opinion of Malthus that, if the currency were reduced to proper proportions, "there is great reason to fear that the country would be absolutely unable to continue the payment of the present interest of the National Debt."[1] In justice a public creditor ought to be paid in paper that is as depreciated as that which he lent; in other words, if the depreciation no longer existed the nominal rate of interest should be correspondingly reduced.[2] This line of argument could hardly carry any weight with a Government which officially denied the underlying assumption that the currency had depreciated. There was also the practical difficulty that most of the loans had been raised in 3 per cents. and offered no margin for conversion. Nothing was actually done until 1822, when Vansittart succeeded in effecting a conversion which relieved the Exchequer of an annual charge of £1,400,000. He chose for this operation the part of the Funded Debt called the Navy 5 per cents. This stock was above par—a necessary condition for an effective conversion—and the holders were given the option of being paid off at par or of receiving for every £100 of old stock £105 in a new issue at 4 per cent. About £150,000,000 were converted, as the holders of a mere fraction—£2,600,000—asked to be paid off.

Thirdly, the debt itself might be extinguished by the adoption of heroic measures. No less a person than Ricardo himself advocated the immediate repayment of the National Debt by means of a general assessment on all property. He pointed out that a temporary sacrifice would remove an evil which militated against the recovery of trade and industry. The country, he held, was quite able to make this effort, and the object was so desirable that it was worth while to grapple with the difficulties it involved. As long as taxation remained at the high level

---

[1] M'Culloch's "Essay on Reduction of Interest," p. 46.

[2] William Cobbett insisted that to allow the holders of stock created during the restriction to benefit from the effect of the resumption was to place an unfair burden on the other taxpayers. He called for the abolition of the National Debt as a preliminary to the return to the gold standard.

which the debt charge necessitated there could be no stabilising of prices and capital would tend to leave the country.[1] It is a curious fact that while Ricardo was expressing these views in the House of Commons Shelley was committing to writing his opinions on reform. He thought that the abolition of the National Debt was an essential preliminary. Shelley contended that if the debt remained unpaid it would be "an eternal rent-charge" levied on industry for the benefit of the fund-holders. It was essentially an obligation contracted by the privileged classes—the actual rulers of the country—to a section of themselves. Consequently, he proposed to value the whole of the property of those who possessed any and to make a levy which would repay the capital of the debt. It would be a mere transfer of wealth among the same individuals. "The payment of the principal of what is called the National Debt, which it is pretended is so difficult a problem," he sums up, "is only difficult to those who do not see who is the debtor, and who the creditor, and who the wretched sufferers from whom they both wring the taxes which under the form of interest is given by the former and accepted by the latter." Shelley even goes so far as to distinguish between wealth gained by legitimate and illegitimate means. All professional persons, as well as all tradesmen who are not monopolists, would stand to benefit from the plan he proposes; for the rest, he conceives the repayment of the debt as a simple matter of cancellation of indebtedness between two sections of the wealthy class. Ricardo's scheme was regarded as one of his crotchets; Shelley's discussion of the subject remained in manuscript for a hundred years.[2] At the time the project of a levy on capital was not seriously considered or even widely canvassed.[3]

---

[1] For a summary of Ricardo's statements on this question *see* Edwin Cannan: "The Economic Outlook," pp. 133–7.

[2] P. B. Shelley: "A Philosophical View of Reform" (first printed in 1920), pp. 55–66.

[3] The idea of a levy on capital was not new. In the reign of George I a member of the House of Commons—Archibald Hutcheson—proposed to pay off the existing National Debt by means of

The question of restoring the currency to a healthy condition attracted a considerable amount of attention. Vansittart was constantly told that his financial difficulties, and even the general public distress, were largely due to the state of the currency. The over-issue of bank notes, it was held, had resulted in their depreciation and there could be no return to normal conditions until the gold standard was restored and the Bank of England required to convert its notes on demand. Consequently the Government was persistently pressed to repeal the Bank Restriction Act and the management of the Bank of England was often severely criticised. Vansittart's attitude towards this question has probably done more to influence the verdict of posterity on his ability as a financier than anything else in his career. After the suspension of cash payments in 1797 the directors of the Bank of England failed to realise that the problem of regulating note-issue had become more complicated. Previously they had contracted their issues when there were signs of an undue outflow of gold from the reserve. This policy, it will be remembered, they had pursued in a mechanical way, which tended to precipitate the crisis they wished to prevent. It was, however, a recognition of the fact that it was dangerous to have a great quantity of notes outstanding when preference was given to gold. But why should preference be given to gold? Firstly, because circumstances might arise in the foreign exchanges which would create a demand for gold. The consequence would be a drain of gold from the country. Secondly, public confidence might be so shaken within the country that a demand for gold might arise. The notes merely represented gold and if there was any indication that they did not represent it perfectly the holders of them would demand their conversion. Granted complete convertibility, there-

---

a contribution of 10 per cent. on all property, real and personal. Proprietors of estates were to be given power to set aside entails and settlements and sell as much as would be required to meet the assessment. David Hume, in his "Essay on Public Credit," noticed some of the difficulties of this plan, particularly that of avoiding inequalities. *See* J. R. M'Culloch, "A Treatise on the Principles and Practical Influence of Taxation and the Funding System," pp. 463–4.

fore, any discrepancy between the value of notes and gold would lead to their return to the Bank.

When the bank notes became inconvertible the directors were launched on an uncharted sea. The old method of regulating issues did not operate—for notes could not be presented for payment—and consequently the gold standard was endangered.[1] For some years a strict limit was set to the issue of notes, but, following a speculative boom, there appeared the peculiar phenomenon of a rise in the price of gold bullion to £4 10s. an ounce. It was accompanied by a fall in the foreign exchanges. What was the explanation of this? Ricardo, in a series of letters to the *Morning Chronicle*, contended that the high price of bullion was a proof that bank notes had depreciated. The state of the exchanges was, he held, a further demonstration of the fact that there had been an over-issue of bank notes. In February Francis Horner[2] raised the question in Parliament and asked for a Select Committee.

---

[1] The gold standard was finally established in Great Britain by the Coinage Act of 1816. It was, however, virtually a recognition of an established fact, for silver had long been relegated to an inferior position in practice. A given quantity of gold of a given fineness was said to be worth so much and on this equation all measurements of value were based, and thus converted into prices. An ounce of 22-carat gold was interchangeable with £3 17s. 6d. The abundance or scarcity of gold would obviously not effect this equation, though it would change the purchasing power of £3 17s. 6d., or, in other words, would raise or lower the general level of prices of other commodities. When the Mint will buy gold offered to it at the above price and there are no restrictions on its export or on its uses in the arts, the standard is as perfect as such a single standard can be.

[2] Francis Horner (1778–1817) was the son of an Edinburgh merchant and was educated at the High School and the University, but he spent two years in England to rid himself of "the disadvantages of a provincial dialect." He was associated with Jeffrey and Brougham in founding the *Edinburgh Review*. Unfortunately his health failed him and he died early in 1817 while in Italy, at the age of thirty-eight. His reputation at Westminster was considerable, but the Bullion Report was his only notable achievement. The remarkable tributes to his ability and character, evoked by his early death, are somewhat marred by the suspicion of patronage. For a brief description of him by one of his friends, *see* Cockburn's "Memorials of His Times," pp. 268–9.

His request was granted and a Committee appointed " to inquire into the cause of the high price of gold bullion, and to take into consideration the state of the circulating medium, and of the exchanges between Great Britain and foreign parts." Its report—the famous Bullion Report[1]—confirmed Ricardo's diagnosis and recommended as a remedy that cash payments should be resumed in two years' time whether the war was over or not. The Committee laid it down that the directors of the Bank ought to " advert to the price of bullion and the foreign exchanges " as the true means of regulating the issue of notes. The directors, however, would not accept these principles. They alleged that there was an actual scarcity of gold, and therefore it had risen in price. To this the Committee replied that the continental markets did not reveal any such scarcity, and at home any amount of gold could be obtained at a price. Even if there were a shortage it would not cause a discrepancy between the market and mint price of gold to emerge, for " the price of gold, being itself measured and expressed in gold, cannot be raised or lowered by an increased or diminished demand for it." Scarcity would be revealed in a fall in the general level of prices. The opponents of the Bullion Committee's analysis sought to explain the fall in the exchanges by the condition of trade and large balance of payments due by Great Britain to other countries. Here it was a question of the extent of the fall. If two countries each have a metallic currency, the exchanges between them can only vary within certain limits. A par of exchange can be established, i.e., the value of the metal in the standard coin of one country can be expressed in terms of the currency of the other. But at normal times payments are not made in coins. The cost of transporting and insuring them is a consideration. Consequently the exchanges may rise above and fall below par. The fall in either country cannot exceed the cost of transporting the precious

1 The Bullion Report is now accessible to students in a convenient form. Professor Cannan reprinted it with a valuable introduction under the title of the " Paper Pound of 1797–1821 " in 1919.

metals themselves in payment. The automatic working of this principle is suspended if the countries, or either of them, adopt a paper currency. The contention of the Bullion Committee was that in such circumstances a fall below par beyond the limit defined above might occur. Close inquiry, it was asserted, showed that this had in fact happened. There was therefore a percentage of the fall which could not be explained by the state of trade and the volume of payments. This proved that bank notes had been over-issued and had consequently depreciated.

That there was an over-issue the directors strenuously denied. They maintained that it could not occur so long as they issued notes to meet solid bills in the course of trade. The old method of making advances was therefore continued, although the check effected by the return of notes and demand for cash was no longer in operation. It is only fair to add that the directors were not alone in their opinion; it was shared by the merchants and by the Government itself. When Horner, in May, 1811, moved a series of resolutions on the lines of the Bullion Report he failed to secure a majority in favour of a single one of them. A few days later Vansittart introduced another set of resolutions, one of which asserted that "the promissory notes of the Bank of England have hitherto been, and are at this time, held in public estimation to be equivalent to the legal coin of the realm, and generally accepted as such in all pecuniary transactions to which such coin is lawfully applicable." These resolutions were passed in spite of the protests of the supporters of the Bullion Committee's theories. One of them—Lord King—determined to put Vansittart's resolutions to the test. He wrote to his tenants requesting them to pay their rent either in guineas or in bank notes for a sufficient sum to buy, at the existing market price, the weight of gold the guineas contained. The challenge was taken up in Parliament, and King defended his action by pointing out that it was only just that his rents should be paid in money of the same intrinsic value as it possessed when he made the agreements with the tenants. Lord Stanhope thought it necessary to meet the challenge by introducing a Bill which would make it illegal to pay more than twenty-one shillings in paper for a guinea, or to receive a note as worth less than its face value. This Bill to prevent the emergence of two prices was supported by the Goverment and became law. What the House of Commons had declared in supporting Vansittart's resolutions to be self-evident was thus enforced by law during the period of the Restriction.

The difference of opinion regarding the effects of the Restriction became even more acute after the war. According to the Restriction Act cash payments should have been resumed six months after the signing of a definitive treaty of peace. The Chancellor of the Exchequer announced in July, 1814, that the notes would become convertible in March of the following year. Lord Liverpool, however, made it clear on a subsequent occasion that his Government did not propose to take this step because of any evil effects of the Restriction; on the contrary, he asserted that it had been the means of bringing the country through the great contest with success and had proved its salvation. In February, as has already been noticed, Vansittart proposed a further extension of the Restriction Act. Horner protested against this course and was told by Vansittart that events had controverted all the opinions of the Bullion Committee. In November, 1816, the directors of the Bank decided to offer gold on demand to the holders of all notes dated earlier than 1812. But they did not continue this policy because a strong drain of bullion to the Continent supervened. Note-issue was again expanded and resumption seemed to be indefinitely postponed. Early in 1819, however, the two Houses of Parliament appointed Secret Committees to inquire into the condition of the Bank. It was arranged that the State should pay off £10,000,000 of Exchequer bills held by the Bank, and that in return the Restriction should completely lapse in 1823. Provision was made for redemption in the meanwhile of large quantities of notes in ingots of bullion at a fixed price in order to prevent a run for coin by holders of small notes. All these precautions proved unnecessary: the Bank sought and obtained permission to resume full cash payment on May 1st, 1821.

The effects of a depreciation of the currency followed by its restoration are clear enough when they are regarded in isolation. Lord King and all others who were obliged to accept payment in the depreciated paper stood to lose if they could not revise former agreements. Similarly, as M'Culloch pointed out, those who lent to the Government during the period of depreciation would gain by the resumption of cash payments. But the part which the Restriction played in the distress of the war and post-war years is more difficult to assess.[1] It is a curious fact that the Bullion Committee merely asserted that there had been a rise in prices, but took no evidence on the question. It was true that prices had risen during the period of Restriction. To what extent this was due to over-issue of paper money was not precisely ascertained. There were obviously other causes in operation. Even in 1810, apart from grain, there were marked indications of a fall in prices. It is well known that this movement became pronounced in 1814, and a steep and almost continuous fall occurred between the end of the war and the resumption of cash payments. Of course, prices might have fallen more had the currency been on a sound basis. The facts, however, go to show that it was misleading to assert that the over-issue was the main factor in price movements. Opponents of the Bullion Committee alleged war conditions as an explanation of the rise. This does not carry the argument to any practical conclusion without a full analysis of what war conditions mean. Joseph Lowe accused the framers of the Report of having no accurate knowledge of the increase of productive industry consequent on the war and the growth of population. He maintained that a large addition to the currency was indispensable to transact

---

[1] Ricardo asserted in the House in 1822 that " to recover from the depreciation the country had found it necessary to undergo a painful process which had been *the cause of a great part of the present distress.* Smart, " Economic Annals," Vol. II, p. 83. Lord Liverpool in 1822 stated that the depreciation of paper had been 25 per cent. in the last three years of the war. Smart, " Economic Annals," Vol. II, p. 71. In his " Present State of England " (1823), p. 56, Joseph Lowe put it at 15 per cent. " in the latter years of the war."

extended business and he minimised the effect of the Restriction. A fuller examination of the effects of war on prices was undertaken by Thomas Tooke in his "History of Prices." As far as the French war was concerned he insisted on the relation between the character of the seasons and the fluctuations of prices. His conclusion was that there were causes in operation, "arising out of the circumstances affecting the cost of production, and the supply of and demand for each commodity, which account fully for the great variations of prices . . . without having recourse to the supposition of alterations in the quantity of money as having been calculated to produce these effects."[1]

Reference has already been made to Vansittart's Budget of 1819;[2] he intended it to be the basis of the permanent peace establishment which his critics were always challenging him to produce. The loan from the Sinking Fund relieved the immediate pressure and left him with a true surplus of £2,000,000. He held, however, that it was essential to secure a balance of £5,000,000 annually for the Sinking Fund, and therefore proposed that a series of new taxes should be levied. These were all indirect—increases of customs duties on a number of articles, additions to the excises on malt, tobacco, and spirits—and proved a disappointment. The failure of the taxes coincided with the beginning of an irresistible demand for remissions. Although Vansittart felt forced to yield, he was quite unable to discover means of compensating the Exchequer for immediate losses.[3] In 1822 he introduced a complicated scheme by which an annual expenditure of £5,000,000 on officers' pensions, retired allowances, etc., was spread over forty-five years by means of annuities.

[1] Thomas Tooke, "History of Prices" (1838), Vol. I, p. 376. His demonstration that the consequences of the Restriction had been exaggerated was complete. M'Culloch was probably right, however, in maintaing that Tooke had pressed the effects of the seasons too far and was in danger of underestimating the part played by the currency. M'Culloch, "Literature of Political Economy," p. 196.

[2] *See* p. 40 *supra*.

[3] The position had been complicated by the consolidation of the Exchequers of Great Britain and Ireland in 1817. According to Article 7 of the Treaty of Union, Ireland was to pay the interest on and provide for the redemption of her pre-Union Debt. For

It was simply a device to lighten the present burden at the expense of the future, and, as was pointed out, both in fact and principle opposed to the Sinking Fund which was at the same time to receive £5,000,000 a year of supposed true surplus. The scheme was to save, nominally at any rate, £2,200,000, that is, this amount was to disappear from the headings of army, navy, and ordnance. But the balance on the £5,000,000 paid on pensions, etc., after this annual charge of £2,200,000 was subtracted, namely, £2,800,000 a year was vested in trustees for forty-five years and they were required to pay the pensions. This really meant that they had to borrow on the security of their future annuities until the pension charge had been considerably reduced by the death of the pensioners. The trustees would be able ultimately to pay off these loans, because after a certain point their annuity of £2,800,000 would exceed the total of pensions still payable. This was Vansittart's last expedient. In 1823 he was transferred to the Chancellorship of the Duchy of Lancaster and elevated to the Second Chamber as Lord Bexley. Already new principles were beginning to influence the Liverpool Administration, and some of its more advanced members were disposed to undertake important fiscal reforms.

---

twenty years following the Union the ordinary expenses of the United Kingdom were to be met jointly by Great Britain and Ireland in the proportion of 15 to 2. For the time the Exchequers were to remain distinct, and the Irish tax system was not to be assimilated to that of Great Britain. All debts incurred after the Union were to be regarded as joint debt and the charge was to be borne in the above proportions, viz., 15 to 2. The war upset these financial arrangements. The average Irish expenditure during the fifteen years before the war was £2,733,000; during the war it was £9,866,000. Less than half of the war expenditure was met by taxation. Ireland could only raise her proportion of the war costs by resorting to borrowing. The Irish Debt therefore grew from £32,215,000 to £112,634,000. By 1816 Irish liabilities under the settlement at the Union amounted to £11,200,000. The separate Irish revenue was less than half that sum. It was obvious that Ireland could not pay her way. Consequently arrangements were made for the consolidation of the Exchequers as from January, 1817. This meant that the revenue of the United Kingdom had to meet the annual deficit. Murray, "Commercial and Financial Relations between England and Ireland," pp. 332–4, 371–9.

(NOTE.—Figures are given to the nearest thousand, and 000's are omitted.)

Year (ending January 5th.)	Exchequer Receipts.	Exchequer Issues.	Surplus(+) or Deficiency (−).	Debt Charge.
	£000	£000	£000	£000
1823	55,664	53,710	+ 1,954	30,143
1824	57,673	56,223	+ 1,450	29,174
1825	59,362	59,232	+ 130	28,988
1826	57,274	61,520	− 4,246	29,415
1827	54,895	55,081	− 186	29,329
1828	54,933	55,787	− 854	29,168
1829	55,187	54,171	+ 1,016	29,068
1830	50,787	51,835	− 1,048	28,326
1831	50,057	49,078	+ 979	28,330
1832	46,424	49,797	− 3,373	28,351
1833	46,989	46,380	+ 609	28,481
1834	46,271	45,782	− 1,489	28,517
1835	46,425	46,678	− 253	29,136
1836	45,893	45,669	+ 224	29,667
1837	48,591	48,093	+ 498	29,537
1838	46,475	49,117	− 2,642	29,433
1839	47,333	47,686	− 353	29,385
1840	47,845	49,358	− 1,513	29,416
1841	47,568	49,162	− 1,594	29,382

(From the "Fourth Report from the Select Committee on Public Income and Expenditure, 1828," the "Return of the Whole Amount of the National Debt, 1691–1857," and "Finance Returns.")

CHAPTER III

A TRANSITIONAL PERIOD—1823–1841

THE seven years immediately following the war exhibit the magnitude of the financial problem which it had bequeathed. Deprived from the outset of the assistance of the income tax, the Chancellor of the Exchequer had been forced to rely on one expedient after another to meet special difficulties as they arose. It was essentially makeshift finance without the slightest indication of a considered policy. The burden of war indebtedness remained. The taxational system, which had to supply the means of reducing it, was unreformed. It was a clumsy instrument, inflicting considerable damage on the community, but of little service to the Chancellor if he wished to increase the revenue. From about 1820 indeed two lines of criticism had begun to make some impression on public opinion. It was dogmatically asserted that the distress of the period was to be traced directly to taxation. It was also claimed that the restrictions on commerce, involved in the complicated tariff, prevented the recovery of industry. These criticisms, although they would both lead to a demand for the remission of taxes, are to be distinguished from one another. The first was particularly associated with the distress in agriculture and took the form of agitating for the repeal of certain taxes; the second embodied a doctrine, namely, the free trade principle that unfettered enterprise would promote prosperity. This the agricultural interest denied. Consequently, while there was a superficial agreement in favour of reduction of taxation, there was a fundamental opposition which was bound ultimately to emerge. The Corn Law of 1815 was intended to guarantee the position of agriculture by protecting it against foreign competition. Any relaxation of the protective system would inevitably raise the whole question of the relative position of agriculture and industry, for if the farmer preserved the home market for his products the manufacturer would find it difficult to gain access to foreign markets.

For the moment, however, there was substantial agreement in favour of reducing taxation. The case of the agricultural interests is simpler and may be taken first. Complaints of distress had been almost continuous since 1815 in spite of the Corn Law. It will be remembered that no foreign wheat was admitted until the home price had reached 80s. a quarter. This price was supposed to be remunerative if wheat were grown on inferior soil, that is, to afford good profits on better land. The farmers, however, seem to have expected an average annual price in the neighbourhood of 80s. The experience of three or four years strengthened their conviction that war conditions were to continue in time of peace. The area under cultivation was well maintained and rents remained high. Then a succession of good harvests revealed the fact that the Corn Law did not prevent a fall in prices. In 1819 and 1820 the home supply, including the heavy shipments from Ireland, caused a glut. A monopoly will not secure uniformly high prices for those who enjoy it if they cannot regulate the supply. The farmers were in the position that an abundant harvest was a disaster to them ; the vagaries of climate being beyond their control. Still a demand was made for more effective protection by raising the price at which importation was to be allowed, a measure which would only accentuate the difficulty by widening the range of speculative farming. It could not safeguard the farmer against a fall in prices in a good year, while it would induce him to resort to inferior land in anticipation of a possible bad year. This meant an increased cost which necessitated high prices. Was it possible to keep inferior soils under the plough by means of an improved Corn Law ? If possible, was it worth while to do so ? The Government, under the influence of the new economic teaching, was inclined to answer both questions in the negative. In 1821, however, in answer to innumerable petitions, it consented to the appointment of a Committee to inquire into the distress of the agricultural interest. Its Report stated that the petitioners were right in asserting that at the existing price of corn the farmer was not adequately remunerated. The explanation was to be found in the high rents, investment of capital in cultivating the waste, and the depression of prices following the return to cash payments. In these circumstances good harvests were ruinous because the farmer's charges exceeded his income. Fluctuations in supply were inevitable and the question was how their effect could be minimised. The Corn Law of 1815, prohibiting the importation of wheat until it reached 80s. and then allowing unlimited foreign competition, certainly did not make for stability of prices. The abandonment of prohibition in favour of a fixed duty recommended itself to the Committee as a sounder principle, but it was not prepared to support its immediate adoption. It is clear that the reasoning of Ricardo and Huskisson had made a strong impression on the Committee.[1] The expression of the doubt whether the prosperity of agriculture was really promoted by prohibition or protection, and the statement that causes were in operation over which legislation could have no control indicate the force of their arguments.

The Committee was a disappointment to the agriculturists. They had clung to the idea that in some way or other the area under cultivation would be maintained—any reduction they regarded as a national disaster—but there now seemed no alternative to making adjustments, including the revision of rents. This led them to throw all their weight in 1822 into the agitation for the repeal of taxes

[1] The Committee included Castlereagh, Robinson, Althorp, Brougham, Huskisson, Parnell, Western and Ricardo. The landed interest ascribed the authorship of the Report to Huskisson and Ricardo, but in some important respects it departed from their opinions. When Huskisson was taxed in the House with being the author he admitted that he had submitted resolutions to the Committee, and, after they had been discussed and amended, he had been asked to draw up the Report. Smart, "Economic Annals," Vol. II, p. 68.

as a means of relief. William Cobbett, who had been denouncing heavy taxation ever since the return to peace, found himself supported by Tory landowners and farmers. He encouraged them to send up petitions, and practically all of them condemned "the overwhelming and all-devouring taxation," as it was called in the widely-noticed Kent petition. An amendment to the address was moved by Joseph Hume,[1] who had now constituted himself the great opponent of taxation, against excessive charges out of all proportion to the reduced value of property. Henry Brougham attempted to detach the country gentry from the Government by tracing the agricultural distress to its financial incompetence. To these criticisms Castlereagh (now Marquis of Londonderry) replied, denying that the distress was so widespread as was alleged, and asserting that the total remission of taxation would not eliminate such distress as did exist. Still he announced economies in public expenditure and the reduction of the malt tax. He also suggested that the Committee of the previous year should be reconstituted. Its second Report was confined to practical proposals for the relief of distress. Although it considered the idea of purchasing the surplus corn by means of Exchequer bills and storing it, the principle of making the Government a dealer in corn was regarded as a dangerous precedent. But it found no objection to inviting farmers to deposit part of their stock in warehouses and advancing money to them on the security of it until prices would recover. It was also recommended that the Corn Law of 1815 should be amended so that wheat should be imported when the price reached 70s. on the payment of a duty which would range from 15s. to 1s. as the price rose from 70s. to 85s. The proposal to make advances on stored corn was withdrawn by the Govern-

[1] Joseph Hume (1777–1855) studied medicine and went to India as a surgeon in the service of the East India Company. He first entered Parliament in 1812 and became leader of the Radicals. His view was that "the more money that was left in the pockets of the people, the stronger would be the Government and the more secure the public credit." It is said that he employed a staff of clerks to analyse the returns of public expenditure.

ment when it met with some opposition in the House. The amendment of the Corn Law, with certain modifications, was accepted and incorporated in the Corn Law of 1822. But a proviso was added that the new Act was not to begin to operate until the home price reached the old level of 80s.; and the consequence of this was that it remained a dead letter, for, in the following years, this price was not reached. The result of the agitation for reduction of taxation was reflected in Vansittart's last Budget with its conversion of the Navy 5 per cents. and the spreading of the pensions charge over a term of years.[1] He was thus enabled to make considerable reductions in the salt and leather taxes. But the presumption in favour of the repeal and reduction of taxes had now become so strong that much more extensive reforms were necessary.

Meanwhile, depression of trade had stimulated a discussion of possible means of re-establishing it on sounder principles. A lead was given by the notable Petition which was drafted by Thomas Tooke for certain London merchants. It laid down principles which are at the basis of free trade: for example, "that freedom from restraint is calculated to give the utmost extension to foreign trade, and the best direction to the capital and industry of the country," and "that the maxim of buying in the cheapest market and selling in the dearest, which regulates every merchant in his individual dealings, is strictly applicable as the best rule for the trade of the whole nation."[2] It called for an investigation into the effects of the restrictive system, as the petitioners believed that it would be found that the distress was aggravated by its operation. The Government received the Petition sympathetically. In the House of Commons Robinson, the President of the

---

[1] *See* pp. 44 and 52-3 *supra*.

[2] The whole of the Merchants' Petition is printed in Smart's "Economic Annals," Vol. I, pp. 744–7, and with slight omissions in Bland, Brown and Tawney, "English Economic History: Select Documents," pp. 698–701. Thomas Tooke (1774–1858) was the author of the "History of Prices," already noticed. He was associated with Ricardo, Malthus, James Mill and others in founding the Political Economy Club in 1821.

Board of Trade, admitted the soundness of the principles it laid down, but pointed out that any change of the commercial system must be gradual. In moving for a Committee in the Lords, Lansdowne ventured to indicate directions in which reforms might be effected. He thought that there ought to be no prohibition or prohibitory duties, that the Navigation Laws ought to be relaxed, and that the duties on timber and silk ought to be revised. To this Liverpool replied that, while unrestricted trade was desirable, it could not be easily attained. Foreign countries would not give any reciprocal advantages so long as their agricultural produce was virtually excluded. They would say, "Admit our agricultural produce and we will admit your manufactures." The country had risen to its present greatness under a restrictive system. Some supposed it had done so in consequence of the system, but he personally agreed with those who thought that it was in spite of it. Still it was utterly impossible with the present debt and taxation suddenly to adopt the principle of free trade. Relaxations in certain directions might perhaps be feasible.

The two Houses appointed Committees on Foreign Trade to explore the whole question. Robinson[1] and Huskisson[2] were on the Commons' Committee and its Report favoured the concession to manufacturers and merchants of "as unlimited a freedom from all interference as may be compatible with what is due to private vested interests that have grown up under the existing system." It recommended a complete revision of the mass of legislation which enforced the restrictions, and a relaxation of the Navigation Laws. The way of the reformers, however, was beset by two formidable obstacles. There was the fear that the revenue would suffer if any

---

[1] Frederick John Robinson (1782–1859) became Viscount Goderich in 1827 and Earl of Ripon in 1833, *see* pp. 72 and 91, and *infra*.

[2] William Huskisson (1770–1830) had attracted some attention by the publication of his "Depreciation of the Currency" in 1810. His loyalty to Canning to some extent retarded his career. He represented Liverpool in the House of Commons. His death was due to an accident at the opening of the Liverpool and Manchester Railway.

extensive changes were made, for there seemed to be no means of guaranteeing the Exchequer against any temporary loss. Then there were the powerful interests which had entrenched themselves behind the restrictions and would suffer from their removal. This issue was raised by the first attempt of the Government to give effect to the new policy. It was proposed that the timber duties should be revised. During the Napoleonic Wars heavy duties had been laid on timber from the Baltic—which was then the chief source of supply—in favour of the North American possessions. These duties had become practically prohibitive and consequently the timber trade had been diverted to Canada. There were strong colonial interests involved as well as those of British shipowners who were engaged in the carrying trade. The Government wished to lower the duties so that, while the colonists enjoyed a certain measure of protection, the consumer might have a fair opportunity of buying the superior kinds of timber which came from the Baltic. It was not a proposal that the convinced free traders could be enthusiastic about because it hardly went far enough. But, moderate as it was, it was bitterly fought by the interests concerned. The Government, however, succeeded in carrying their Bill. In the following year the revision of the Navigation Laws was undertaken. They were intended to encourage the growth of English shipping. As far back as the reign of Richard II the attempt had been made to limit the carrying trade to native vessels. In practice this restriction had constantly to be relaxed to meet the requirements of other interests. The seventeenth century witnessed such an expansion of the maritime power of Holland that the old policy was revived and strengthened with the purpose of countering it. Goods were only to be imported into England in English and colonial ships, or in those of the country of origin. Since the Dutch were mainly carriers, the aim of these provisions was perfectly obvious. Contemporaries differed as to whether the purpose was being achieved, but it is now generally agreed that little or no damage was actually done to the Dutch. The Acts, however, were retained and elaborated, particularly with respect to the colonial trade. Adam Smith, as is well known, approved of the Navigation Acts as a device dictated by considerations of national defence. He made it quite clear that they were unfavourable to the development of foreign trade and he condemned their operation as far as the colonies were concerned. It was possible for Huskisson to contend that the political argument in favour of the system was no longer relevant. He proposed to make a number of modifications in the Acts, repealing the clauses which had fallen into disuse, consolidating more recent regulations, and relaxing the rule that foreign ships should only carry to this country the produce or manufactures of their own. His main object was to substitute the principle of reciprocity for that of prohibition by entering into agreements with other States on the basis of mutual concessions.

Events now conspired to give the exponents of more liberal views a dominating influence in the Liverpool Ministry. In August Londonderry committed suicide and Canning succeeded him at the Foreign Office. Sidmouth had retired from the Home Office earlier in the year and Robert Peel took his place. When Vansittart resigned the Exchequer, Robinson was promoted from the Board of Trade to the Chancellorship, and the vacancy thus created was filled by the appointment of Huskisson. Robinson was an aristocrat, good-natured and liberal-minded, but not possessed of the higher qualities of leadership. The promotion of Canning, Peel, and Huskisson, however, strengthened an important element in the Government; they were not merely enlightened, each understood the point of view of the new industrial middle class better than the older statesmen did. Canning's attention was for the time concentrated on questions of foreign policy in which he vigorously asserted Great Britain's independence of action against reactionary forces on the Continent. His brilliancy contrasted sharply with the more solid qualities of Peel, who was slowly building up a reputation by the competent discharge of his official duties. His name was mostly associated with the Act of 1819, which required the resumption of cash payments—

for, characteristically enough, he had promoted the Bill and publicly acknowledged that the vote he had given against Horner's resolutions in 1811 was a mistake. For the present he devoted himself to the reform of the criminal law, a task which was much overdue. Huskisson's opinions had been well advertised in the discussions of the last two years. He combined a firm grasp of the principles of the new political economy with an unrivalled knowledge of trade and commerce. As a parliamentarian he was not a striking success, for his voice and manner were against him. But, when the circumstances of the time are considered, his achievements in the next four years are a great testimony to his strength of purpose and ability to conciliate opposition.

Huskisson's reforms constitute the first phase of the movement towards free trade. It must not be supposed, however, that he was a thorough-going free trader.[1] There was ample scope for reforming the tariff by abolishing prohibitions and reducing duties to reasonable proportions without raising fundamental issues. Huskisson was in favour of retaining a degree of protection, for manufactures at any rate; and, even had he not been, the profession of any desire to break completely with the protective system would have jeopardised his prospects of attaining the immediate objects he had in view. His ideas had, for the most part, to find expression through the annual financial expositions with which it was Robinson's practice to prepare the way for his Budget statements.

---

[1] This is put very well by Sir Henry Parnell in his treatise "On Financial Reform": "No greater error can be made than supposing that Mr. Huskisson established free trade in this country. In his speeches in 1825, he certainly proclaimed and proved the policy of this system; but he did no more than strike a balance between the Free Traders and the Prohibitionists in taking a duty of 30 per cent. as the standard of regulation. . . . He uniformly maintained that the rates of duty he selected were high enough to prevent the foreign from coming into competition with the English manufacturer. . . . It must not, however, be forgotten that he was, in a great measure, forced into this course by the prejudices and interests he had to deal with." Parnell, "On Financial Reform," Fourth Edition, 1832, pp. 72–3.

The co-operation between the two appears to have been complete. They were undoubtedly fortunate in that their accession to office happened to coincide with a great improvement in trade and industry—even the perennial complaint of depression in agriculture was almost hushed in 1824—and consequently opinion was better disposed towards innovations. The Budget of 1823 must be regarded as a preliminary survey of the field in order to find a foundation for the new schemes. Robinson put in the forefront reduction in the burden of taxation, which was made possible by economies in expenditure and the prospective improvement in the yield of the taxes due to returning prosperity. He estimated that there would be a surplus of over £7,000,000, and proposed to set aside £5,000,000 for reduction of debt and to remit taxes to the extent of the balance. These remissions were confined to the Assessed Taxes and amounted to a reduction of 50 per cent. on windows, horses, carriages and servants in Great Britain, while these taxes were completely repealed in Ireland. Robinson's exposition was well received in the House, though some of his critics suggested that he would have done greater immediate service to the country if he had used the whole surplus for the relief of taxation. His contention was that an efficient Sinking Fund was necessary to maintain the public credit. Consequently, he proposed to abandon the recent practice of paying over a large sum to a nominal Sinking Fund and then diverting it to other purposes. The principle of Pitt's original scheme was to be restored in its purity, namely, the sum was to be handed to the Commissioners to be expended quarterly in purchasing stock, which they were to hold until the interest on it amounted to 1 per cent. on the total debt.

By 1824 Robinson and Huskisson had matured their plans. The Budget proposals were original and far-reaching. Apart from the £5,000,000 for the reduction of debt there was a surplus of £1,450,000 on the past year, and there was likely to be a similar surplus of £1,052,000 in the coming year.[1] He intended to augment this by (1)

[1] Part of the surplus was due to the payment of £2,500,000 by the Emperor in discharge of the Austrian Loan (*see* p. 19 *supra*). As

effecting a conversion of the 4 per cents. to 3½ per cents., thus saving an annual charge of £375,000, (2) by allowing the bounties on whale-fishing and fish-curing to lapse at the end of the year, and (3) by providing for the gradual extinction of the linen bounties. Instead of using this surplus for the reduction of the debt, he proposed to give precedence to the remission of taxation by employing it "as a means of commencing a system of alteration in the fiscal and commercial regulations of the country." In the first place, he announced an important change with regard to wool. There had long been a prohibition on the export of raw wool in order to ensure an ample supply for the home industry. The farmers naturally complained of this restriction, but their interest was to some extent consulted by the imposition of a duty of a penny a pound on imported wool. In 1819 Vansittart had raised the duty to sixpence to give them more effective protection. Robinson's proposal rather cleverly met the demands of both parties by means of a compromise; the duty on the import of foreign wool was reduced to the original figure of one penny to suit the manufacturers, while the farmers were given the right of export on the payment of the same charge. A long-standing prohibition on export was thus removed, and foreign wool was admitted on the same conditions as home wool was exported. This arrangement was accepted without serious opposition. Secondly, Robinson grappled with the much more contentious question of the protection afforded to the silk industry. It was admitted to be the extreme example of an industry maintained by artificial means.[1] There were duties on the importation of raw silk, thrown silk was highly protected, and the importation

this was a windfall it was devoted to special purposes, including the building of the National Gallery. The Emperor's debt, capital and interest, was estimated at £22,000,000. His "bankruptcy" was the subject of much comment.

[1] In a review of the state of industry, Lord Liverpool had, in 1820, expressed the wish that there had never been a silk manufactory in England for it was completely artificial, but, as there was much capital invested in it and it employed 50,000 persons, he could not see how it could be abandoned. Smart, "Economic Annals," Vol. I, p. 754.

or use of foreign manufactured silk goods was strictly prohibited by law. The Government wished to reduce the duties on the importation of raw and thrown silk—a step which would, of course, meet with the approval of the manufacturers—but it combined with this a proposal that silk goods should be admitted on the payment of a duty of 30 per cent. *ad valorem*. There was an immediate outcry. The industry, it was alleged, was peculiarly in need of a monopoly of the home market. It was exotic and enjoyed no natural advantages. France would prove a formidable rival, partly because labour and the cost of living were much cheaper there, and partly because fashion would certainly show a preference for the finer French fabrics if they could be obtained. To these arguments Huskisson replied himself. Cotton, he pointed out, was exotic, but it had made phenomenal progress since it had been freed from restrictions. It had also led the way in adopting new inventions. That the silk industry could not compete with the French trade was due to the monopoly it had enjoyed, for that had "a chilling and benumbing effect" on enterprise. Fashion certainly did show a preference and the result was the wholesale smuggling of French goods into the country.[1] This evil, which represented nothing but loss to the revenue, would be removed by the admission of the goods at a reasonable rate. In the end it was agreed that the reduction of the import duty on raw material should be adopted at once, while the prohibition on the import of manufactured goods should not be removed until July, 1826, so that the manufacturers might have an opportunity of preparing for competition.

In 1825 Robinson was able to announce that the reforms of the previous year so far from involving the Exchequer in loss had been followed by the yield of a larger surplus than he had expected. He proposed to use it with a view to the extension of commerce, restriction of smuggling,

[1] Robinson drew the attention of the House to the fact that Joseph Hume had "produced his bandana handkerchief even in this place, and, having triumphantly unfurled the standard of smuggling, blew his nose in it, and deliberately returned it to his pocket."

and the relief of the burden of direct taxation. The prohibitory duty on the import of bar iron was reduced and the high duties on hemp, coffee, cocoa, and wines were moderated. The Assessed Taxes were simplified by dropping a number of unimportant items, and poorer householders were relieved by the remission of the Inhabited House Duty on houses below £10 rental, and of the Window Duty on houses of not more than seven windows. Huskisson himself dealt with the Government's commercial proposals. He took up, first, the question of Colonial Policy and met the criticism that the colonial establishments were a burden on the Mother Country by adumbrating a new attitude towards the Colonies. He held that the monopoly principle must be abandoned, because the restrictions on colonial trade were harmful both to Great Britain and the Colonies. All friendly foreign states were to be allowed to trade directly with the Colonies, their imports to pay duties which would afford a measure of preference to the products of the Mother Country and yield a revenue to the Colonies. Second, he dealt with British protective duties in a comprehensive way. Taking the most important industries he examined what protection they had, and suggested a lowering of the tariff in each case. Cotton, although Britain had no serious rival, was actually protected by import duties ranging from 50 to 75 per cent.; this was reduced to a uniform duty of 10 per cent. on all cotton manufactured goods. Wool was given a protective duty of 15, and linen of 25 per cent. In no case was an article to have a higher protective duty than 30 per cent.[1]

[1] In consequence the codification of the Customs laws had to be undertaken. It was performed by James Deacon Hume. "Mr. Hume's labour was the greatest codification of Customs law that had ever been attempted. It is thus described in the first Customs Report: 'The importance and utility of the work can never be sufficiently appreciated. In a short time it will cease to be known that in the interval between the 1st and 53rd, George III, there were 1,300 laws of the Customs passed, whereof 600 passed in the eighteen years between 1797 and 1815. In June, 1815, there were 1,100 Customs Acts in force. All these, with the additions between 1815 and 1825 were repealed on July 5th, 1825, by one Act (6 Geo. IV., c. 105), in which 443 Statutes were enumerated and the rest

The argument for this maximum was cogently stated. "If the article be not manufactured much cheaper or much better abroad than at home, such a duty is ample protection. If it be manufactured so much cheaper, or so much better abroad, as to render £30 per cent. insufficient, my answer is, firstly, that a greater protection is only a premium to the smuggler; and, secondly, that there is no wisdom in attempting to bolster up a competition which this degree of protection will not sustain. Let the State have the tax, which is now the reward of the smuggler, and let the consumer have a better and cheaper article, without the painful consciousness that he is consulting his own convenience at the expense of daily violating the laws of his country."

The chief plea in favour of the removal of restrictions on commerce—and also in favour of Government economy and reduction of taxation—was that individual enterprise should enjoy greater freedom, the assumption being that by this means the prosperity and well-being of the country would be promoted. The very remarkable recovery in 1823, followed by the feverish activity of 1824 and 1825, seemed to be an immediate justification of the new policy of the Government. Ministers were inclined to regard it in this light and therefore were slow to realise that there were real dangers ahead. There can be no doubt that there was in the country a considerable amount of capital seeking investment. It had been augmented by the remission of taxation and also by the successive conversions of Government stock which tended to make fund-holders seek more profitable openings for their money elsewhere. Commercial reforms tended to stimulate foreign trade, the Continental States were recovering from the effects of the long wars, and the recent establishment of the independent Latin Republics of South America seemed to open up prospects of most lucrative speculation. At the same time the

---

repealed by a general definition; thus sweeping away all the laws of the Customs accumulated during the space of 550 years.'" "Customs Tariffs of the United Kingdom," 1800–1897, C. 8706 (1897), p. 38.

progress of the Industrial Revolution called for large capital outlay at home; not only were the new machine industries rapidly developing, but the ports needed docks, and already about £14,000,000 had been invested in canal and navigation schemes.[1] In these circumstances everything depended on the direction which investment would take and the ability of the credit economy to stand the strain of extensive operations.

The direction which investments took was governed by the special inducements of the moment, and was, unfortunately, not controlled by the normal amount of prudence. When the speculative mania was at its worst the companies which promised an early and large return were preferred to those of a more solid nature. Large sums were invested in foreign loans, and companies to promote mining in Mexico, Chili, Peru and Brazil were especially favoured. The most optimistic opinions of the quantities of manufactured articles which could be disposed of inspired increased production and purely speculative trans-shipment to likely markets. In 1825 all the characteristics of a trade boom emerged: credit was inflated, prices rose, and the exchanges became unfavourable. The inevitable collapse came in December; the failure of Sir Peter Pole & Co. beginning a panic which involved nearly seventy banks.[2] The drain of gold for shipment abroad had so depleted the reserve of the Bank of England that it suggested a restriction on payment. To this the Government was opposed and, with the support of London merchants who declared their confidence in its solvency, the Bank faced and weathered the crisis by freely discounting all solid bills offered to it. When Parliament assembled in 1826 it was expected to relieve the existing distress and take precautions against any future disaster of the same nature. The demand that the Government should advance loans on security in the form of Exchequer bills was resisted by the Ministry, but an

[1] E. A. Pratt: "History of Inland Transport and Communications in England," p. 234.

[2] Peter Pole & Co. acted as agents for about forty country banks.

arrangement was made with the Bank of England by which it agreed to lend assistance to individuals against goods and other securities, and this proved sufficient to restore confidence. It was one thing to have averted complete disaster by emergency measures, it was another to lay down principles which would prevent it occurring again. A remedy must be based on a complete analysis of the causes. This was hardly possible, for the ramifications of the movement defied precise statement. The most obvious feature was the general spirit of unreasoning speculation. How could this be restrained in the future? The Government's answer was simple. Speculation had been fostered, supported and encouraged by the country banks with their excessive issue of one-pound notes. It was therefore necessary to place banking on a firmer foundation and to forbid the issue of notes for low denominations. The Government held that the credit system was inadequately organised to meet the requirements of the country, the restriction of country banks to six partners allowing "any small tradesman, a cheesemonger, a butcher, or a shoemaker, to open a country bank, while persons with a fortune sufficient to carry on the concern were not permitted to do so."[1] Any modification of this rule meant a departure from the monopoly enjoyed by the Bank of England, and could not be forced upon that institution until its Charter was due to be renewed. In the end, however, a compromise was arranged by which the six partners restriction was removed on condition that the Bank of England should retain its rights within a radius of sixty-five miles of London. This understanding was embodied in an Act (7 Geo. IV, c. 46), and the foundation of joint-stock banks with the right of note-issue became possible. The alleged danger of one-pound notes was met by forbidding the circulation of notes for less than five pounds.[2]

---

[1] Lord Liverpool's statement, *see* Smart, "Economic Annals," Vol. II, p. 350.

[2] The proposal to extend the prohibition to Scotland was strenuously resisted by Sir Walter Scott. Under the pseudonym of Malachi Malagrowther he wrote to the *Edinburgh Weekly Journal* ridiculing the passion for uniformity in the two kingdoms.

The question was also raised whether the terms of the Bank Charter Act of 1742 made it impossible to establish joint-stock banks in London itself, provided they were not banks of issue. The London private banks confined themselves to deposit banking,[1] and it was contended that such banks might become joint-stock without any infringement of the privileges of the Bank of England. The Act of 1826 did not settle this question. An agitation in favour of the reform was maintained until the Bank Act of 1833 fully recognised the claim. The exclusive privileges of the Bank of England applied to it as a bank of issue. In the next year the first London deposit joint-stock bank—the London and Westminster—was founded.

The crisis of 1825 naturally encouraged the opponents of Huskisson's policy to accuse him of precipitating it by pursuing a mistaken course. He was urged to take advantage of the fact that the prohibition on the import of manufactured silk goods had not yet been removed to abandon that measure. To this special plea he replied that there was no reason to believe that the silk industry had suffered more than others in the depression, and the Government did not propose to return to the principle of prohibition which it had been destroying. He recalled to the memory of the House the underlying basis of the recent reforms by reading the Merchants' Petition, which he insisted did not emanate from the much disparaged economists but from practical men of high standing in the commercial world. The maximum protective duty of 30 per cent. was sufficient in the hardest cases, and he did not intend to accept any revisions. This firm attitude defeated the instinctive reaction against the recent reforms and disappointed the hopes of the vested interests. The manufacturers, however, could retaliate by challenging the Government to relieve the general distress by modifying the Corn Laws. Why should prohibition of imports be maintained in this case and not in others? Huskisson answered

[1] The cheque and deposit system had become well established among London private bankers in the course of the eighteenth century.

that there was not time to go into the whole question of the Corn Laws that session. The Prime Minister, however, sought special power for the King in Council to deal with any emergency in view of the approaching dissolution of Parliament. The main question was thus shelved. In September an Order in Council threw open the ports to cereals, other than wheat, at a fixed duty. The new Parliament—the General Election had taken place in July and had returned the Government to office—was summoned in November to confirm the action of the executive. Liverpool promised that in the following year the Corn Laws themselves would be considered.

On February 17th, 1827, Lord Liverpool had a sudden seizure from the effects of which he never recovered. The Ministry which he had so long held together showed immediate signs of dissolution. It fell to Canning to introduce the new Corn Bill. Taking the averages for past years the Government came to the conclusion that 60s. was the price which it should aim at securing. The proposal therefore was that a protective duty of 24s. 8d. should be imposed when the price stood at 60s., the duty rising by 2s. for every shilling fall in price, and falling by 2s. for every shilling rise in price up to 70s., after which wheat was to enter on paying a registration duty of 1s. only. In spite of strong opposition the Bill passed the Commons, but the Government was defeated in the Lords on an amendment moved by the Duke of Wellington. Robinson, who had been created Lord Goderich and appointed Secretary for the Colonies in the Canning Adminstration, intimated that the Bill would be dropped.[1] A Bill of a temporary nature was then substituted, the subject to come up for discussion in 1828. Canning, who had been struggling against ill-health for some months died on August 8th at the age of fifty-seven. Goderich

[1] Canning formed a Ministry in April, but he failed to retain the distinctively Tory elements, Eldon, Wellington and Peel refusing to serve under him. Huskisson, always a loyal follower of Canning, remained at the Board of Trade; Canning himself filled the office of Chancellor of the Exchequer. He secured the co-operation of the Whigs.

tried to hold the Ministry together, but abandoned the task before Parliament reassembled. The Duke of Wellington was then induced to form an administration of a predominantly Tory nature, though Huskisson and three other Canningites agreed to join him. It was announced in the King's Speech that the new Ministry intended to fulfil the promise made by Canning, and introduce a Corn Bill on the same principles as that of the previous session. It is a tribute to Huskisson's strength of purpose that the Wellington Administration should have made itself responsible for a Bill which incorporated his idea of a sliding-scale. That the scale should be more definitely protective than that proposed in 1827 was the price he had to pay for his success. When home wheat stood at 66s. the duty was to be 20s. 8d., rising by one shilling as the price fell by that amount, and falling by one shilling for every shilling rise in price to 66s., then by two shillings to 69s., by three shillings to 71s., and by four shillings to 73s., when it became 1s. The Bill was passed without amendment, and thus became the Corn Law against which the great Anti-Corn Law agitation was launched ten years later.[1] Huskisson saw the Bill through

[1] The Act 9 Geo. IV, c. 60, repealed that of 1815 and established the following sliding scale:

When the average home price of *Wheat* was:				Bill of 1827
66/– and under	67/–	the duty was to be	20/8 a quarter.	(12/8)
67/– ,, ,,	68/–	,, ,,	18/8 ,,	(10/8)
68/– ,, ,,	69/–	,, ,,	16/8 ,,	(6/8)
69/– ,, ,,	70/–	,, ,,	13/8 ,,	(4/8)
70/– ,, ,,	71/–	,, ,,	10/8 ,,	(2/8)
71/– ,, ,,	72/–	,, ,,	6/8 ,,	(1/–)
72/– ,, ,,	73/–	,, ,,	2/8 ,,	
at and above	73/–	,, ,,	1/– ,,	

When the price was under 66/– the duty was to be increased from 20/8 by 1/– for every shilling or part of a shilling in the fall. Similar sliding scales were drawn up for barley, oats, rye, pease and beans. The weekly average prices were to be sent to the officers of the Customs at each port, and on these the duties were to be assessed.

The differences between the Act of 1828 and the Bill which was defeated in 1827 are shown in brackets. In the Bill, however, the duty was to be increased by 2/– for every fall in the price below 66/–, i.e., when the price was 52/– the duty would have been 40/8.

the Commons, but differences with his colleagues led him to vote against the Government on a question of transferring a borough franchise, and formally to submit his resignation to the Duke. Wellington, who found the Canningites troublesome, promptly accepted it.

The passing of the Corn Law of 1828 marks the end of the movement initiated and guided by Huskisson. Henry Goulbourn,[1] Wellington's Chancellor of the Exchequer, returned to the narrower questions of financial reform, in which he was assisted by the appointment of a new Finance Committee. His most notable achievement was the repeal of all previous legislation dealing with the Sinking Fund—thus sweeping away the last remnants of Pitt's scheme—and the foundation of what came to be known as the Old Sinking Fund, based on the actual realised surplus of each year.[2] The promises of recovery in 1827 were disappointed, and by 1829 there were complaints of general and acute distress. Economy was urged upon the Ministry from all sides. Goulbourn effected considerable reductions in the charges of the Army and Navy and also in the Civil Service estimates. In 1830 he admitted that he was faced by the alternative of meeting the persistent demands for remission of taxes, either by reductions of existing taxes, which would represent an absolute loss to the Exchequer, or by

---

[1] Henry Goulbourn (1784–1856) had been Irish Secretary and, like Peel, he resigned on the succession of Canning. He was Home Secretary in Peel's 1834 ministry. In 1841 he returned to the Exchequer, but the fact that Peel introduced the important Budgets himself tended to obscure Goulburn's achievements. He was an intimate friend of Peel and supported him loyally in the crisis of 1845–6.

[2] This form of Sinking Fund was recommended in the "Fourth Report from the Select Committe on Public Income and Expenditure: 1828," pp. 23–5. The Committee expressed the opinion that it was a sound policy to apply "a surplus revenue perseveringly" to the reduction of the Debt. They added that they would have recommended that the resolution made in 1819, that £5,000,000 should be annually devoted to this object, should be persisted in, had not experience shown that it involved additional borrowing. There was no clear surplus to that amount, nor any immediate prospect of such a surplus arising. Consequently, they fell back on the realised surplus and abandoned the idea of a fixed amount.

a redistribution of the burden, which might be effected through a tax on income or property. The Government had decided against the latter course, though Goulbourn was careful not to condemn the principle. His problem was how to give relief to those who most needed it without seriously impairing the yield of the taxes. He had to weigh the interests of the Exchequer against those of the taxpayers, that is, he had to decide what remissions would be likely to be most beneficial to the latter, while he was precluded from seeking compensation for loss to the former by imposing a new tax. Consequently he fixed upon indirect taxes which fell on articles generally consumed, and the cost of collection of which took much more out of the pockets of the consumers than reached the Exchequer. He announced that the tax on beer would be entirely repealed; this involved a loss of £3,000,000 to the Exchequer, but amounted to much greater relief to the taxpayers as the restrictions on manufacture and the expenses of collection would lapse with it. The same considerations applied to the duty on cider and the surviving portion of the leather tax. In all he estimated that he was giving real relief to the extent of £5,000,000 at the cost of about £3,500,000. The Chancellor's statement suggested—though he did not follow up the idea—that the time was come for the equalisation of taxation. In the discussion however, the old sectional view, that each tax should be considered on its merits and not as part of a general scheme for distributing the burden according to ability to pay, still predominated. The objection was made that reduction of the debt should take precedence of further remission of taxes. But Althorp reiterated his opinion that the debt was a perpetual charge which the State had to meet each year and not a capital amount to be paid off.[1] He was becoming, through his membership of the Finance Committee, the leading spokesman of the Whigs on financial questions. His contention was, that

[1] Althorp had expressed this opinion in 1825. Smart, "Economic Annals," Vol. II, p. 270. John Charles Spencer, Viscount Althorp, (1782-1845) succeeded to Earldom in 1834.

any surplus should be employed to reduce taxation, a process which would be followed by the increased yield of the taxes retained through the greater prosperity of the country. Goulbourn, however, succeeded in reducing the debt charge by means of a conversion of the 4 per cents. which had been created in 1822. They now became 3½ per cents., irredeemable for ten years. The operation involved about £175,000,000, and the claims of the dissentients did not come to more than £3,000,000.

The Wellington Administration sealed its fate by its declaration of opposition to Parliamentary reform. It was defeated in November, 1830, on a motion of Sir Henry Parnell for a Select Committee to inquire into the details of the Civil List. Earl Grey consented to form a Ministry on condition that Parliamentary reform was undertaken, and the Whigs at last returned to power. Their financial policy was one of retrenchment and was destined to prove to be the weakest side of their work. Althorp, who now became Chancellor of the Exchequer, had already fully expressed his views in the House of Commons, and he had the assistance of Poulett Thomson,[1] who was appointed Vice-President of the Board of Trade, in attempting to put them into practice. Poulett Thomson combined experience as a merchant with knowledge of the teaching of Ricardo and had more than once made a valuable contribution to the discussion of financial questions. They were both greatly influenced by the opinions of Sir Henry Parnell, who had been Chairman of the Finance Committee. He published in 1830 his comprehensive treatise "On Financial Reform," which might well have been accepted as their programme. In spite of all their apparent advantages, however, the Whigs during eleven years of almost continuous enjoyment of office effected little in financial reform, and finally drifted into annual deficits. The explanation of this failure, which contrasts very sharply with their activities in other directions, is fairly obvious.

[1] Charles Edward Poulett Thomson (1799–1844) had been in business in Russia; he was subsequently Governor-General of Canada and was raised to the peerage as Baron Sydenham.

The truth is that repeal and remission had gone so far that any further reform depended on a reconsideration of the whole basis of taxation. It was full time to turn from an agitation against particular taxes to the establishment of new principles. Reduction of taxation had become something of a fetish, while the problem of its incidence had been overlooked. The Whigs had used the old cry, and when they were returned to office they found themselves unable to fulfil popular expectations. Althorp was handicapped partly by his past record and partly by the diffidence which prevented him from advocating the proper remedy. As far back as 1822 he had traced distress to excessive taxation and had suggested that the Sinking Fund should be suspended in order to effect reductions. In Budget debates he had asked for the repeal of the leather tax, the window tax and other duties, maintaining that all surpluses should be used for such purposes. His future colleague, Poulett Thomson, was more interested in Huskisson's financial measures and wished to remove the taxes which hampered the development of trade and industry. His point of view is clearly indicated in a speech he made on Goulbourn's proposals in 1830. The Chancellor of the Exchequer, he contended, had given too much weight to the complaints against the amount of taxation and not enough thought to the nature of it. It was raised in such a way as to check industry; for instance, raw materials were taxed on coming into the country, and manufactures paid such charges that their consumption was restricted. Turning to the possible loss to the Exchequer if these taxes were repealed he argued that Government expenditure could be reduced and better taxes discovered. After enumerating several possibilities he said that he was personally in favour of a direct tax on income. Althorp apparently agreed with him in principle but was afraid to declare himself. Grey and other Whig chiefs, on the other hand, were strongly opposed to the income tax, and consequently no comprehensive reforms were possible.

The practical ruling-out of the income tax meant that, while Althorp and Poulett Thomson wished to follow the programme sketched in detail by Parnell, they were deprived of the means which he considered essential. "If an income tax were imposed," he writes,[1] "and if, at the same time, Government made those retrenchments which it has the power of making without any difficulty, a reduction of some millions of taxes might be attempted in the first year; and if the business of retrenchment were steadily and vigorously persevered in, a further reduction of one or two millions of taxes might be effected in each subsequent year, till the whole plan of reform might be carried into execution." He laid down the important principle that "the securing of a sufficiency of revenue should never be a matter of doubt," and the provision of it should be a condition precedent to a thoroughgoing reform. That the income tax alone would serve this purpose was demonstrated by the fate of Althorp's first Budget. He proposed extensive repeals—of the taxes on coal and slate, printed calicoes and cotton, tallow candles and glass—and reductions in the duties on newspapers and advertisements. The whole amounted to an estimated loss of £3,170,000. To compensate the Exchequer he suggested new taxes, the chief of which fell on the transfer of real and personal property, the exportation of coal, travelling by steamboat, and additions to the duties on Canadian timber and wines. They were estimated to yield £2,740,000. But the new taxes were so severely criticised that Althorp had to withdraw them. Peel pointed out that the tax on transfers, in as far as it applied to the Public Funds, was contrary to the terms of the Loan Acts. Others showed that the remaining proposals were ill-considered. The Budget had, therefore, to be completely revised. The failure of this ambitious effort reacted throughout the whole period.

In the Reformed Parliament Althorp had to meet the demand for reduction in taxation, and in the Budget of 1833 applied the surplus of £1,571,000 to that purpose. He refused to repeal the malt tax on the ground that the increased yield showed that remission was not urgently

[1] Parnell: "On Financial Reform," p. 270.

needed, and he postponed dealing with the newspaper duty until he could afford its total repeal. The relief he offered to industry was reduction and repeal of a variety of minor taxes, for instance, the duty on property insured against loss at sea, on agricultural stock insured against risk of fire, on windows, on advertisements, on tiles, and on soap. This did not satisfy influential sections in the House: an amendment in favour of the repeal of the malt tax was carried against the Government, and a strong movement was set afoot against the continuation of the window and inhabited house taxes. Althorp decided to meet the situation by asking the House to agree that such repeals would involve a change in the whole financial system of the country which at the present was inexpedient, as it would necessitate a general tax on property. This resolution was carried by 355 votes to 157. The presentation of the unacceptable alternative, however, merely won a temporary respite. Althorp was still strongly urged to repeal the inhabited house duty. In 1834 he felt that he had to choose between the window and inhabited house tax as he could not repeal them both. The window tax, although objectionable in principle, was levied so as to fall more heavily on the wealthy; the house tax was assessed on such a basis that it was comparatively light on very large houses. On this ground Althorp decided to submit to the clamour and repeal the inhabited house tax, although his first intention was to abandon the window tax. Thus he forfeited another £1,200,000 of revenue.

It was Althorp's misfortune that previous administrations had left him little scope for the policy of repeal and remission; and he was not equal to the carrying out of a new scheme of taxation. It should also be remembered that he was one of the main supports of his party, and his time was occupied with the general reform programme which it promoted. He did not care for public life and had been persuaded to accept the Chancellorship against his own inclination. It is, however, a tribute to his ability and influence that both Grey and Melbourne in turn felt that they could not go on without his assistance as leader of the Commons. But the death of his father, Lord

Spencer, in 1834, removed him to the Upper House. In the reconstruction of the Whig Administration, which followed Peel's failure to gain a working majority in 1835, Spring Rice became Chancellor of the Exchequer. He had to face the fact that during the past five years taxes which had yielded £7,000,000 had been repealed. In his second year he actually managed to reduce the duties on paper and on newspapers, but this was the last considerable reduction. Expenditure, particularly on the Army and Navy, began to rise, and a succession of bad harvests impaired the produce of the taxes. The Government was involved in annual deficits of over £2,500,000 in 1837–8, of nearly £500,000 in 1838–9, of over £1,500,000 in 1839–40, and of rather more in 1840–1. Francis Baring, who succeeded Spring Rice in 1840, tried to remove the deficit by means of a general increase of 5 per cent. in the Customs and Excise duties. This expedient proved a disappointment. In the next year he resolved to attempt to find additional revenue by lowering the protective duties on timber and sugar in order to increase consumption. The Government was defeated on the Sugar Duty Bill. Lord John Russell's announcement that he was in favour of a fixed duty of 8s. a quarter on wheat in place of the sliding scale gave the Opposition its opportunity. Peel carried a vote of no confidence and Melbourne resigned. The Whigs had long lost whatever reforming energy they had ever possessed, and were drifting when circumstances demanded action. Already the promulgation of the People's Charter and the foundation of the Anti-Corn Law League had challenged the rulers of the country to reconsider fundamental principles.[1]

[1] The Charter was drafted in 1838, the same year in which the Anti-Corn Law League was founded. Both the Chartists and the supporters of the League drew particular attention to the general distress of the period.

(NOTE.—The figures are to the nearest thousand, and 000's are omitted.)

Year (ending January 5th.)	Exchequer Receipts.	Exchequer Issues.	Surplus(+) or Deficiency (−).	Debt Charge.
	£000	£000	£000	£000
1842	48,084	50,186	− 2,102	29,450
1843	46,966	50,945	− 3,979	29,428
1844	52,583	51,140	+ 1,443	29,269
1845	54,004	50,648	+ 3,356	30,496
1846	53,060	49,243	+ 3,817	28,254
1847	53,790	50,944	+ 2,846	28,078
1848	51,546	54,503	− 2,957	28,141
1849	53,389	54,185	− 796	28,563
1850	52,952	50,854	+ 2,098	28,324
1851	52,811	50,232	+ 2,579	28,092
1852	52,233	49,507	+ 2,726	28,017

(From the "Statistical Abstract," First Number, 1854.)

CHAPTER IV

FISCAL AND FINANCIAL REFORM—1842–1852

THE achievements of the Reformed Parliament in other directions have served to obscure its weakness in the management of finance. This was present from the first, but became obvious from 1837 onwards. By that time only the most strenuous efforts could have availed to re-establish public confidence, for then a series of bad harvests and acute depression in trade created a position which demanded heroic measures. The crisis, however, revealed the incompetence of the Whigs and called into being an opposition, official and other, before which they at last succumbed. Sir Robert Peel was summoned to grapple with problems of the first magnitude. The manner in which he dealt with them invested fiscal and financial questions with a dramatic interest which has never been paralleled in our history. He entered upon his task backed by a strong majority, but determined that he would not remain in power unless it allowed him freedom to pursue his own course. At the moment the triumph of the Tories, or Conservatives as they now came to be called, seemed sufficiently decisive to crush all misgivings as to what their leader's assertion of independence might eventually mean. Lord John Russell had declared in favour of amending the Corn Laws by adopting a fixed duty and had been hopelessly defeated. The victory at the polls was generally regarded by the agricultural interest as a guarantee against any such change of policy. The agitation of the Anti-Corn Law League, which, under the leadership of Cobden, had been making alarming progress in the north, seemed to have been successfully countered. The general situation in the country was admittedly bad; but Peel was particularly strong in finance and would doubtless find a solution. What was not realised was that Peel would not be hampered by any prejudices when he came to deal with the facts. His past record was a proof of this. He had voted against the adoption of the recommendations of the Bullion Report in 1811, and yet in 1819 was responsible for the Bill which required the resumption of cash payments by the Bank of England. Nor did he avail himself of the specious plea that circumstances had changed and that he was enlightened enough to recognise the fact. He said frankly that he had been wrong; that he had now read the Bullion Report with the same attention as he would read the proof of a proposition in mathematics and could find no defect in the argument. This example of his candour might have appeared quixotic to politicians, but it did not constitute any breach of party understandings. There was a more serious change of opinion. Peel had differed from Canning on the question of Catholic Emancipation and had refused to serve under him on this ground. Yet he had changed his mind by 1829, and was a prominent member of Wellington's Ministry when this reform was carried. He might have voted against the resumption of cash payments in 1811 because he had not closely considered the question. But he had been the most notable opponent of Catholic Emancipation, and had allowed that issue to govern his public conduct. In this case he did not admit a change in his convictions, but pleaded that it was no longer expedient to oppose the demand. And, had his supporters examined with attention his utterances on the Corn Laws, they would have been somewhat shaken in their confidence that this was a question on which he could be trusted to resist amendment. It is true that he had been in office when the 1815 and 1828 Acts were passed and he had fully approved of both. He voted as a protectionist and paid little attention to the theoretical basis of his belief until he was faced by a practical issue. Then on this, as on other questions, he weighed the facts without reference to his preconceived antipathies. In supporting the sliding scale in 1828 he pointed out that, with the growth of population, the country would come to depend more largely on foreign supplies of food. Later he justified protection to agriculture on the ground that other interests enjoyed protection and heavy national burdens fell on the land. By 1839, however, he was prepared to admit that agriculture ought not to have any advantages which were inconsistent with the general interests of the community, especially with those of the labouring classes.

Some conception of the man is essential to the understanding of the method in which he performed his task. Peel was by nature an administrator with no instinct for or interest in abstract theories, apart from the guidance they afforded in the solution of practical difficulties when they arose. He had a great capacity for work, and when a question was forced on his attention, always dealt with it comprehensively. The failure of a line of policy made as great an impression on his mind as the success which attended an experiment. Failure and success alike indicated the limits of the practicable. When he had envisaged a problem he tested every solution, discarded those which were ruled out by practical objections, and accepted that which seemed best, even if it involved a break with his past professions and imposed an almost intolerable strain on the loyalty of his party. Having decided on his course he kept to it without thought of compromise or concern for consequences. While he enjoyed the implicit confidence of a small group of lieutenants, he had no gift for disarming criticism by personal charm or apparent accommodation to the views of others. He was sensitive and, under the strain of office, irritable and taciturn. But his chief characteristic was his straightforwardness; in opposition he was never factious, when in power his chief ambition was to get that done which a wide survey of the position proved to be necessary, and in the way which promised the surest and best results. Approaching his problems with the knowledge that the country had put its confidence in him, he took time to inquire into the facts and to mature his plans. He assumed office in September, 1841, but did not expound his financial proposals until the following March. His first duty, however, was to define his attitude towards the Corn Laws, for the agitation in the country had been carried on with renewed vigour by the Anti-Corn Law League during the winter. He deprecated the opinion that the Corn Laws were the special cause of the general distress, pointing out that the country was suffering from the consequences of the commercial crisis of 1837–8, and expressing the belief that a manufacturing country could not avoid the depression which followed a period of undue activity. It seemed to him that the agricultural interest bore special public burdens, and he could not contemplate without misgiving the extension of the country's dependence on foreign food supplies. But he felt that there was a strong case for a revision of the sliding scale. The 1828 scale was steep, and dealers in foreign corn were tempted to hold back supplies to get higher prices. Peel therefore proposed a scale which would present less opportunity for speculative dealing, and, at the same time, secure a remunerative price for home-grown corn. This two-fold purpose he thought would be attained if the scale was made less steep and had two "rests." Average prices for the last series of years showed that wheat could be profitably grown for about 56s. a quarter. These considerations led to the conclusion that the scale should range between 20s. when wheat was under 51s. to 1s. when it rose above 73s., with a "rest" from 52s. to 55s. at a duty of 18s., and from 66s. to 69s. at a duty of 6s.[1] Against these proposals

[1] 5 and 6 Vict. c 14 repealed the Act of 1828 and imposed the new scale. For Wheat it worked out as follows:

When under 51/- a quarter at home,	20/- duty.	On the importation of *Wheat* from foreign countries.
51/- and under 52/-	19/- ,,	
*52/- ,, ,, 55/-	18/- ,,	
55/- ,, ,, 56/-	17/- ,,	
56/- ,, ,, 57/-	16/- ,,	
57/- ,, ,, 58/-	15/- ,,	
58/- ,, ,, 59/-	14/- ,,	
59/- ,, ,, 60/-	13/- ,,	
60/- ,, ,, 61/-	12/- ,,	
61/- ,, ,, 62/-	11/- ,,	

Other cereals on a corresponding but lower scale.

Lord John Russell moved the official Whig amendment in favour of a fixed duty which, as he claimed, would rule out speculative dealing. Charles P. Villiers also moved his annual motion in favour of the total repeal of the Corn Laws. But both Whig and Radical were defeated by overwhelming majorities, and Peel's revision of the sliding scale was accepted. The retention of the sliding scale, although greatly modified, did not satisfy the Anti-Corn League, and their propaganda was immediately turned to the exposure of its weaknesses.

Having disposed, temporarily at any rate, of the most contentious issue, Peel turned to the pressing question of the revenue. He realised that everything depended on the success which attended his attempt to escape from the annual deficits which had begun in 1837. How was this to be done? It was obvious that the deficit was not accidental; it was becoming chronic. Peel satisfied himself that it could not be eliminated by economies in expenditure. He repudiated "the wretched expedient of continued loans." So he was thrown back on increased taxation. Here the experiments made by his predecessor offered a warning against the effort to adjust income and expenditure by any manipulation of the existing system of taxes. In 1840 Baring had tried a general increase of the custom and excise duties, and it had not produced what he had expected. This Peel took as a demonstration that the limits of taxation on articles of consumption had been reached. The following year Baring had adopted the opposite principle—so closely associated with the reforms of Robinson and Huskisson—of reducing duties

62/-	and under	63/-	10/- duty	On the importation of *Wheat* from foreign countries.
63/-	,, ,,	64/-	9/- ,,	
64/-	,, ,,	65/-	8/- ,,	
65/-	,, ,,	66/-	7/- ,,	
*66/-	,, ,,	69/-	6/- ,,	
69/-	,, ,,	70/-	5/- ,,	
70/-	,, ,,	71/-	4/- ,,	
71/-	,, ,,	72/-	3/- ,,	
72/-	,, ,,	73/-	2/- ,,	
73/-	and upwards		1/- ,,	

Other cereals on a corresponding but lower scale.

in the hope that increased consumption would more than compensate the Exchequer for loss. Peel was convinced of the soundness of the general principle, but, after a survey of the effects of previous reductions, was able to demonstrate that a considerable time had to elapse before the Exchequer reaped the full advantage of its application. The very fact that it had been done so often also restricted the field for its further operation. Moreover, the emergency precluded the possibility of waiting on events. It was not that he was opposed to remission and reduction of taxes—in fact, he wished to undertake such reform on a more comprehensive scale than any of his predecessors in order to stimulate a revival of trade—but he put in the first place the maintenance of public credit and the securing of a surplus revenue. The conclusion to which his analysis of the whole problem had driven him, since it is the most momentous decision in the history of the nineteenth century taxational policy, must be given in his own words: "I propose for a time at least—(and I never had occasion to make a proposition with a more thorough conviction of its being one which the public interest of the country required)—I propose that, for a time to be limited, the income of this country should be called on to contribute a certain sum for the purpose of remedying this mighty and growing evil [i.e., *the deficit*]. I propose that the income of this country should bear a charge not exceeding 7d. in the pound, which will not amount to £3 per cent., but, speaking accurately, £2 18s. 4d. per cent., for the purpose of not only supplying the deficiency in the revenue, but of enabling me, with confidence and satisfaction, to propose great commercial reforms, which will afford a hope of reviving commerce, and such an improvement in the manufacturing interests as will react on every other interest in the country; and, by diminishing the prices of the articles of consumption, and the cost of living, will, in the pecuniary point of view, compensate you for your present sacrifices; whilst you will be, at the same time, relieved from the contemplation of a great public evil."

The long abeyance of the income tax in spite of the financial difficulties of successive Governments is some measure of Peel's courage in proposing to impose it even for a limited period in time of peace. Since the publication of Parnell's treatise on financial reform in 1830 the case for the income tax had become generally known. Still the old objections seemed to have lost none of their weight. Peel himself fully shared the feeling that the tax ought to be avoided. He had, indeed, never shown any disposition to accept it. On the contrary, he had declared himself against its adoption on more than one occasion. When Huskisson stated that he thought that the substitution of a direct tax on income in place of the innumerable indirect taxes would be beneficial to industry, Peel expressed his doubts as to the effects of such a step and asserted that the Government had, after full consideration, decided against it. That he was not merely voicing the opinion of the majority in the Cabinet is proved by the fact that in 1833, when in opposition, he commended Althorp for not proposing an income tax, and went on to say that only extreme necessity would justify its imposition in time of peace. Two years later he warned the agricultural interest not to press for a repeal of the malt tax as it might lead to the infliction of "the scourge of a property tax." He made the same point when the Whigs introduced the penny post in 1839 and thus threatened to destroy all profit arising out of the Post Office, though then he, for the first time, showed an inclination to accept an income tax in certain circumstances. But, in the following year, he approved of Baring's policy of attempting to remove the deficit by increasing indirect taxation. It is clear therefore that Peel began with the conventional view about the income tax and only abandoned it when he had satisfied himself that an emergency had arisen which demanded a new policy. There could be no greater error, however, than to suppose that he had adopted the principle of direct as against indirect taxation, or that he wished to effect a redistribution of the burden of taxation. He was severely practical. Every way of escape from the annual deficits had been explored and the income tax alone promised to be successful. That is why he adopted it, and to him it was essentially a means of escape; when the income tax had served its turn it was to be abandoned. At first he contemplated asking Parliament to agree to the retention of the tax for five years, for inquiry revealed the fact that such a period was required to allow increased consumption to reward the Exchequer for reducing indirect taxes. In the end, however, he decided on a limitation to three years. The main principles of the tax were identical with those of the war income tax which had been repealed in 1816. The rate was 7d. in the pound, and a deduction of £150 was allowed on all incomes. The tax was not extended to Ireland as there was no machinery for its assessment and collection, and it was not worth while to improvise it for a temporary tax. But additional revenue was to be raised in Ireland by increasing the duties on spirits and stamps.

It will be remembered that Peel wished to revive the income tax not only to meet the deficit but to undertake extensive fiscal reforms, which he hoped would lead to greater prosperity, that is, it was to wipe out the old deficit and to provide against the emergence of a new one as an immediate result of the simplification of the tariff. He had been convinced that the recovery of industry was in some degree retarded by the existence of a complicated network of prohibitive and protective duties. Although still nominally a protectionist he thought that a movement in the free trade direction was imperatively demanded by the circumstances of the time. The abstract arguments of the economists were calculated to make much less impression on his mind than the detailed evidence presented before the Committee on Import Duties which had been appointed in 1840 on the motion of Joseph Hume. The testimony of James Deacon Hume[1] and George Richardson Porter,[2] who were officials of the Board of Trade,

[1] James Deacon Hume (1774–1842) as Controller of the Customs undertook the consolidation of the laws relating to the tariff, *see* note, pp. 67–8*n supra*. He was appointed Joint Secretary of the Board of Trade in 1828.

[2] George Richardson Porter (1792–1852) was the head of the Statistical Department of the Board of Trade. He was the author of the well-known " Progress of the Nation."

was particularly impressive. They showed that the system handicapped the trader by its complexity and consequently discouraged enterprise and competition. It was expensive to work and conferred no benefit on producer, consumer, or taxpayer. The Report of the Committee revealed how much remained to be done in spite of all the efforts of Huskisson and Poulett Thomson when they were at the Board of Trade. From the revenue point of view the Committee stated that of the whole customs receipts £20,800,000 out of £22,120,000 was yielded by eighty-two articles, and £18,600,000 of this by nine articles only. It therefore recommended that duties should be charged on a small number of productive articles so as to "facilitate the transactions of commerce, benefit the revenue, diminish the cost of collection, and remove the multitudinous sources of complaint and vexation." The Report, issued in 1840, had exercised some influence on the Whigs and, in a tentative way, they began to adjust their policy in accordance with its recommendations. Peel, however, determined to deal with the question on comprehensive lines.[1] He had appointed the Earl of Ripon (formerly Viscount Goderich) as President of the Board of Trade, but he relied mainly on the assistance of W. E. Gladstone, whom he had chosen as Vice-President. On him the burden of reviewing the tariff fell, and he admitted in after years that the task involved six times the labour that he expended on the three subsequent revisions of 1845, 1853, and 1860 put together. The principles on which the new tariff was constructed were: (1) The removal of prohibitions and the relaxation of prohibitory duties; (2) The reduction of the duties on the import of raw materials of manufacture to a point not exceeding five per cent. *ad valorem;* (3) The reduction of the duty on partially manufactured articles to a point not exceeding 12 per cent. *ad valorem;* (4) The reduction of the duties on manufactured articles to a point not exceeding 20 per cent. Gladstone found that the revision

[1] Peel himself had not read the Report in December, 1841. C. S. Parker: "Peel," Vol. II, p. 509.

necessitated changes in the rates charged on some 750 out of a total of 1,200 articles on which duties were paid. It was claimed that these reductions would lower the general cost of living while they did not expose home industries to unfair competition. Taking them altogether they would represent an estimated loss to the Exchequer of £3,780,000.

The Government's proposals for the reform of the tariff were, on the whole, well received. Their supporters may, indeed, have felt uneasy about the future but they could hardly convict either Peel or Gladstone of actual departure from protectionist principles. On the other hand, the convinced free traders, while they welcomed the simplification of the tariff, had to recognise that a moderate system of protection might offer a more serious resistance to their assaults than one which was disfigured by anomalies and absurdities. But the confidence felt in Peel's judgment was strong enough to ensure the acceptance of a reform for which the discussion of the past year or so had prepared the way. It was the means by which he proposed to attain his end that aroused the strongest opposition. All the old arguments against the income tax were restated. It was "inquisitorial," "oppressive," and "unjust." The Whigs opposed it in the Commons and Lords. Lord John Russell fought the proposal at every stage in the former, while Brougham, aroused by the prospect of seeing his victory of 1816 reversed, brought forward a long series of resolutions in the latter. Peel met all the criticisms by asserting that, in his opinion, the income tax was essential to the financial stability of the country. There was a general agreement that an end had to be put to the annual deficits. Additional indirect taxation was condemned by the experience of 1840: a simplification of tariff might, in time, effect a balance of income and expenditure, but previous experiments had proved that the Exchequer would suffer an immediate loss. Therefore the income tax was the keystone of the arch. Without it the deficits could not be stopped, nor could industry be relieved from the pressure of a heavy and clumsy tariff. The House of Commons eventually accepted the whole scheme by a majority of 106.

It is a curious fact that the Budget of 1842, although the income tax yielded more than was expected, did not produce the surplus which Peel had anticipated, but actually resulted in a deficit of £3,979,000. This was partly due to the overlooking of an obvious and perfectly simple administrative detail. The income tax was to be collected half-yearly, and Peel had taken credit for a full year's yield without noticing that the second instalment would not be available within the period. There had also been an over-estimate of the amount which the Customs duties would produce and the Excise had suffered from the fall in the consumption of malt. The shrinkage of the indirect taxes, however, confirmed Peel's wisdom in resorting to the income tax. Its productiveness, taking the two payments of the first year together, was most gratifying. Peel had estimated it at £3,770,000; it proved to be £5,100,000. Consequently he was content to allow the principles of the 1842 Budget to mature, particularly as there were indications of an improvement in trade. His Chancellor of the Exchequer—Goulburn—confined himself to a few necessary adjustments to meet the unexpected deficit. This course was justified by the yield of the taxes in the year 1843-4. There was a surplus of £4,165,000 which left a considerable sum in hand when the deficit of the previous year had been wiped out. Goulburn also estimated that 1844-5 would give him a surplus of £2,376,000. Of this he proposed to employ £400,000 for the remission of taxes, reducing the duties on coffee, currants, and certain kinds of glass. He also abolished the protective duties on raw wool which Huskisson had substituted for the prohibitive duties in 1825.[1] A serious crisis was almost precipitated by the Government's attempt to deal with the sugar duties on the same lines as those on other imports. In 1841 the Whigs had been defeated on a motion to admit sugar on the payment of a protective duty of 12s. per cwt., partly on the ground that it would place British West Indian planters, who were precluded from using slave labour, at a disadvantage in

---

[1] *See* p. 65 *supra*.

competing with those rivals outside the Empire, who were under no such restriction. Foreign grown sugar therefore continued to be charged the prohibitive rate of 63s. a cwt while Colonial sugar paid 24s. In pursuance of their general policy the Government proposed to remove the prohibitive duty and to reduce the protection to a reasonable amount. After their attitude towards slave-labour sugar in 1841, when they were in opposition, they had to limit the concession to foreign free-labour sugar. They now proposed to admit it at 34s. per cwt., arguing that the differential duty of 10s. was sufficient protection for the West Indies. Goulburn declared the object of the Government was to secure larger and cheaper supplies of what was now recognised as a necessary, without thereby abandoning opposition to the slave trade. The West Indian interest was aroused by the prospect of the competition of foreign free-labour sources of supply. The Whigs criticised the distinction between free and slave sugar, contending that a tariff should not be framed on considerations of morality. An amendment was carried against the Government, but Peel refused either to abandon the new scale of duties or resign. He moved the restoration of the original clause and, in spite of the protests of Lord John Russell, reinforced by the sarcasms of Disraeli who now openly opposed the Government,[1] he carried his amendment by a majority of twenty-two.

It will be noticed that Goulburn devoted a relatively small proportion of his surplus to the reduction or remission of taxes. The rest was employed to strengthen public credit. Deficiency bills were all paid, the Exchequer balances were augmented so that the Government had no need to resort to the Bank of England for advances in anticipation of the taxes, and the amount of Exchequer bills in circulation was reduced to modest proportions. Consols reflected the result of this policy. They had

[1] Disraeli had spoken in favour of the commercial reforms of 1842 and sought to prove that free trade was the traditional policy of the Tory Party. Later he had drifted into criticism of the Government on other issues and did not receive the Prime Minister's whip on the assembling of Parliament in 1844.

risen from 89 in 1841 to 99 in 1844. The promise of revival of trade and industry in 1843 was more than fulfilled in the following year. To what degree this was due to the financial policy of the Government it is impossible to say. But it may be contended that Peel had contributed to the establishment of confidence, and he certainly took the opportunity which the favourable condition of the money market afforded to lighten the burden of the National Debt. In 1844 was carried through a conversion of dimensions hitherto unprecedented. Some £250,000,000 of stock standing at 3½ per cent. was reduced to 3¼ per cent. for ten years, to be followed by a further reduction to 3 per cent. in 1854, with a guarantee that no change would then be made for twenty years when the debt was redeemable. This meant a saving of £625,000 annually for the first ten years, and of £1,250,000 annually for the next twenty. The operation was completed by Goulburn with remarkable success. He had, of course, to pay off all dissentients, but their claims did not amount to more than £250,000, and this charge he was able to meet out of his surplus revenue.

The chief interest in the year 1844, however, will always centre round the Bank Charter Act. To Peel's mind it was the complement to the Act of 1819, which required the Bank to resume cash payments and restored the gold standard. At that time the convertibility of notes seemed to be a sufficient guarantee against their over-issue. In the crises of 1825 and 1836–9 experience went to show that this belief was ill-founded. The banks were allowed to exercise their own discretion about the amount of gold they held against their issues, the obligation to cash their notes on demand being supposed to act as a check. But the country banks were tempted to expand their issues even when the state of the exchanges and the drain on the reserve of the Bank of England gave cause for anxiety. Failures had been frequent and disastrous. It appeared therefore that it was necessary to prevent the banks from indulging in an excessive issue of notes when a boom in trade presented them with apparently sound opportunities for advancing credit. For, if they went beyond a certain point, the convertibility of their notes was merely nominal.

The question was primarily a currency question. If absolute convertibility was, in certain circumstances, endangered, Peel thought that it was the business of the Government to devise a method of safeguarding it. It was not, he claimed, any interference with ordinary banking transactions but a perfectly legitimate attempt to regulate the currency. Banks enjoyed the right of note-issue as a privilege from the State and consequently the Government might justly define its conditions. The discussion of this question had been going on for some years before Peel announced in 1844 that he intended to take advantage of a clause in the Bank Charter Act of 1833, which empowered the Government to suspend the Charter at the end of twelve years. He proposed to introduce another Act which would incorporate the new principles he had adopted.

Controversy had revealed two distinct schools of thought. The one maintained what is usually called the Banking Principle, namely, that there was no danger of over-issue so long as the notes were always convertible; the other upheld the Currency Principle, namely, that the issue of notes must be regarded as an addition to the currency and for that reason strictly regulated. The exponents of the Banking Principle argued that the number of notes put into circulation would depend on the course of business, for they would only be issued in making advances against securities. Thomas Tooke, who argued strongly in favour of this view, denied that it was in the power of the banks to make any direct addition to the amount of notes in circulation. They would be guided by the needs of their customers, which was an index to the state of trade. The theoretical exposition of the Currency Principle is to be found in the pamphlets of Samuel Jones Loyd.[1] In its simplest form his contention was that if the currency of the world was entirely gold each country would get its share by the operation of a natural law. When it became scarce

[1] Samuel Jones Loyd (1796–1883) was the son of a Welsh Nonconformist minister who became a banker in Manchester. The son succeeded to his father's position and also entered Parliament in 1816. He exercised a great influence in financial affairs. In 1850 he became Lord Overstone.

in a particular country it would appreciate in value, prices would fall, imports decrease and exports increase, a process which would continue until a proper proportion of gold had been secured. If gold was abundant the opposite process would redress the balance. Suppose, however, one country adopted paper money. Then the process might be hindered, for a drain of gold might be accompanied by an issue of notes to fill the void thus created, prices would not fall, and the natural adjustment would not take place. The problem, therefore, was to regulate the issue of notes in such a way that they would be susceptible to the movements of gold. Loyd proposed to attain this automatic fluctuation by a limitation of note-issue to a certain amount, all additions to be covered by the deposit of an equivalent of coin or bullion in the reserve.

Peel's own conclusions on the question were summarised by him in an important Cabinet memorandum.[1] In characteristic fashion he asked his colleagues to consider the possible courses of action. He pointed out that the maintenance of the existing system would satisfy both the interests and the prejudices of the majority, but it would be discreditable to the Government to acquiesce in its continuance when they knew of its imperfections and dangers in order to please their supporters. It was obvious that the Bank of England had a very imperfect control over note-issues for, even when it recognised that contraction was necessary, it could not count on other issuers following its example. Nominal convertibility into gold, where there was unlimited competition as to issue, did not ensure the value and practical convertibility of the paper. Since the Government could not honourably evade its responsibility it might be urged that the opportunity should be seized to prohibit the issue of paper payable on demand by the Bank of England and all other banks. The issue of money is the prerogative of Sovereignty ; such paper possesses the character of money ; the Sovereign has to protect the holders of it from the consequences of its depreciation and should enjoy all profits on its issue.

[1] It will be found in C. S. Parker's " Peel," Vol. III, pp. 134–9.

In theory, all this was incontrovertible. Peel held, however, that anyone responsible for the conduct of public affairs would shrink from proposing this course as a practical measure. They were not beginning with a new state of society; use and wont could not be disregarded. There was no uniformity of practice throughout the British Isles, and a purely Government paper would, in times of political danger be more likely to be distrusted than that issued by private banks. On these and other grounds he recommended a middle course. No new banks of issue should be established. The existing ones should be subjected to strict regulations in the exercise of their privilege of note-issue. In every case such publicity should be secured that the public would be able to judge of the soundness of the bank. The Bank of England was the centre of the English system—he did not propose to deal with Scotland and Ireland at the moment[1]—and it should separate its issue department from its other business. Constant publicity should be demanded as to the notes in circulation, and the quantity of coin, bullion, and securities held against them.

The Bank Charter Act gave legislative effect to these recommendations. The Bank of England was divided into the Issue and Banking Departments. Special regulations were applied to the former. It was allowed to issue notes against public securities to the extent of £14,000,000; beyond that amount, notes could only be issued against coin or bullion. Weekly accounts in a specified form were to be submitted to the Government for publication in the *London Gazette*. The problem of the country banks was met (1) by confining the right of note-issue to those which already enjoyed it, (2) by limiting their issue to the average of the twelve weeks preceding April 27th, 1844, and (3) by

1 The circulation of the Scottish Banks was regulated in the following year. Existing banks of issue were allowed to retain an authorised circulation equal to the average during the year ending May 1st, 1845, i.e., no particular bank was given a predominant position. In the same year similar restrictions were applied to the Irish banks of issue, though the Bank of Ireland was to have the right of increasing its note issue if any other bank surrendered it.

providing that their notes should not be legal tender. In certain circumstances a country bank would lose its right of note-issue, for instance, by amalgamation with another bank, and the Bank of England could then increase its issue against securities to the extent of two-thirds of the lapsed issue. The result has been that the issue of the country banks has become almost negligible, while the "uncovered" issue of the Bank of England has been augmented.[1] It may be said therefore that the Act gave legislative effect to the contentions of the exponents of the Currency Principle as far as that was compatible with a recognition of the practical questions involved. The currency system of the country rested on the foundation laid down by Peel until 1914. Controversy has never ceased to rage round the merits and demerits of its principles. Here it is only necessary to notice that Peel shared the belief of the currency school, that a limitation on note-issue would restrict the expansion of credit. No doubt an exaggerated importance was attached to notes. The limitation of note-issue by no means prevented over-trading. Crises continued to occur. In 1847, 1857 and 1866 the Government thought it necessary to suspend the Bank Charter Act, that is, it allowed the Bank of England to disregard the limit on note-issue which the law had imposed. Step by step, however, the technique of banking was improved and the effect of raising the Bank rate as a check on undue speculation was more fully recognised.

The fact that the income tax was due to expire in 1845 made it necessary for Peel to review the effects of the Budget of 1842 and to indicate his proposals for the future. The Queen's Speech at the opening of the session had prepared the way for the renewal of the tax and had naturally aroused the widest interest. Peel took the earliest opportunity to introduce the Budget himself.[2] He pointed out that his measures had met with success, and there was every prospect of a surplus of about £5,000,000

[1] By the recent absorption of Messrs. Fox, Fowler & Co. (established 1787) by Lloyds Bank, the process has been completed.
[2] On February, 17th, 1845.

in the current year. This was roughly the amount yielded by the income tax. In the year 1845–6 he anticipated that there would be a balance even if the income tax was allowed to lapse. The increase of expenditure, however, would in that case probably involve a deficit in the following year. He held that it would be imprudent to allow such a contingency to arise, and therefore recommended the renewal of the income tax for another three years. In 1842 he had calculated that it would take five years for the reform of the tariff to compensate the Exchequer for the reductions then made. It would have been possible to plead that three years had proved insufficient and to ask for an extension on that ground. But Peel's real object was not merely to make sure of the tax until the ordinary income had fully recovered; he was now convinced that the experiment of 1842 had demonstrated that a more extensive reform of the tariff was desirable. He wanted a renewal of the tax to cover this operation. His policy had undergone a subtle change in the last three years; he had come to regard the mass of indirect taxes as unprofitable and even harmful, while the income tax had revealed itself to be highly satisfactory. He did not contemplate that it would become a permanent part of the revenue, but its usefulness for a special purpose had been amply demonstrated. Its success had made a similar impression on the Opposition. Lord John Russell and his followers repeated their objections to the tax, but they did not refuse to vote for its continuance.[1]

If Peel's belief in the income tax had been strengthened by the experience of the past three years, his attitude towards the tariff had also hardened. In 1842 he had confined himself to reductions of duties; he was now prepared to undertake repeals on an extensive scale. The issue of direct as against indirect taxes was clearly involved. It has been well said that the Parliament of 1845 deliber-

[1] The Prince Consort expressed the case very well in a note to Peel on February 18th. "You got the income tax voted yesterday with an extraordinary majority. It is evident that everybody wants you to bear the abuse of it and still to have the five millions in case of getting into office." Parker's "Peel," Vol. III, p. 170.

ately adopted the income tax—for other arrangements were quite feasible—" at a time when the tax was not proposed as a measure of urgency, as in 1798, or even in 1842; but when it was calmly weighed in the balance against cheap sugar, cheap glass, cheap cotton, and the rest, and found to be a price worth paying for these countervailing benefits."[1] No wonder the country gentlemen in the Commons were becoming restive; Peel's approach to free trade could no longer be disguised. The reformed tariff of 1845 was a very considerable advance on that of 1842 because of the number of articles which were now struck off. All duties on exports, including that on coal, were abolished. Some 430 articles, mostly the raw materials of manufactures—such as silk, flax, furniture woods, animal and vegetable oils, minerals, and dyes—were to be imported duty free. The sugar duties were further reduced at a loss to the revenue of about £1,300,000, which meant that the consumer would have it 1½d. per lb. cheaper. The excise duty on glass was abolished, to the great advantage of the industry.[2] Peel also dropped the duty on property sold by auction, which had been in existence since 1777, partly because it was a burden on the transfer of property in a particular manner and partly because fraudulent evasion was common. Altogether Peel made remissions and reductions amounting to £3,338,000, that is, nearly three times as much as in 1842. But neither on Customs nor Excise did he lose so much in the first year as he expected. The estimated surplus on the year 1845–6 was £672,000; the actual, £3,817,000.

The Budget had been introduced on February 17th, and on March 20th Peel was able to announce to the Queen that his most sanguine expectations had been fulfilled. " The Income Tax Bill, the Sugar Duties Bill, and the Tariff," he wrote,[3] " have been passed by the House of Commons before Easter." He might well have reflected

[1] Northcote: " Twenty Years of Financial Policy," p. 77.

[2] Buxton suggests that the subsequent development of the industry made it possible to construct the Crystal Palace for the Great Exhibition of 1851. " Finance and Politics," Vol. I, p. 61.

[3] Parker: " Peel," Vol. III, p. 171.

that he had carried his party as far as he could along the lines of tariff reform and that it was now necessary to allow the new system time to consolidate itself. Public credit had completely recovered and the country was enjoying the benefits of a revival in trade and industry. A succession of good harvests had enabled him to maintain the Corn Law of 1842 in spite of the agitation of the Anti-Corn Law League. Peel, however, had his misgivings. The speculation in railways, which led many to commit themselves to an ultimate capital obligation quite beyond their means, seemed to him to threaten a collapse of the market. He realised that a renewed outbreak of distress would have far-reaching consequences. "I shudder," he wrote to an intimate correspondent, "I shudder at the recurrence of such a winter and spring as those of 1841–2." This was written at the end of August.[1] A damp summer was then turning into a drenching autumn. Peel knew very well that a failure of the harvest would immediately precipitate the question of the Corn Laws. For his own part the success of the application of free trade principles to other commodities and the cogency of Cobden's arguments in favour of extending them to corn had convinced him that agriculture could not be protected much longer. But his party was intimately concerned with this interest and the proposal to repeal the Corn Laws could hardly fail to shatter it. The crisis, however, proved to be much more acute, and in its consequences much more appalling than Peel's worst apprehensions. When the corn was rotting in the ear reports came from Ireland that a blight had fallen on the potatoes. The meaning of this was obvious enough to one at all well acquainted with Irish conditions.[2] The Irish peasantry lived largely on potatoes, bargaining to work for farmers in return for a piece of land on which to grow them. Failure of the potato crop demanded immediate precautions against famine. Peel fully realised all that was involved. "The remedy," he

---

[1] Parker: "Peel," Vol. III, p. 194.

[2] It will be remembered that Peel had been Chief Secretary for Ireland (1812–19).

wrote to the Lord Lieutenant,[1] "is the removal of all impediments to the import of all kinds of human food; that is, the total and absolute repeal for ever of all duties on all articles of subsistence. You might remit nominally for one year. But who will re-establish the Corn Laws once abrogated, though from a casual and temporary pressure?" The fact that he wrote this on October 15th is sufficient proof that his future conduct was not dictated by the course of political events.

Peel summoned his Cabinet at the end of the month and insisted that it was necessary to decide whether they would recommend Parliament—which, he thought, ought to assemble before Christmas—to maintain, modify, or suspend the Corn Laws. He declared himself in favour of suspension. His view was accepted by only three of his colleagues,[2] and the country became aware from the frequent and apparently fruitless deliberations of the Cabinet that there were acute differences. Lord John Russell was watching events from Edinburgh. On November 22nd he wrote a letter to his constituents in the City of London condemning the indecision of the Government in the face of a serious crisis and abandoning his advocacy of a fixed duty in favour of the total repeal of the Corn Laws.[3] Peel admitted that this was a dexterous blow; for, as he said, it left the Government no option but either to do nothing or to act in apparent conformity with the advice of the leader of the Opposition. A majority in the Cabinet now rallied to the support of the Prime Minister, but Lord Stanley remained unconvinced. As the position seemed untenable, Peel decided to resign. Lord John, however, failed to form a Ministry, and the Queen commanded Peel to withdraw his resignation. He reconstructed his Cabinet[4] and appeared at the head of a free trade Government when Parliament assembled on January 19th, 1846. Then ensued the

---

[1] Parker: "Peel," Vol. III, p. 224.

[2] Lord Aberdeen, Sir James Graham and Sidney Herbert.

[3] The letter appeared in *The Times* on November 27th.

[4] Gladstone, who had resigned on the Maynooth question in January, 1845, now accepted the Colonial Secretaryship.

culminating incident in his career. He had undertaken to carry the repeal of the Corn Laws through a House of Commons which had been elected to maintain the protection of agriculture. The irony of his position led Peel to attempt to tack on the corn question to the wider issue of tariff reform. Writing to Goulburn on December 27th, 1845, he said: "My wish would be not to give undue prominence to corn, but to cover corn by continued operation on the Customs tariff; expunging all articles which are not worth retaining either for revenue or protection; diminishing duties which have been—though not so intended—prohibitory or nearly so; reducing, as far as it may be safe, all protections where there is no special case to be made out for retaining them; and thus applying to corn a principle of nearly universal application. . . . I attach great importance to *our doing*, and doing now, what yet remains to be done. Let us put the finishing stroke to the good work."[1]

Peel's proposals therefore were presented to the Commons as "the continued and more extensive application of those principles which governed the introduction of the tariff in 1842." He definitely professed his intention to deprive the agriculturist of the argument that he was entitled to protection because the manufacturer was protected. Protective duties, he told the House, were, abstractedly and on principle, open to objection, and could only be defended on some special ground of public policy or justice. The last three years had demonstrated that reduced protection was the means of increasing revenue, the demand for labour, commerce, comfort, and public contentment. For these ends all interests ought to be prepared to make present sacrifices. He appealed to the manufacturers, in the first place, to do so, announcing the removal of the remaining protection enjoyed by the linen, cotton, and woollen industries, and the general adoption of a duty of 10 per cent. (in lieu of the 20 per cent. of the 1842 tariff) on the importation of foreign manufactured articles. Even Disraeli could not refrain from paying a

[1] Parker: "Peel," Vol. III, p. 294.

tribute to the skill with which Peel dealt with the House. "And to-night the manner in which he proceeded to deal with the duties on candles and soap, while all were thinking of the duties on something else; the bland and conciliatory air with which he announced a reduction of the impost on boot-fronts and shoe leather; the intrepid plausibility with which he entered into a dissertation on the duties on foreign brandy and foreign sugar; while visions of deserted villages and reduced rentals were torturing his neighbours, were all characteristic of his command over himself and those whom he addressed."[1] When he came to the vital question he tried to moderate the blow by postponing the complete repeal of the Corn Laws for three years, retaining, in the meanwhile, a revised sliding scale.[2] Nothing was gained by this tactful method of approach. The protectionists thought that they had been betrayed and, under the leadership of Lord George Bentinck, they fought the proposals with the greatest pertinacity and bitterness. Disraeli skilfully directed their parliamentary manœuvres, and, although Peel was able, with the assistance of the Whigs and the Cobdenites, to carry the third reading in the Commons by a majority of ninety-eight, and the Lords acquiesced in the decision, his enemies were determined to be avenged. On the night that the Corn Law Bill passed its third reading in the House of Lords the protectionists voted with the Opposition against the Government's Irish Coercion Bill. Peel was defeated by

---

[1] Disraeli's "Lord George Bentinck: A Political Biography," pp. 69–70.

[2] By 9 and 10 Vict., c. 22 the duties on corn were altered on June 26th, 1846, to the following scale to continue until February 1st, 1849:

When under 48/- a quarter at home,	10/- duty.	On the importation of *Wheat* from foreign countries.
48/- and under 49/-	9/- "	
49/- " " 50/-	8/- "	
50/- " " 51/-	7/- "	
51/- " " 52/-	6/- "	
52/- " " 53/-	5/- "	
53/- and upwards	4/- "	

With corresponding modifications for other cereals.

seventy-three. Three days later—June 29th—he resigned, expressing the hope in the concluding words of his speech that his name would sometimes be remembered in the homes of those whose lot it is to labour and to earn their daily bread by the sweat of their brow.

The next six years are in the nature of an epilogue. Political parties did not recover from the strain exerted on them in 1846. Lord John Russell's Administration, which succeeded Peel's, survived until 1851 because the Peelites did not wish to endanger the cause of free trade. But it was weak in the Commons and the Lords were often hostile. When Russell was at last forced to resign in February, 1852, Stanley—now Lord Derby—formed a Government of the defenders of protection, but his appeal to the country in the summer proved that a return to the old system was out of the question. Disraeli, who was now Chancellor of the Exchequer, recognised that it was "obsolete." The maintenance of Peel's reforms is therefore the most significant fact of this period. In itself the Whig finance hardly deserves the condemnation which has usually been meted out to it. The difficulties of the years immediately following 1846 were formidable. With famine in Ireland, a serious financial crisis in England, and continued bad harvests, any Government might have been seriously embarrassed. Despite the protests that it was not the business of Government to interfere with the laws of supply and demand, relief measures had to be undertaken in Ireland, and these involved an expenditure of £2,000,000 out of Exchequer balances, as well as a loan for an additional £8,000,000. The consequences of the "railway mania" of the previous years contributed to bring about the acute crisis in the money market which threatened to become a disastrous panic in the autumn of 1847. The Government had to consent to a suspension of the Bank Charter Act to prevent a complete collapse. Even as it was the failures are said to have amounted to a total loss of £30,000,000. The revenue naturally suffered from these disasters. Lord John Russell anticipated a deficit of over £3,000,000 in the year 1848–9, even provided that the income tax were renewed. But it was now due to expire at the end of the second three years. The Government, however, held that it was indispensable and proposed that it should be extended for another five years; for the first two at 1s. and the remaining three at the existing rate of 7d. in the pound. This proposal was so strongly resisted in the Commons that it had to be abandoned in favour of a renewal for three years at the old rate.

The year 1849 is notable on account of the lapse of the Corn Laws under the provisions of the Act of 1846. It also witnessed the repeal of the Navigation Laws. There is a real connection between the two events. Owing to the shortage of cereals it had been necessary to suspend the limitations on importation in 1847 so as to allow foreign ships to take part in the trade. The contention that this competition would mean lower freights—and consequently cheaper corn—would obviously support the plea for their complete abolition. The Conservatives fought to retain the power of negotiating separate treaties of a reciprocal nature on the general lines laid down by Huskisson in the 'twenties. Free traders pointed out that Great Britain had not waited for other countries to abolish their duties against her manufactures before she admitted their corn. Reciprocity is based on the assumption that restrictions benefit the country which adopts them. This the free traders denied and, in the words of Sir James Graham, they were opposed to any principle "which makes the folly of others the limit of our own wisdom." Sir Robert Peel regarded the abolition of the Navigation Laws as the necessary corollory of his free trade policy.[1] In the House of Commons he and his followers gave full support to the Government. Lord Stanley led the opposition in the Lords but, through the good offices of the Duke of Wellington,

[1] After his defeat in 1846 Peel declared that he would not again accept office. He was ungrudging in the assistance he gave his successor. Peel was thrown from his horse at Constitution Hill and died as a result of his injuries on July 2nd, 1850.

the Bill secured a majority of ten. The next three sessions afford little of interest except the growing strength of the movement for economy. In 1851 the window tax was repealed and a house tax imposed in its place, thus reversing Althorp's decision in 1834. Controversy still turned round the income tax. The Government declared in 1851—when it was again due to determine—that it could neither do without it nor find a substitute. Lord Stanley protested against it being allowed to degenerate into a permanent tax, recalling the circumstances in which the House had consented to its imposition in 1842, and contending that its renewal in 1845 was merely a carrying out of Peel's original scheme. It had been retained in 1848 to support the credit of the country after the disasters of the previous year. When the Bill to continue the tax for three years was in committee Joseph Hume succeeded in carrying an amendment which limited it to one year in order to refer the whole question of assessment and collection to a Select Committee. The next year, as has already been stated, Stanley (now Earl of Derby) formed a Ministry with Disraeli as Chancellor of the Exchequer. In his Budget statement Disraeli spoke of the need of reviewing the basis of taxation and establishing the principles according to which the revenue should be raised. As a provisional arrangement he proposed to retain the income tax for still another year. The subsequent Dissolution and General Election did not give Derby a working majority independent of Whigs and Peelites. In December, 1852, Disraeli introduced his second Budget. The financial position forced him to recommend the retention of the income tax for three years, but he attempted to give compensation to the interests which had suffered from the reforms of the tariff—a matter on which he had always held Peel had not redeemed his promises.[1] The Budget,

---

1 The claim was also made that the method of local rating imposed an undue burden on the classes which had suffered from the repeal of the Corn Laws. An Act of 1840 had definitely settled the question that rates could not be levied on movable property. It was therefore argued that grants should be made from the Exchequer to assist in meeting the charges of Local Government, for that was

however, was rejected by the House of Commons by a majority of nineteen after it had been submitted to damaging criticism by Gladstone.

---

the only means of securing some contribution from personal property and industrial incomes. Disraeli pressed for such an arrangement in 1850 and 1851. Already Parliament voted certain annual amounts towards the cost of administration of justice and poor relief. Later the improvements in sanitation and education were held to strengthen the case for grants in aid, *see* pp. 150–154, and 163–4 *infra*.

(NOTE.—Figures are given to the nearest thousand, and 000's are omitted.)

Year (ending Jan. 5th 1853–4 and Mar. 31st thereafter).	Exchequer Receipts.	Exchequer Issues.	Surplus(+) or Deficiency (—).	Debt Charge.
	£	£	£	£
1853	53,210	50,792	+ 2,418	27,935
1854	54,430	51,175	+ 3,256	27,805
1855*	76,568	83,187	— 6,616	35,431
1856	70,397	93,121	—22,724	28,113
1857	72,963	76,218	— 3,255	28,681
1858	67,882	68,129	— 247	28,745
1859	65,477	64,664	+ 813	28,673
1860	71,090	69,502	+ 1,587	28,754
1861	70,284	72,792	— 2,508	26,335
1862	69,674	71,116	— 1,442	26,331
1863	70,604	69,302	+ 1,302	26,232
1864	70,209	67,056	+ 3,153	26,212
1865	70,313	66,462	+ 3,851	26,369

* In 1854 a new method of keeping the public accounts was introduced. The whole gross revenue was brought into the Exchequer, i.e., no reductions were made for the costs of collection, these being met in future by votes in supply on account of the revenue departments. It should also be noticed that there was a change in the financial year, which was to end on March 31st and not on January 5th as hitherto. The figures given for 1855 above are therefore not only gross but also for the five quarters between January, 1854 and April, 1855.

CHAPTER V

THE COMPLETION OF FREE TRADE—1853–1865

FOR six years after the repeal of the Corn Laws those who had followed Peel on that issue had been out of office. The split in the Tory ranks had led to the formation of a Whig Government which, after effecting some important reforms, seemed to be drifting back to that condition of financial ineptitude which had called for the intervention of Peel in 1842. Lord Derby, however, found it impossible to emulate the example of Peel when the defeat of the Whigs in 1852 at last gave him his opportunity. His Ministry consisted of untried men, and its hold on the House of Commons was precarious. He was hampered by the protectionist traditions of his party, which put the Peelites on their guard against a possible reversal of policy. His appeal to the country in July also proved that the electorate had no desire to undo the work of Sir Robert Peel. Derby was, therefore, presented with the problem of how to arrive at financial stability without departing from general free trade principles or unduly disappointing the expectations of his immediate followers. To this Disraeli addressed himself. He admitted, when Parliament assembled, that the country did not wish to return to protection. But he could not entirely overlook the demands of the agricultural interest. As has been noticed, he proposed compensations ; he suggested that the malt tax and the hop duty should be reduced by one-half, and that farmers should be assessed for income tax on one-third instead of one-half of their rent. He combined with this a considerable increase in the house tax, which was calculated to impose a heavier burden on the towns. The defeat of the Government on these Budget proposals brought to a head a suggestion which had already been informally discussed—a possible coalition of Whigs and Peelites. After much negotiation a Ministry was formed under the leadership of a Peelite—Lord Aberdeen—and with five others in the Cabinet, although their party only numbered thirty in the House of Commons. Gladstone was appointed Chancellor of the Exchequer.

Finance has rarely so completely dominated the political situation as it did in 1853. The two traditional parties had failed to find any permanent basis for taxation, or to enunciate principles which had won any wide acceptance. On one ground or another they had contrived to secure the temporary continuation of the income tax, while protesting that it was not to be considered as an integral part of the revenue. When and by what means it could be dispensed with, neither party had clearly indicated. Meanwhile the Committee, which Hume had moved for in 1851, had examined a great number of witnesses with a view to discovering whether the income tax could be so reformed that its more objectionable features might be eliminated. Special attention was paid to the question of differentiating the rate according to the kind of income on which it was charged. It seemed obviously unjust that a temporary income, such as that derived from a profession, should pay at the same rate as a permanent income, such as that secured from the ownership of land. In the former case a provision would have to be made for old age and for the support of members of the family out of current income which would not be necessary in the latter. Actuaries suggested that all kinds of incomes should be capitalised and then assessed on that basis, but this recommendation presented serious practical difficulties.[1] There was, however, a strong body of opinion in favour of differentiation,

[1] J. S. Mill, who gave evidence before the Committee in favour of differentiation, also maintained that their arguments were fallacious. His point was that it was misleading to capitalise the income and to omit to capitalise the payments, i.e., if allowance be made because an income is terminable, the fact that it pays the tax for a limited period must also be taken into account. *See* Mill's "Principles of Political Economy," Book V, Chap. II, § 4.

though, in the end, the Committee had to confess its failure to arrive at an agreement as to the method of making it by submitting the evidence it had taken to Parliament without any recommendations. Gladstone was therefore faced with the necessity of defining his attitude to the income tax. He recognised that the whole of his Budget would have to rest on his decision with regard to it.

The Budget was introduced on April 18th in a speech which lasted nearly five hours and revealed a remarkable grasp of detail as well as a real unity of conception. The proposals with respect to the income tax Gladstone declared to be the corner-stone of the whole financial plan. His first object was to remove the feeling of uncertainty. "We think it unfortunate," he declared,[1] "that political circumstances have, for the last two or three years, led to a state of doubt in regard to the continuation of the tax and have even begotten by degrees a feeling on the part of the public, that the country is about to be entrapped unawares into its perpetuation." He had decided to arrest the movement towards the retention of the tax simply as a means of balancing the annual accounts. The income tax was a special instrument hitherto employed for special purposes. In an historical retrospect Gladstone showed what Pitt had achieved by using it as a "fiscal reserve," and how, when its object had been secured, it was allowed to lapse. It was also for a definite purpose that Peel had "called forth from repose this giant, who had once shielded us in war, to come and assist our industrious toils in peace."[2] Consequently he held that the tax was neither intended nor suited to be a permanent portion of the ordinary financial system. Even those who wished to retain it agreed that its inequalities ought to be removed by undertaking its reconstruction. To any alteration of the existing basis of the tax, however, he was strongly opposed. Relinquishment, he urged, was a possible course; when an emergency arose the weapon could be

---

[1] Gladstone's "Financial Statements," p. 48.
[2] *Ibid*, p. 18.

taken down from the shelf and used as formerly for the ends of honour and of duty. But to break up the basis of the tax by revising the schedules and extending the exemptions on one ground or another was to impair its possible usefulness in the future. "Whatever you do in regard to the income tax," he concluded,[1] "you must be bold, you must be intelligible, you must be decisive. You must not tamper with it. . . . I believe it to be of vital importance, whether you keep this tax or whether you part with it, that you either should keep it or should leave it, in a state in which it will be fit for service on an emergency; and this it will be impossible to do, if you break up the basis of your income tax."

The income tax was due to lapse. Should the Government allow it to do so? Gladstone asserted that it was a possible course to take. By means of a tax on real property, a universal system of trade licences, and a change in the levy of legacy duties, a sufficient sum could be raised to dispense with the income tax at once. But there were serious objections. The threefold substitute would cause more dissatisfaction than the income tax itself, and it would arrest the beneficial reform of taxation. He therefore proposed that, having marked out the income tax as essentially a temporary expedient, and having preserved it from amendments which would detract from its effectiveness in a possible future emergency, the House should agree to its extension for another seven years; for two years at 7d., for another two years at 6d., and for a final three years at 5d. in the pound. It was then to expire on April 5th, 1860. The merit of this plan was, that by taking a sufficiently long period it was possible to adjust the taxational system to meet the loss of the income tax. As long as it was renewed from year to year a comprehensive view was out of the question. The certainty that it would be levied for seven years also made it worth while to consider extensions of the tax, for the argument against any alteration of the basis obviously did not apply to an enlargement of its scope. Gladstone therefore proposed

[1] "Financial Statements," p. 47.

that incomes between £100 and £150—which had been exempt—should pay at the rate of 5d. in the pound for the whole seven years. He justified this lowering of the exemption level by contending that the class thereby included had benefited considerably from the revision of indirect taxes which had been effected by means of the income tax. On the same ground he argued that the exemption which Ireland had hitherto enjoyed ought to be removed. In 1842 Peel had intended to secure an equivalent to the income tax in Ireland by raising the spirits duty and augmenting the stamp charges.[1] The former had never been done, and the latter had only operated until 1850, when the stamp duties were reduced. There had been some opposition in the Cabinet to Gladstone's present proposal, but it was finally overruled by the decision to forego the repayment by Ireland of the £4,500,000 of consolidated annuities, a debt which had been incurred in the extension of the Poor Law to Ireland and in relieving the distress caused by the Famine.

Gladstone was also quite prepared to consider the inequalities of the income tax provided that the basis was left intact. He agreed that intelligence and skill paid too much and property too little, but he refused to vary the rate according to the source of income. It was possible and desirable in his opinion to effect an equalising of burdens by other means. To the plea that a man ought to be able to invest his savings, he replied that the suggestion was impracticable, except in one form, which the Government had decided to accept. If the savings, to the extent of one-seventh of the annual income, were invested in a deferred annuity or life assurance, it was to be exempt. While this concession was offered to all classes Gladstone argued that in actual practice it would benefit those who earned their incomes by their own exertions. He also allowed the recipient of an income from a profession the privilege, already enjoyed by traders, of assessing themselves on the average of three years instead of on each year separately. But his main effort to equalise

[1] *See* p. 90 *supra*.

burdens fell completely outside the structure of the income tax. He proposed to do so by reforming and extending the existing legacy duty. From the time when it had been imposed by Pitt in 1796, the duty had been anomalous, for his attempt to levy it on all collateral successions to property, real and personal, had failed; real property remaining exempt. In 1805 the duty had been applied to direct succession to personal property by bequest or inheritance, though personalty passing under the trusts of a settlement was not charged. Bequests payable out of real property were subject to duty, but real property passing by settlement or inheritance was not. As it stood, therefore, the legacy duty was manifestly unfair. It presented Gladstone with an opportunity to remove a number of injustices and at the same time to construct a tax on property which would redress the balance between the undue charge on incomes derived from professions as compared with that on incomes arising from property. He proposed to apply the legacy duty to all successions without distinction. But he did not intend to charge the same rate in every instance. Some property had to meet several other public charges—Gladstone suggested that it might be called "rateable property" because it included more than the term real property—and therefore ought not to pay so much as the kinds of personal property which escaped such charges. He laid down the general principle that the successor to rateable property should only pay on the estimated value of his life interest. The duty was also to fall more lightly on direct succession than on that of more remote relatives or strangers.

It was an essential part of Gladstone's argument that the income tax should serve some special purpose. He therefore proposed to associate it, in the seven years of its extension, with the remission of duties, "in order to bring to completion the noble work of commercial reform"; in other words, he wished to continue the policy of Sir Robert Peel, and to employ the same means for that end. He undertook a further general revision of the Customs tariff. The duties on 123 articles were abolished, and those on 133 reduced. Revision was based on the general principles that semi-manufactured goods should enter the country duty free, while manufactured goods, if retained in the tariff, should not be charged more than 10 per cent. *ad valorem.* The estimated loss to the Exchequer was over £1,250,000. One important effect of the reduction of the tariff on manufactured goods was that the preference hitherto given to Colonial manufactures by differential rates was eliminated. Gladstone was convinced of the merits of simplification, and insisted that indirect taxes should fall heavily on a limited number of commodities rather than more lightly on a much wider range. The other reductions and remissions, which fell outside the Customs tariff, also aimed at simplification. He repealed the excise duty on soap at a loss of over £1,000,000. In place of stamp duties on receipts, graduated according to the amount, he introduced a uniform rate of a penny for £2 and upwards. The Assessed Taxes were reformed by abolishing the progressive scales, compositions, and exemptions which had rendered them extremely complicated. Gladstone hoped by this means to make the charges "few, simple, and as nearly as possible, uniform." All the reforms did not come into immediate effect, but it was estimated that, when they did, they would amount to a total loss of more than five millions. This, it was hoped, would be more than compensated for by increased consumption before the income tax was due to lapse.

The Budget of 1853 was primarily conceived as the basis of a policy which would, if pursued for seven years, stabilise the system of public finance. Considered as an effort to group a mass of complicated details by the application to them of considered principles, it was a great essay in financial reconstruction. Everything, however, depended on what happened within the prescribed period. Had it been one of normal development Gladstone's hopes would probably have been realised. But it must be admitted that he had his disappointments before the outbreak of the Crimean War completely upset his calculations. His purpose in the intervening seven years was to find a secure tax income and to effect economies in expenditure so that the income tax could become a "reserve" after 1860. The chief new sources of income on which he relied were the legacy duty and the increased yield of the articles retained in the simplified tariff. In the latter his expectations were more than realised,[1] but his estimates with regard to the former proved to be very wide of the mark. He anticipated that it would bring in by the end of four years, when it would be in full operation, an additional £2,000,000 to the revenue. As a matter of fact it did not produce more than £600,000. The error seems to have arisen from the assumption that the property which became chargeable to the new tax would be as valuable as that which paid the old legacy duty.[2] But Gladstone met with a more serious failure in his attempt to reduce the annual charge of the National Debt by carrying through a conversion. Previous reductions of the rate of interest on Government securities had left little margin for the operation unless an effort was made to create 2½ per cents. Gladstone admitted that 3 per cent. had been taken in the past as the lowest possible limit, but he thought the general fall in the rate of interest presented him with an opportunity which ought not to be lost. The prevalent opinion at the time, indeed, was that interest had fallen permanently; in some unexplained way it had settled down after the violent fluctuations of the past. If this was so, it was the clear duty of the Chancellor to effect a reduction in the annual debt charge. He therefore decided to undertake a conversion which presented difficulties of considerable magnitude. Goulburn had, in 1844, dealt with £250,000,000—an operation without precedent at that time—but Gladstone proposed to deal with nearly twice that amount. The stock in

---

[1] The Customs amounted to £20,552,000 in 1852–3, and £23,306,000 in 1860–1.

[2] The opponents of the tax believed, or affected to believe, that Gladstone underestimated its yield in 1853. They spoke of four millions; probably to secure support in resisting what Lord Morley calls "the first rudimentary breach in the ramparts of the territorial system." For a discussion of the reason for the miscalculation *see* Northcote, "Twenty Years of Financial Policy," pp. 207–10.

question was, for the most part, either 3 per cent. "consolidated" or "reduced" annuities, and, under the terms on which they were held, twelve months' notice had to be given before they could be redeemed. It was impossible to announce that the interest would be reduced and dissentients paid off at the termination of the notice, for the Government would thus pledge itself to a course which might prove a bad bargain. Gladstone's plan was conceived in order to induce holders voluntarily to yield their 3 per cents. for new stock. It was a highly ingenious scheme. They were offered three options: (1) The holders of 3 per cents.—then standing at par—could exchange them for new 3½ per cents., secure against redemption for forty years, by giving £100 of the old stock for £82 10s. of the new. This involved a reduction both in the capital and the interest. (2) As an alternative they could exchange their 3 per cents. for 2½ per cents., each £100 of the old stock to purchase £110 of the new. The capital was in this case increased, but the interest was reduced. This, it was expected, would prove very attractive, for there was no margin for future conversion, and it thus seemed to offer a permanent form of irredeemable stock. Consequently Gladstone limited the issue of 2½ per cents. to a total of £30,000,000. (3) In addition to these alternatives there was a third option of a different nature. Exchequer bonds were introduced bearing a fixed rate of interest—2¾ for ten years, and 2½ for the following thirty years—and redeemable at par. These terms were offered to the holders of certain eighteenth century stocks, such as South Sea stock, as well as to those who had "consolidated" and "reduced," but the former were warned that unless they took advantage of the offer they would be paid off in January, 1854. They objected to the terms. As the year wore on it became increasingly obvious that Gladstone had misread the situation when he propounded his conversion scheme in the spring. The international outlook was threatening, and the harvest happened to be a bad one. Government securities fell below par, and consequently the set of options lost all their attractiveness. Less than £3,000,000 were converted under all the options put together. Fortunately the Government had not committed itself to pay off the holders of any stocks except those already mentioned. When January came round consols were down to 91, and the dissenting holders of South Sea stock and other old annuities had to be paid off at par, for which £8,000,000 had to be taken from the Exchequer balances. Gladstone afterwards acknowledged that he had committed an error in not discerning the signs of the times. He failed to see that the high-water was just past and that, although the tide had not perceptibly fallen, yet it was going to fall.[1] But the reception which the proposals received in financial circles proves that his scheme was not regarded as rash or ill-considered when he introduced it. The blame does not attach to the financier, but to the statesman. Gladstone, it is alleged, ought to have known that the country was about to be drawn into a continental war. This criticism is easy to make after the event. It was, indeed, inevitable that his opponents should fasten upon the failure of the conversion and the consequent depletion of the Exchequer balances in the financial discussions of the following year. This miscalculation, however, did not affect the merits of the 1853 Budget. The country entered upon the Crimean War with its financial stability well established, and in this department at any rate it revealed its real strength. Had not Gladstone laid the foundations of a comprehensive scheme the outbreak of war would have contributed to the growing financial confusion.

The Budget of 1854 was introduced on March 6th, a few weeks before the actual declaration of war against Russia, but the estimates were already seriously affected by the increased military charges. Although the reforms of the previous year had met with a gratifying success, Gladstone anticipated a deficit of over two and a half millions. He pointed out that it would be possible to meet this by going back on some of the resolutions of 1853, as, for

[1] Letter of March 8th, 1861, printed in Morley's "Gladstone," Vol. I, p. 473; *see also* short memorandum in Appendix of same volume, pp. 647–8.

instance, by reimposing the excise on soap and suspending the reduction on tea. At the moment, however, he saw no reason for revising their previous decisions, or indeed, for resorting to any additional indirect taxation. Nor did he propose to raise a loan. He urged that it was highly desirable to pay the expenses of the war by means of taxes and, as far as he could see at present, by direct taxes. His proposal was that the income tax should be doubled for the first half of the year, which would give him a surplus of nearly £500,000. This was admittedly provisional. The declaration of war opened up the whole question again, and Gladstone presented a second financial statement on May 8th. His new estimates required some £6,850,000 more than he had asked for in March. In accordance with his contention that the war, in its early stages at any rate, should be paid for by means of taxes, he proposed to secure the whole amount by this method, so distributing the burden that it would fall equally on all classes. In the first place, the doubling of the income tax was to be extended to the second part of the financial year and to remain as the war rate until the conclusion of hostilities. Secondly, there was to be a further rise in the duties on Scottish and Irish spirits. Thirdly, the duties on different kinds of sugar were to be revised so that the finer qualities should pay at a higher rate than the coarser. Fourthly, the malt duty was to be raised from 2s. 8½d. to 4s, a bushel. Since the money was needed before the taxes would be collected, Gladstone issued Exchequer bonds in anticipation of their yield. He contended that this was not a departure from the principle he had already laid down, because the bonds would be redeemed in a comparatively short time by the proceeds of taxes which had been voted. This, however, was hardly a safe assumption. War is usually progressively more expensive. It was probable that when the bonds fell due the whole available tax yield would be necessary for the conduct of the war, and the Chancellor of the Exchequer would be faced by the alternative of increasing taxation or of renewing the bonds for a new period. Gladstone was not justified in ignoring the possibility that he was making a considerable addition to the unfunded debt by the method he adopted.

It has often been pointed out that Gladstone unnecessarily embarrassed himself by enunciating broad general principles. A practical politician, it is argued, should avoid generalisations, because he will find the deductions from them highly inconvenient at some subsequent stage of his public career. As a matter of fact, Gladstone was not so reckless in this matter as some have supposed. There is usually some reservation behind his most sweeping statements. But he certainly had the gift of focussing attention on the main principle so effectively that, when he pointed out the more or less implicit qualifications, he was accused of casuistry. In 1854 he provoked a great deal of discussion by his assertion that wars should be paid for by present taxation and not by loans which shifted the burden on to posterity. His argument in support of this thesis was partly based on moral considerations and partly on economic. "The expenses of a war," he declared, "are a moral check which it has pleased the Almighty to impose upon the ambition and lust of conquest, that are inherent in so many nations. . . . The necessity of meeting from year to year the expenditure which it entails is a salutary and wholesome check, making them measure the cost of the benefit upon which they may calculate." This doctrine finds little confirmation in history. The risks of war are sufficiently appalling, it might appear, to deter the nations from embarking upon it without insisting on the additional terrors of high taxation. War, however, is not contemplated, even by those nations in which ambition and lust of conquest are supposed to be inherent, as a nicely calculated affair of material benefits. At the worst, there is the belief that the advantages will greatly outweight the costs. More usually each side is able to convince itself that war is an inevitable outcome of the machinations of the other. The fear of increased taxation will not dispel international suspicions or mitigate racial animosities. To contemporaries, however, it was the preaching of this doctrine by a member of the Government engaged in the prosecution of a war that seemed incongruous. Why should he want to check the warlike ardour of the people by throwing the whole cost on the present and by safeguarding the interests of future generations? Was it not his business to proclaim that no expense was too lavish to achieve the ends for which the country had gone to war? Was not national honour involved? Gladstone did not seem to realise that to talk of moral checks was to arouse some suspicion of the strength of his patriotism.

The economic reasons adduced for and against the practice of borrowing reveal some confusion of mind. Gladstone spoke as though the Government had the alternative of imposing the burden of war cost on posterity, if it wished. He also seemed to regard loans as subscribed out of accumulations of capital, thereby diverting it to unproductive purposes and damaging the position of the working classes. His opponents, of whom Newmarch[1] was the most notable, were content to argue that heavier taxation would ultimately encroach on capital, but that there was sufficient capital to meet any loans that were likely to be floated without diminishing the amount profitably employed in productive industry. Stafford Northcote similarly contends that there are certain conditions of national existence under which it is less injurious to part with capital than with earnings, the assumption being that taxes would fall on the latter and borrowing would secure the former. This capital he conceives as withdrawn from the market, thus reducing the fund which supports labour. He thinks, however, that heavy taxation, would hit the workers harder than this diminution in

1 William Newmarch, in his essay "On the Loans raised by Mr. Pitt," already referred to on p. 16*n. supra*, is obviously dealing with Gladstone's arguments, although he does not mention his name. His idea that there were sufficient "overflowings of the National Capital" to float loans without doing any damage to the fund is taken from Mill, "Principles of Political Economy," Book V, Chap. VII. Northcote, "Twenty Years of Financial Policy," pp. 259–262, is also concerned about the effects on the wages-fund. The theory, which caused some of the confusion in the arguments noticed in this passage, was ultimately abandoned by Mill in 1869.

the wages-fund. The antithesis between capital and present earnings or current production is unreal, and the idea that posterity can lend any assistance misses the real point. A war must be carried on by means of existing resources, whether they be commodities or services. The question is whether the State should secure command of these means by acquiring purchasing power through taxation or through borrowing. Whichever method it employs it limits the amount available for other purposes. By taxation it imposes economies on those who are obliged to pay; by borrowing it induces persons to limit their present demand in consideration of a future payment. Taxation differs from borrowing in that it does not involve any future charge. At the time, however, both taxation and borrowing are means of gaining a lien on present production. Gladstone was certainly right in suspecting the results of the fatally easy method of borrowing. It always tends, when proper banking facilities exist, to be partly based on credit and not on current savings. When this happens purchasing power is manufactured which is not represented by any increased production. Prices tend to rise, and what is in effect disguised taxation of general consumption results. To impose additional taxation at the beginning of a war is a sound policy. If once the opportunity is missed experience has demonstrated again and again that it is impossible to recover lost ground.

How Gladstone would have met the financial problems of the later stages of the war can only be inferred from his subsequent statements. The Aberdeen Ministry fell in January as a result of the outcry against the mismanagement in the Crimea, and, although he accepted office in the reconstituted Government under the leadership of Lord Palmerston, Gladstone (and his Peelite colleagues) resigned when the Prime Minister agreed to the appointment of a Committee of Inquiry into the conduct of the war. He was succeeded at the Exchequer by Sir George Cornewall Lewis.[1] The Budget was intro-

[1] Sir George Cornewall Lewis (1806–1863) was a native of Radnorshire. He was Financial Secretary to the Treasury from 1850 to 1852.

duced on April 20th, 1855; the new Chancellor had so recently assumed office that he followed the main lines which his predecessor had intended to propose. There was an estimated deficiency of £23,000,000 to be provided for in the coming year, and a loan was inevitable. Lewis contracted with Messrs. Rothschild for a loan of £16,000,000 and issued £3,000,000 of Exchequer bills; the remaining £4,000,000 required he raised by taxation, chiefly indirect, falling on sugar, tea, coffee, and spirits. He added twopence in the pound to the income tax, thus raising it to 1s. 4d. It is possible that Gladstone would have attempted to impose heavier taxation in 1855, but it is quite clear that he would have been unable to avoid a loan. The costs of the war continued to outrun the estimates and Lewis had to supplement them from time to time. Still the country stood the financial strain with comparative ease, a fact which was largely due to the unimpaired prosperity of trade and industry, and the special effort to meet the war charges out of current income. Gladstone's insistence on increased taxation in 1854 was fully justified. The total cost of the war was computed by Lewis on the basis of a comparison of the years 1851–1854 and 1854–1857, which gives a general indication of the rise in public income and expenditure. He showed that the war had involved the net addition of over £32,000,000 to the National Debt, and a special taxational effort amounting to about £38,000,000. Of the latter the yield of direct taxes was about 65 per cent. of the whole. It would, however, be misleading to suppose that, even from the narrow point of view here taken, that the Crimean War merely represented the spending of £70,000,000; there was no return to the scale of public expenditure in 1851–1854, for the war had broken the European peace and ushered in a period of international unrest which resulted in a general increase of armaments.

The Budget of 1856, although it was brought forward after the conclusion of peace, was to all intents and purposes a war Budget. Retaining all the war taxes, the Chancellor had still to borrow £5,000,000 in order to avoid a deficit. He submitted that, apart from the charge of the debt, the country's expenditure per head of the population was not greater than that of other nations. But the necessity for economy was insisted upon by both Disraeli and Gladstone. The former argued that the maintenance of a considerable military establishment in time of peace so far from strengthening the country, would impair its resources should another crisis arise; the latter regretted that more stringent reductions had not been proposed. There was already an indication of the differences of opinion which were to shape the financial discussions of the next three years. The hopes that had been placed in the year 1860 had by no means been dissipated by the Crimean War. It was still expected to mark an era in finance, and the problem was how to secure that excess of income over expenditure which would enable the Chancellor to dispense with the income tax in accorddance with the plan of 1853. Neither Lewis nor his opponents faced the fact that the Crimean War had so upset calculations that the prospect of adhering to that plan was hardly worth contemplating. They differed as to the method which ought to be pursued in order to attain an end about which they were in agreement. Lewis wished to continue the war taxes as far as practicable so as to pay off part of the debt recently contracted by meeting the Exchequer bonds on maturity and maintaining a special Sinking Fund. Disraeli expressed the popular feeling against the retention of war taxation in time of peace. His protest was supported by Gladstone, who insisted that economy in expenditure was an urgent necessity. The Chancellor's critics did less than justice to his efforts to reduce the National Debt, and thereby to lighten the annual charge as soon as possible. They represented the issue as a choice between high taxation accompanied by high expenditure, and remission of war taxation with a corresponding revision of the estimates. In 1857 Lewis proposed to retain the income tax at 7d. in the pound until 1860—instead of the 5d. rate provided for by the arrangement of 1853—and to reduce the duties on tea and sugar from the war figure, but not so low as had been originally intended. But he resisted other demands for remissions and aroused

Gladstone's indignation by associating himself with the eighteenth century doctrine, that a good system should press lightly on a number of points and heavily on none.[1] This reduction of taxation, however, meant a smaller surplus in the coming year, and seemed to threaten a deficit in the following two years, when it would take full effect, for there was not a corresponding revision of expenditure. Disraeli drew attention to this danger, pointing out that it would probably make the removal of the income tax in 1860 impossible.

The assumption that the Government could, if it wished, return to the standard of expenditure in 1853 was groundless. War in Persia and China, and reconstruction of dockyards and building of the new battleships meant increased estimates. The General Election of 1857 showed that the country approved of Palmerston's policy, and inferentially, of the expenditure it involved. Consequently the opposition to the estimates had to be modified and Lewis's Budget accepted. His calculations, however, were upset by the unexpected costs of operations in the East and the complication introduced by the outbreak of the Indian Mutiny. Still more serious was the financial collapse which came in the autumn. This crisis had its origin in the United States, where speculation had been stimulated by the recent gold discoveries. Banks had advanced credit for the construction of railways to such an extent that many of them could not meet their liabilities when the failure of the Ohio Life Insurance and Trust Company precipitated a panic. The effect was immediately felt in Great Britain, for some £80,000,000, it was estimated, had been invested in American stock. The Western Bank and the City of Glasgow Bank had to suspend payment. So strong was the drain on the reserve of the Bank of England that the discount rate was advanced to 10 per cent. Still the demand for accommodation continued until by November

[1] He declared that Arthur Young's opinion that "simplicity in taxation is the greatest additional weight that can be given to taxes" was full of wisdom and a useful practical guide in the arrangement of a system of taxation.

11th the stock of coin and bullion had fallen so low that it was impossible to make any further advances. At this point the Chancellor of the Exchequer intimated to the Directors of the Bank that, if they were unable to meet the demands for advances on good securities without exceeding the limits of note circulation defined by the Act of 1844, the Government was prepared to propose a Bill of Indemnity to cover a breach of its provisions. This announcement restored confidence, though, in this instance, the Bank had actually to issue notes to the extent of £2,000,000 beyond the statutory limit.[1]

The financial outlook in 1858 was not so bright as it had been at the beginning of the previous year. The money market had been through a period of acute strain and needed time to recuperate. With its commitments in the East the Government had little opportunity for retrenchment in expenditure. But the year 1860 was drawing near and it was hard to abandon the hopes which had been built on it. By a peculiar irony the accidents of politics called to the Exchequer in the two remaining years Lewis's leading critics—Disraeli and Gladstone—and they had in turn to put forward their practical proposals. Palmerston was defeated in February on the Conspiracy Bill. He was succeeded by Lord Derby, who found himself as in 1852, at the head of a Government which did not command a majority in the House of Commons. His Chancellor—Disraeli—could plead that the estimates had been prepared before he assumed office, and that the delicate balance of parties greatly restricted his action. He had also identified himself while in opposition, with the general demand for reduction of taxation. The estimated expenditure of the year was over £67,000,000, but of this £3,500,000 was due to the arrangements which had been made for the redemption of the war debt. Since he held that there was an obligation to reduce the income tax to 5d.—the rate contemplated by the "compact" of 1853—he had to face the alternative of increasing taxation

[1] This is the only instance in which it was found necessary to exceed the limit. But *see* p. 207*n. infra.*

or abandoning the attempt to redeem the debt. He chose the latter, proposing the repeal of the War Sinking Fund Act and renewing the Exchequer bonds which were falling due. By this means he converted an estimated deficit of £4,000,000 into one of £500,000. To meet this he raised the spirit duties in Ireland to the English level[1] and imposed a penny stamp duty on bankers' cheques. Disraeli, in preferring to prepare for the removal of the income tax rather than to continue the redemption of the debt, was no doubt giving expression to the popular feeling on the question; but a broader survey reveals that it was a mistake. In 1859 the Derby Ministry was defeated on its Reform Bill and, on appeal to the country, failed to secure a majority. The Whigs, Peelites, and Radicals came to an understanding, and Palmerston returned to power. He now conceived a strong suspicion of the designs of Napoleon III, and the country supported him in preparing by the building of ships and the construction of defences for any eventualities. There was a consequent increase in the naval and military estimates which defeated the hopes for economy. Gladstone, when he introduced his Budget in June, had to announce an estimated deficit of nearly £4,500,000. It was too late in the year to contemplate anything more than a provisional arrangement. He was as opposed as ever to the policy of borrowing, and the indirect taxes still remained at their war level. Necessity compelled him to resort to the income tax which he proposed to raise to 9d. in the pound. As this would fall short of what was needed, he also reduced the length of the credit period allowed to maltsters, which would have the effect of bringing an additional three-quarters of a million of the duty within the current financial year.

The time had now arrived to put the hopes so persistently centred in 1860 to the test. Gladstone took the unusual

[1] There had been a considerable difference between the duties on spirits in England, Scotland and Ireland. Gladstone raised the Scottish and Irish duties in 1853, and again in 1854. Sir George Lewis assimilated the Scottish and English duties in 1855, and in 1858 Disraeli removed the remaining difference by bringing up the Irish duty to the same level.

course of presenting his Budget as early as February 10th, for he was anxious to explain the details of a scheme which was even more comprehensive than that of 1853. With his wonted skill he put in the foreground the facts which gave a peculiar significance to the coming financial year. There was the unprecedented relief to the annual charge of the National Debt caused by the falling in of annuities to the amount of £2,146,000. As the law stood, the duties on tea and sugar, yielding nearly £12,000,000, would lapse on March 31st. At the same time the income tax would terminate and thus deprive the Chancellor of between £9,000,000 and £10,000,000. On the side of revenue the House seemed to have the opportunity of making decisions of far-reaching importance. Gladstone maintained the illusion. He estimated the income for 1860–1 on the basis of the understanding of 1853—omitting the income tax and taking the tea and sugar duties at the minimum rates—in order to demonstrate the extent of the deficit and allow his hearers to exercise the largest and freest choice as to the means they would adopt to meet it. The total income would be £60,700,000 ; he estimated the expenditure at £70,100,000—leaving a deficit of £9,400,000. A simple solution of the problem, he suggested, would be to renew the tea and sugar duties at the existing "war" rates and impose an income tax of 9d. in the pound. But this would be a curious sequel to the calculations of 1853. In an interesting digression he showed where those calculations had broken down. The succession duty had been a disappointment, and the Crimean War had not only wiped out the annual surpluses which would have reduced the National Debt, but had also considerably increased it. Additional taxation of the war period, however, was sufficient to meet these charges and make the abandonment of the income tax possible. The real difficulty was the steep rise in expenditure. In 1853 estimates of future expenses were based on the fact that there had been hardly any increase for about twenty-five years. The assumption that there would be no perceptible rise in the seven years had been completely falsified, and the principle of economy could not be drastically applied.

To accept increased expenditure and then make the requisite additions to taxation was not Gladstone's method. As a financier he sought for some unifying principle as the basis of his Budgets. In 1853 it was the provision for the ultimate extinction of the income tax accompanied by commercial reform as a justification for its temporary retention. The key stone in 1860 was the Commercial Treaty with France. Everything fell into its place with respect to it. He was profoundly dissatisfied with the rapid growth of public expenditure. The only hope of abating it was to remove the suspicion of French motives, which was inspiring the outlay on forts and ships. "For this panic," he wrote at a later date,[1] "the treaty of commerce with France was the only sedative. It was, in fact, a counter-irritant; and it aroused the sense of commercial interest to counteract the war passion." The Treaty also made it possible to continue the task of reforming the tariff which had been suspended for seven years. The very fact that expenditure had reached such a high level was, he urged, a reason for persevering in that course. Former revisions had enabled the country to bear an increased burden of taxation without staggering under it. There was every cause to believe that a further simplification would contribute to the general prosperity and thereby strengthen the resources of the community. Further, the continuation of the policy of commercial reform would justify the retention of the income tax, for it would again be associated with the work which Peel had ascribed to it. In short, the Treaty with France enabled the Government to complete the process which had been initiated in 1842, and continued in 1845, 1846, and 1853; it opened up the prospect of economy in public expenditure; and it promised such an adjustment of revenue and expenditure that ultimately it might be possible to dispense with the income tax.

The suggestion of a commercial understanding with France had been thrown out by John Bright during a

[1] *See* undated memorandum quoted in Morley's "Gladstone," Vol. II, p. 23.

speech on expenditure and taxation in the previous session.[1] It had come to the notice of the French economist, Michel Chevalier, who wrote to Cobden urging him to take up the question. Cobden discussed it with Gladstone, and came to an agreement that he should get into touch with the French supporters of the project in Paris, where he had already arranged to spend a holiday. He found that the French Minister of Commerce, Eugène Rouher, was well disposed to free trade ideas. The Emperor himself also entered into the discussions. It is clear, however, that he was much less influenced by the commercial aspects of the proposal than by the possible political advantage of better relations with Great Britain. He was somewhat chary of arousing the opposition of the strong protectionist interests in France, and it was only after much vacillation that he ultimately decided in favour of a treaty. Under the constitution of the Second Empire Napoleon claimed that he had the power to amend the tariff in a foreign treaty without reference to the French Chamber. But Cobden had to contend with many other serious difficulties before the details of the scheme were finally adjusted. He made it a fundamental principle that Great Britain should not grant France any exclusive privileges. This meant that, as far as Great Britain was concerned, the concessions given to France were to be offered to all other countries. But what the concessions were to be was the subject of negotiation between the two contracting parties. In this way Great Britain did not depart from its free trade attitude, though it was taking the final step in that direction, with the help of an agreement with another State. To doctrinaire free traders this seemed a departure from strict principles, for they held that the country ought to remove its tariffs without consultation with, or guarantee from, any other. Cobden's view was that practical considerations in this instance outweighed mere theoretical objections. Great Britain's offer was simple. She proposed to abolish immediately and totally all duties on manufactured goods, to reduce the duty on

[1] G. M. Trevelyan : "Life of John Bright," p. 285.

brandy to the colonial level, and to adopt a lower scale on the importation of wines. These were, in fact, concessions to France, though they were also freely offered to all other countries without any conditions. France, however, limited her concessions to Great Britain only. She engaged to reduce the duty on British coal and coke, bar and pig iron, steel, tools and machinery, yarns, and flax and hemp manufactures. From October 1st, 1861, she agreed to remove all prohibitions and to reduce high duties to 30 per cent. or less *ad valorem*. After 1864 the maximum was to be 25 per cent., and an arrangement was made for the conversion of *ad valorem* into specific duties by further negotiation. The treaty was signed on January 23rd, and was to run for ten years in the first instance. Within that period its influence became more potent than its authors had anticipated, for it included a most favoured nation clause, by means of which any further concessions made by one of the parties to another State automatically accrued to the other. France entered upon a period of commercial negotiations, and Great Britain secured a further reduction of duties on many articles as a result.[1]

Gladstone estimated the loss to the revenue of the first year's operation of the Commercial Treaty at £1,190,000. He also proposed to abolish the duties on a variety of articles quite apart from the treaty—including butter, eggs, cheese, nuts and tallow—at a further loss of nearly £1,000,000. The tariff was thus reduced to forty-eight articles and, except for the remaining nominal duties on timber and corn, was not in any sense protective. To effect these commercial reforms the income tax was raised from 9d. to 10d. in the pound for one year. This naturally aroused opposition, and in the discussion of the Budget proposals the issue was narrowed down to the extra penny which, it was alleged, was necessitated by the suggested repeal of the paper duty. The case against the duty as one of the surviving Excise charges on manufactures was peculiarly

[1] *See* C. J. Fuch's "Trade Policy of Great Britain," Chap. I; P. Ashley, "Modern Tariff History," Part III, Chap. III; and J. A. Hobson, "Richard Cobden, the International Man," Chap. X.

strong; it was expensive to collect, it tended to prevent improvement in manufacture, and it was, as its critics insisted, a "tax on knowledge," for a uniform charge on all qualities of paper affected the price of all publications. But the capitalists interested in the industry did not wish competition to be introduced, and their original objections were soon converted into more general terms. The Government's majority in the House of Commons fell to nine, and when the Paper Duty Abolition Bill reached the Lords it was so successfully identified with the increase of the income tax that the Second Chamber rejected it. This interference with a money Bill led to a strong remonstrance from the Commons; but the matter was allowed to drop for the moment.

The Budget Speech of 1861 is remarkable for the space given to an analysis of the financial history of the past year. It was, Gladstone freely admitted, an unfavourable statement. Taxation and expenditure had reached the highest point known in time of peace. The harvest had been one of the worst for the last half-century. There was a deficiency of £2,000,000 on the estimated receipts. He demonstrated, however, that the reforms in the tariff had been followed by increased consumption, and had therefore been fully justified. The presentation of his argument was a complete contrast from that of the previous year. Then he wished to bring the deficiency of revenue into relief, and did so by assuming that the taxes which were about to expire could not be counted on. Now he took for granted that the income tax at 10d. and the sugar and tea duties were to be continued, and by this means he produced a prospective surplus of nearly £2,000,000. This was too much to keep in hand, and consequently he proposed remission of taxation. The surplus was not sufficient to enable him to do anything effective with the sugar and tea duties. Besides, the income tax had the prior claim. His plan was therefore to take the penny off the income tax at the loss of rather more than £1,000,000 and to associate it with the repeal of the paper duty, which had been defeated in the previous year. The Opposition had so closely connected the extra penny with the proposed repeal of the paper duty that Gladstone was in a position to gain his end by admitting their argument that the two were linked together. He also took occasion to repudiate the idea that he was opposed to indirect taxation as such, and to point out that the free trade movement had meant the extensive repeal of indirect taxes and the concentration of the burden on a few productive indirect taxes. As to the opinion that it was peculiarly his duty to abolish the income tax because of the promises of 1853 he pleaded that it was imposing an impossible task on him in the existing circumstances. " I should like very much," he added,[1] " to be the man who could abolish the income tax. I do not abandon altogether the hope that the time may come."

From the beginning of the Palmerston Ministry Gladstone had never disguised his uneasiness about the high level of expenditure. At first he had to struggle as best he could against popular opinion which supported the Prime Minister's efforts to strengthen the national defences. It is a tribute to his courage and resourcefulness that, in spite of the increasing estimates of the first three years, Gladstone was able to carry through the Budget scheme of 1860. After 1862 he began to reap his reward. In that year he had such a limited surplus that, in view of the complications arising out of the American Civil War, he decided that he could neither remit any taxation, nor did he think it necessary to impose any. The only important alteration of the year was the commutation of the hop duty for a new scale of brewers' licences. It proved to be the turning-point. The international situation became easier, and the principle of economy won general acceptance. Year after year the Chancellor had substantial surpluses. The last four of his series of eight consecutive Budgets are characterised by reduction of expenditure and remission of taxation. He tried to balance the relief given to direct and indirect taxes so as to distribute it as evenly as possible. In 1863 he reduced the income tax to 7d. in the pound and the duty on tea to 1s. In the following year the

[1] Gladstone's " Financial Statements," p. 244.

income tax was brought down to 6d., and the complicated question of the sugar duties was taken in hand. Gladstone not only effected a reduction, but also simplified the duties by adopting a new system of classifying the different kinds of sugar. The changes he made removed the last remnants of the "war" duty on the commodity. In the Budget of 1865 he employed a handsome surplus to reduce the income tax to 4d.—the lowest point it had ever touched—and the tea duty to 6d. The legislative inactivity of the Palmerston Ministry brought out into sharper relief the work of its Chancellor. So, when its seven years had run it was no wonder that its appeal to the country secured a vote of confidence. In the new Parliament Gladstone was able to announce another surplus. He completed his work by repealing the duty of 1s. the load on timber which, though low, was distinctively protective. But the death of Palmerston reopened the question of Parliamentary Reform, and on this issue the Government resigned in June, 1866.

(Note.—Figures are given to the nearest thousand, and 000's are omitted.)

Year (ending 31st March).	Ex-chequer Receipts.	Ex-chequer Issues.	Surplus(+) or Deficiency (—).	Debt Charge.
	£000	£000	£000	£000
1866	67,812	65,914	+ 1,898	26,233
1867	69,435	67,780	+ 2,655	26,082
1868	69,600	71,236[1]	— 1,636	26,572
1869	72,592	74,973[1]	— 2,381	26,618
1870	75,434	68,865	+ 6,569	27,054
	(73,681)[2]	(67,111)		
1871	69,945	69,548	+ 397	26,826
	(68,174)	(67,778)		
1872	74,708	71,490	+ 3,218	26,840
	(73,088)	(69,870)		
1873	76,609	70,714	+ 5,895	26,805
	(74,722)	(68,828)[3]		
1874	77,336	76,467	+ 869	26,707
	(75,474)	(74,605)		
1875	74,921	74,328	+ 593	27,094
	(73,599)	(73,005)		
1876	77,132	76,622	+ 510	27,444[4]
	(75,488)	(74,978)		(280)
1877	78,565	78,125	+ 440	27,993
	(76,769)	(76,330)		(625)
1878	79,763	82,403	— 2,640	28,413
	(77,740)	(80,380)		(765)
1879	83,116	85,408	— 2,292	28,644
	(81,155)	(83,446)		(634)
1880	81,265	84,106	— 2,841	28,763
	(79,344)	(82,185)		(651)
1881	84,041	83,108	+ 933	29,575
	(81,872)	(80,939)		(351)

[1] Including Supplementary Votes for the Abyssinian Expedition, etc.
[2] See note [1] on next page.
[3] Including £3,200,000 for the *Alabama* claims.
[4] From 1876 the amount of the New Sinking Fund — which is included in the Debt Charge—is given in brackets in each year. It was suspended in 1886 and 1887.

(NOTE.—Figures are given to the nearest thousand, and 000's are omitted.)

Year (ending 31st March).	Exchequer Receipts.	Intercepted for Local Taxation Accounts	Exchequer Issues.	Surplus(+) or Deficiency (—).	Debt Charge.
	£000	£000	£000	£000	£000
1882	85,822 (83,955)		85,473 (83,606)	+ 349	29,665 (270)
1883	89,814 (87,387)		89,716 (87,288)	+ 98	29,679 (214)
1884	88,085 (86,160)		87,880 (85,954)	+ 205	29,652 (600)
1885	90,043 (87,988)		91,093 (89,038)	— 1,050	29,548 (508)
1886	89,581[1]		92,224	— 2,643	23,450
1887	90,773		89,997	+ 776	27,958
1888	89,802		87,424	+ 2,379	26,214 (679)
1889[2]	88,473	1,400	87,684[3]	+ 789	26,225 (1,164)
1890	89,304	5,186	86,083	+ 3,221	25,227 (700)
1891	89,489	6,974	87,733	+ 1,756	25,207 (1,272)
1892	90,995	7,582	89,928	+ 1,067	25,200 (1,542)

[1] In comparing the figures of 1886 and subsequent years with those of previous years it should be noticed that in the former the Army and Navy Extra Receipts and the Contributions by India for Military Charges are excluded. The revision which is necessary to make the figures comparable has been carried back as far as 1870, the revised amount being given in brackets, *see* "Statistical Abstract," Thirty-second Number, 1885.

[2] From 1889 part of the yield of certain taxes (Customs, Excise and Death Duties) was paid to Local Taxation Accounts and did not appear—although collected by the Imperial Government—in the Exchequer Receipts, *see* p. 234*n.*, for details.

[3] Inclusive of expenditure incurred under the National Debt Conversion Act, 1888, which amounted to £2,009,958, and which though not in the Budget Estimate was met out of revenue.

CHAPTER VI

STRAINS AND STRESSES—1866–1892

I

SIR ROBERT GIFFEN expressed the opinion that Gladstone was preparing for another great *coup* in the series of Budgets from 1863 to 1866.[1] The annual expenditure had been reduced from £72,792,000 in 1861 to £65,914,000 in 1866. The income tax stood at 4d. in the pound, and the duties on tea and sugar were moderate. Still the revenue was proving elastic and further surpluses seemed certain. What was to be the next step ? Would Gladstone take the favourable opportunity to consign the income tax to the "reserve" of which he had spoken in 1853 ? Or would he retain it in order to effect reforms in the taxational system ? It was clear enough that the policy of reduction of direct and indirect taxes would reach a point when it would be necessary to adopt a more positive course. A comprehensive survey and consolidation of the existing taxes was a task which would have made a peculiar appeal to Gladstone. But the *coup* which Giffen surmises was in contemplation was not to be brought off at this juncture. The years from 1863 to 1866, with their remarkable surpluses, did not prove to be the inauguration of a new period. They were in many ways highly exceptional. The Chancellor had a real passion for economy, and public opinion had rallied to his support. A wave of prosperity was passing over the country and the public revenue was

[1] Giffen: "Essays in Finance," first series, p. 223. Giffen's essay on "Mr. Gladstone's Work in Finance" was written in 1869.

rising. Appearances might well encourage the hope that Gladstone would attain the object he had set before himself in 1853. The year 1866, however, dispelled the illusion. It was not only that the Government resigned in June—though the breach in continuity was important. Gladstone had been able to accomplish so much because he had been at the Exchequer for eight years; his successor could hardly be expected to have the same grasp of details. But, altogether apart from personal considerations, 1866 was a critical year. The prosperity of the previous years had stimulated speculation to a dangerous extent. Recent legislation had also contributed to assist in the inflation of credit. In 1862 the amended Companies Act had facilitated the formation of joint stock enterprises with limited liability. Immediate advantage was taken of this law to found a great variety of new companies as well as to reconstruct old companies on the new basis. In order to dispose of the stock issued by these companies the practice of "financing" was generally adopted, i.e., instead of waiting until its stock was placed among subscribers a new company would hand its securities over to a finance company which would make an acceptance in its favour. It was then possible to raise money at once on the credit of the finance company. The finance companies themselves obtained their funds by placing their shares at high prices. This arrangement had considerable advantages (for instance, a railway company could begin construction at once), but it obviously depended on the sound management of the finance company and the ultimate success of the enterprises which they were backing. The real question was that of their ability to meet their acceptances when they fell due. One of the most important of the finance houses was that of Overend, Gurney & Co. It financed railways in Great Britain, cotton in the United States, and also had investments in India. Such was the confidence in its operations that money was pressed on it by the public and, as long as the speculative mania continued, it had little difficulty in finding outlets for it. The crash came on May 10th, 1866, when Overend, Gurney & Co. suspended payment with liabilities amounting to nearly £19,000,000. It was a failure on an unprecedented scale and led to a collapse of confidence. On May 11th—"Black Friday"—there was a general run on the banks, and conditions of complete panic prevailed. The Bank of England did what it could by advancing £4,000,000 in the course of the day.[1] But its reserve was so depleted that it had to intimate the position to the Government. The suspension of the Bank Charter Act was authorised with the proviso that the Bank was to maintain the rate of discount at 10 per cent. The announcement of this decision allayed the panic and the Bank did not require to exceed the legal limit of its note issue. But the crisis left an acute feeling of uneasiness and the money market was slow in recovering from its consequences. The damage to trade and industry, however, was not serious, because it had been essentially a credit crisis. Unfortunately it coincided with the visitation of the rinderpest, which caused the loss of farm stock of the estimated value of £3,000,000, as well as the temporary intermission of the cattle trade. The harvest also proved unsatisfactory. In these circumstances the revenue lost that elasticity which had characterised the past few years.

In June, 1866, Lord Derby assumed office for the third time without a party majority in the House of Commons. Disraeli again became the Chancellor of the Exchequer. There was no professed change in financial policy. The new Government was as committed as its predecessor to the principles of free trade, and in introducing supplementary estimates in July, Disraeli declared that it was his intention to observe the precepts of public economy which he had preached while in opposition. England's real strength, he insisted, was her financial reserve and not her actual fighting forces. Accordingly, when the time came for the presentation of the Budget of 1867, it included no novel features. In spite of the Chancellor's good intentions

[1] The Bank of England had reluctantly refused to advance £400,000 to Overend, Gurney & Company because the security offered was not sufficient. Andréadès: "History of Bank of England," p. 358.

there was a rise of considerably more than £1,000,000 in the estimated expenditure of the coming year. But he anticipated a surplus of £1,200,000, most of which was to be applied to the scheme of debt reduction. This was following the lead which Gladstone had given in the previous year. Events had conspired to draw attention to the fact that, considering the increase of national wealth and the buoyancy of the revenue, very little had been done to reduce the debt charge. Preference had been given to the remission of taxes, a course which offered the greatest possible present relief but did not lighten the burden which posterity would have to bear. The question was asked whether they would be likely to be able to meet the charge. On this serious doubts were expressed. It was pointed out that the country's industrial supremacy was based on its coal supplies, and they would be exhausted within a comparatively short time.[1] Instead of remitting taxes in face of the increasing annual yield, prudence demanded that the large surpluses should be devoted to the repayment of the debt. There were also suggestions that the Government should acquire railway debentures, or even invest in ordinary or preference railway stock, in order to secure the means to pay it off. The actual plan adopted by Gladstone was much less ambitious. It was that of turning part of the funded debt into terminable annuities, i.e., of cancelling debt on which interest had to be paid in perpetuity in favour of debt which would be wiped out in a fixed number of years by annual payments which included interest and return of capital. These annual payments were, of course, heavier than the interest on the funded debt, and consequently the annual charge of the debt was temporarily increased. But when the annuities terminated there would be a considerable relief.

[1] William Stanley Jevons had drawn attention to the matter in his "Coal Question" (1865), and a Commission was appointed to go into the whole problem.

John Stuart Mill, who had been returned for Westminster in 1865, made a speech in which he insisted on the duty of paying off the National Debt before the coal supplies were exhausted. "Autobiography," p. 165.

It was really a method of creating a practically inviolable sinking fund. The difficulty about terminable annuities was that they offered very little attraction to the public. As a matter of fact, however, they were not offered directly to individual investors. There had accumulated at the Post Office Savings Bank a considerable surplus representing the excess of deposits over withdrawals. This was invested in Government stock. The Chancellor of the Exchequer could convert this stock into terminable annuities. By this means he would pay to the Savings Bank a larger annual sum for a fixed number of years. In all probability the capital portion of the annuity, i.e., the amount by which it exceeded the interest the Savings Bank would have received on the stock had it not been converted into terminable annuities, would be available for reinvestment in the funds. So that, at the end of the period, the Savings Bank would hold as much stock as at the beginning, and the whole operation had enabled the Government to extinguish part of the permanent debt.

Owing to the change of Government Gladstone had not carried through his debt reduction scheme of 1866. But Disraeli took it up in the following year on the same general lines. He proposed to convert £24,000,000 of Savings Bank stock into terminable annuities to run until 1885. The interest on this stock had been £720,000, while the annuity was to cost £1,760,000; in other words, the annual charge was to be increased by £1,040,000 until 1885, when it was to terminate. As it happened, other annuities—those created by Vansittart in 1822[1]—fell in this year, and they represented a saving of £586,000; so that Disraeli was only faced with an increase of £454,000 in the debt charge. Since he could not anticipate anything more than a moderate surplus in the year 1867–8 it was fortunate that the creation of new annuities coincided with the extinction of old ones. The estimates for the year, however, were upset by an unexpected turn of events. The King of Abyssinia had committed certain British subjects to prison, and, prolonged

[1] Pp. 52–3 *supra*.

negotiations having failed to secure their release, the Government reluctantly came to the conclusion that it would be necessary to send an expedition. To meet the probable charge an autumn session was held. The expense of the expedition was estimated at £3,500,000. It was proposed to raise part of this by an additional penny to the income tax in the current year, the balance being postponed to the next financial year, for the Indian Government was bearing the cost in the first instance. The Abyssinian expedition was successfully conducted, but the estimated expenditure proved to be very wide of the mark. It actually amounted to £8,750,000. In 1868–9 the income tax was raised by another penny, but this did not prove sufficient. There was a general increase in expenditure accompanied by a failure of several items of taxation to show the usual buoyancy. The result was that the high-water mark of expenditure of 1861 was again reached, and there was a deficit of over £1,500,000. With the income tax at sixpence and the reduction in expenditure effected by Gladstone in his last four Budgets wiped out, it seemed necessary to review the whole financial position. The Government depended on the divisions between their opponents in the House of Commons. In February Derby resigned and Disraeli became Prime Minister, Ward Hunt[1] succeeding to the Chancellorship of the Exchequer. Gladstone defeated the Government on the Irish Church question in April, and Disraeli decided not to resign but to dissolve Parliament. In the subsequent General Election the Conservatives experienced the fate of 1852 and 1858. Gladstone now formed an Administration, which entered upon office pledged to promote far-reaching reforms.

Retrenchment was the key-note in finance. Gladstone himself declared that he could see no justification for the recent additions to expenditure. The new Chancellor of the Exchequer—Robert Lowe[2]—was determined to effect

[1] George Ward Hunt (1825–1877) had been Financial Secretary to the Treasury in the Ministry. In 1874 he was given the post of First Lord of the Admiralty, *see* p. 152*n.*, *infra*.

[2] Robert Lowe (1811–1892), first Viscount Sherbrooke, had spent

reductions. As usual, the Army and Navy as the great spending departments seemed to offer the best opportunities for economy. But the cry that the Government is impairing the efficiency of the services is one which is more likely than any other to endanger its popularity. The issue, however, was complicated by the simultaneous reforms effected in the Army and Navy. Forces were withdrawn from the Colonies and concentrated at home, short service followed by a period in the reserve was introduced, and the system of purchase of commissions abolished. These changes naturally involved new expenditure, but at first they made it possible to reduce the number of men serving with the colours, and therefore lessened the total cost. A similar policy was pursued by the Admiralty; foreign squadrons were reduced, a system of compulsory retirement for officers introduced, and the dockyards reorganised. In both services many vested interests were disturbed by the rigorous application of the principle of economy, and the Government had to bear the opprobrium of the blunders which could hardly be avoided in attempting to accomplish so much. Here it is only necessary to notice that economies were secured and that the Government was not responsible for the turn shortly to be given to events by the outbreak of war on the Continent. In the new circumstances the expenditure on the services again rose considerably. It should also be remembered that Gladstone's first Administration differed in an important respect from Palmerston's last. In the first part of the sixties there was comparatively little legislation. The passage of the Reform Act of 1867 inaugurated a new period. There was a quite unprecedented legislative activity, and the State was beginning to assume responsibilities, as, for instance, for the health and education of its subjects, which were bound to mean greater outlay.

Lowe's first Budget was in many ways a remarkable

---

some years in Australia. He is chiefly remembered as a Liberal opponent of reform and the leading spirit in the "Cave of Adullam." He was inclined, as Bright complained, to take "a Botany Bay view of the great bulk of his countrymen."

achievement. In presenting it, he drew a dark picture of the public revenue. He stated that it showed no sign of elasticity, and that the decline in the yield of the Customs went to prove that the spending power of large sections of the community had decreased. But by means of economy he thought that he could secure a balance of accounts in the coming year if the income tax was retained at sixpence. Like Gladstone in 1860, he presented an alternative course, which was as depressing as it was obvious, in order to bring out the full significance of his real proposals. To produce a surplus of £3,350,000, not only without imposing any new taxation, but actually while making considerable remissions, seemed something of a conjuring trick. Lowe proposed to do, on a much more extensive scale, what Gladstone had done in 1859 and 1860 with the malt and hop credits, that is, he put forward a scheme by which the collection of certain taxes should be advanced and thus bring within the financial year more than their normal yield. It was in its very nature an operation which could not be repeated; but it did not prejudice the revenue of subsequent years, for each would make the same claim on its successor, though how the question would be settled at the end of the world Lowe confessed he was at a loss to know. The income tax was to be collected in one sum in January instead of three times a year.[1] Under the existing system the last quarterly payment fell outside the financial year in which it was charged; the whole was to be brought within the year, and the transition from the one method of collecting to the other meant that 1869-70 had the advantage of the deferred quarter of 1868–9 as well as the four quarters which properly belonged to it. For the Assessed Taxes Lowe substituted licence duties, to be paid prospectively. The old method was to charge the tax on a return which the taxpayer was under an obligation to make in April in respect to the previous year. Under the new system he was required to declare what dutiable

[1] The tax was normally imposed in April, two quarters were paid in October, a third in January, and the fourth in the following April. In Scotland, however, it was already paid in one lump sum.

articles he intended to keep or use in the coming year, and was assessed accordingly. Here again the effect was to bring additional revenue within the financial year 1869–70. Finally the land tax and the house duty were to be paid annually in January instead of in two instalments falling in October and April. The reforms proved convenient to the taxpayer and also enabled the State to economise on the cost of collection. They placed the Chancellor in a position to contemplate the reduction of taxation. He decided to take a penny off the income tax, to repeal the duty on fire insurance (which Gladstone condemned in 1853 and reduced in 1864), and to abolish the corn registration duty. The last was the only survival of the Corn Laws. It was a nominal duty which had been retained as a means of registering the importation of foreign corn. When the home harvest was deficient it ran up to £800,000 or £900,000. Although it was a low duty it could not be defended on strict free trade principles, and it was the only remaining customs duty which had no corresponding excise duty on the home-produced commodity. As a practical question Lowe pointed out registration was quite possible without imposing a duty. The Budget of 1869 was followed by a notable recovery of the revenue. Lowe had a surplus of £3,570,000 at the end of the year.

Except for one miscalculation the Chancellor might have been regarded as one of the most fortunate occupants of the office. He enjoyed year by year unprecedented surpluses, and consequently was able to make substantial remissions of taxation. In 1870 he took another penny off the income tax and reduced the sugar duties by half. He also consolidated the stamp duties and made them less onerous. But the outbreak of war between Prussia and France in the summer introduced an element of uncertainty which Lowe found it difficult to assess. Great Britain was under certain treaty obligations to Belgium which, in the event of the violation of the neutrality of that country by one of the belligerents, might necessitate intervention. In the circumstances, therefore, prudence demanded that the Army and Navy should be prepared for events. The

Government asked for a vote of credit for £2,000,000, and the economies which had been effected in the services disappeared. These consequences of the Franco-German War, however, were more than counterbalanced by the advantages Great Britain reaped as a neutral. But Lowe took a pessimistic view. He thought that the revenue in 1871–2 would reveal an actual decrease in the yield of the taxes. He estimated the expenditure at £72,300,000 and the revenue at £69,600,000; he therefore proposed to provide for a deficiency of £2,700,000. As the past policy had been to relieve direct and indirect taxation by conceding the claims of each in making remissions, so he endeavoured to apportion the additional burden between them. His plan was ambitious and raised a storm of opposition. As an indirect tax he proposed to impose one on the manufacture of matches, calculated to produce over £500,000. The additions to direct taxation were to be divided between property passing by death and the income tax. The probate and administration duty was to be extended in its scope, and the rate of charges in the legacy and succession duties was to be raised. As the yield of these additional taxes would leave only £1,950,000 to be provided by the income tax Lowe was faced by a difficulty. The practice had been to add to or take a penny off the tax as occasion required. A penny meant rather more than £1,500,000, i.e., Lowe wanted something between a penny and twopence. To meet the difficulty he proposed to adopt a percentage instead of the penny in the pound method. This would enable a Chancellor of the Exchequer to operate on a much more manageable scale and to adjust the income tax charge to the necessities of the moment with considerable precision. But there was no general desire to meet the convenience of the Chancellor in this direction, for it would tend to confirm the permanence of the tax. The whole Budget aroused so much criticism—and Lowe had no gift for conciliating opponents—that it had to be entirely recast. In the end the simple device of adding twopence to the income tax was adopted. The failure seriously damaged the Chancellor's financial reputation. As it turned out, his apprehensions of a fall in the revenue were ill-founded. There was, at the end of the year, a surplus exceeding in amount the yield of the additional twopence on the income tax which was supposed to be necessary to effect a bare balance.

The country was now beginning to experience the effects of one of the greatest trade booms of the century. Confidence had at last recovered from the shock of 1866. Speculation again became rife and innumerable joint stock companies were formed to take advantage of the increasing demand for commodities. Investment in foreign loans became especially attractive, and reacted particularly on the coal and iron industries, because the loans were mostly raised in order to lay down or extend railway systems. The opening of the Suez Canal also stimulated new shipping enterprise. Prosperity was reflected in the rapid rise in prices which was followed by an increase of wages in a surprisingly short time. Abroad there were indications that the foundations of this great trade activity were none too secure; but for the time there were no serious apprehensions of a collapse at home. The result of the growing volume of trade on the Exchequer receipts might well have suggested that the time had arrived for the financial *coup* which Gladstone had not yet been able to make. Lowe, however, acted with caution. He could not overlook the fact that expenditure, in spite of strict economy, had not fallen to the old level, though, when allowance is made for the rise in prices, it cannot be denied that he achieved some success in his efforts. With a surplus of over £3,000,000 in 1871–2 he took the twopence off the income tax, which he had imposed in the previous year, and accompanied it with the reduction by half of the duties on coffee and chicory. In spite of these heavy remissions the realised surplus of the year was £5,895,000. In the Budget of 1873—his last—Lowe continued his two-fold principle of remission: the income tax was reduced from fourpence to threepence, and the sugar duties were again halved. He also proposed to meet half of the compensation which was due to the United States under the arbitration award, for the damage done by the *Alabama*, i.e., £1,600,000.[1] Before the year had closed a special charge of £800,000 was incurred by the Ashantee War. The taxes, however, still showed such an increasing yield that it proved possible to meet this charge and the whole of the *Alabama* award out of the surplus on the year without completely exhausting it.

The Government had long outlived the popularity with which it had entered upon its legislative programme in 1869. Its majority was breaking up under the strain to which its component parts had been subjected when the Ministry tried to redeem its election promises. The by-elections were going steadily against it, and the Irish University Bill led to a defeat in the House of Commons. Disraeli refused to form a Ministry while the existing Parliament remained. Consequently Gladstone continued in office until the beginning of 1874. He tried to strengthen his position by reconstructing the Cabinet and, recognising that Lowe's unpopularity was one source of weakness, he transferred him to the Home Office and assumed the Chancellorship of the Exchequer himself. This step seemed highly significant. When he took it Gladstone was merely deferring to the opinion of his colleagues but, reflecting on the embarrassments of the Ministry, he came to see that he had an opportunity of rehabilitating it by appealing to the country with a programme of financial reform. The idea of recommending a dissolution was conceived early in January; the decision was made public on the 24th, when the Prime Minister issued an election address to his constituents. His purpose was to precipitate a contest on finance. He anticipated a surplus in the coming year of rather more than £5,000,000. He suggested that it should be employed, (1) to assist local taxation on the condition that certain reforms in local government were effected, (2) to repeal the income tax,

---

[1] The *Alabama*, which was building on the Mersey, was allowed to put to sea, although it was evident that she was intended for the assistance of the Southern States in the American Civil War. It was eventually agreed that Great Britain should refer this alleged relaxation of her neutrality to arbitration. The Geneva Tribunal granted America heavy damages.

and (3) to remove the tax on some article of popular consumption. He hinted that these great remissions would necessitate a "judicious adjustment of existing taxes," and added that he would not be a member of a Government which did not practise economy. The address was a bold stroke. Apparently it was decided upon with confidence that it would be successful. Had the subsequent General Election turned upon finance it might have been. But the Prime Minister could not impose that condition. Disraeli cleverly evaded the direct issue. The surplus, he declared, would be used by either party to remit taxation, and the abolition of the income tax and the relief of local charges had always been favoured by the Conservative Party. The impression was created that whichever party won the election, the income tax would lapse. So wider questions of policy were discussed in the contest and the Liberals were defeated. Whether Gladstone was justified or not in attempting to force an election on financial reform cannot be discussed here. He chose his ground and lost; but, had he won, he would have been able to redeem his promises. That fact makes the juncture an important one. There was a momentary chance of realising the aim of 1853. The goal which he had consistently kept in view and more than once had approached seemed to be reached at last; his ambition to be the Chancellor who would abolish the income tax was almost attained.

II

Gladstone's failure to carry the country with him in 1874 may be said to mark the close of that great period of financial policy which was opened by Peel's reforms of 1842. The income tax had then been adopted as a means to an end, and the retention of it in 1853 and 1860 had been justified on the ground that it had not fully achieved its purpose. But it had come to be employed as a convenient make-weight in taxation, though Gladstone's contention that its basis ought not to be interfered with because it was a temporary tax had served to prevent any attempt to remove its alleged inequalities. The economies of 1862 to 1865 and the surpluses of 1870 to 1873 seemed to be preparing the way for the relinquishment of the tax, which Gladstone had argued in 1853 was the honourable course. Circumstances, however, did not prove propitious. The direct issue was not raised in 1866, but the result of the 1874 election was decisive; the prospect of repeal faded away and, for his own part, Gladstone felt that he was absolved from the promise of 1853. The defeat of the Liberals also marked the transition to a new attitude. They had been dominated by the idea of reducing public expenditure to a standard which made little or no allowance for the extension of State action. While it is true that their successors mainly drove up expenditure through their active foreign policy, the additional charges for education and public health—accompanied by assistance to local authorities—indicate that social policy was already beginning to make heavier demands. The severe trade depression of the later seventies further complicated the position by raising doubts about the wisdom of the free trade principles which had hitherto seemed to be reinforced, in practice, by the prosperity with which their application had been attended.

The Conservative Government of 1874–80 had a serviceable majority. Disraeli invited Sir Stafford Northcote to accept the Chancellorship of the Exchequer. He had already served as President of the Board of Trade and Secretary for India. His "Twenty Years of Financial Policy," published in 1862, had revealed his interest in and grasp of financial questions.[1] Northcote was necessarily influenced by Gladstone's January pronouncement. He had the surplus of £5,500,000 in contemplation and had to decide how he would dispose of it. On the ground that he had not had enough time to consider the problem in all

[1] Disraeli, when he became Prime Minister in 1868, would have given his post at the Exchequer to Northcote had he not felt it necessary to retain him at the India Office during the Abyssinian War. So the appointment went to Ward Hunt. Buckle, "Life of Disraeli," Vol. IV, p. 595. Northcote (1818–1887) became Earl of Iddesleigh in 1885.

its bearings, he promised to introduce a comprehensive scheme in the following year. His Budget was therefore intended to be a preliminary treatment of the question. It effected one important change in the method of presenting the annual financial statement. Gladstone, in arguing in favour of his plan, had adopted the course of estimating the future yield of the taxes on the basis of a normal increase year by year. It had become the custom to take the receipts of the previous year for the purpose—hence the large realised surpluses under Lowe. To ignore the probable increased yield, when the taxes revealed great elasticity, was a safe but hardly a businesslike way of making estimates. It had, however, one advantage; the estimated was much smaller than the realised surplus, and consequently the rate of taxation was maintained for the current year and a much larger sum was available for the redemption of the debt under the operation of the Old Sinking Fund. But the large realised surplus then constituted a case for remission of taxation, although here again the extent of the relief would be limited by omitting to consider the probable increased return from the taxes in the next year. Northcote abandoned the old system by allowing for an annual increment in the estimates. He recognised that this would tell against the efficiency of the Old Sinking Fund, and in 1875 he introduced new proposals for expediting the paying off of the debt. His first Budget, however, was dominated by the surplus which the election had brought to the notice of the public. What was he to do with it? A thorough review of the fiscal position was, as has been noticed, postponed; consequently his proposals were not to prejudice the future. Repeal of the income tax would necessitate other adjustments—Gladstone had alluded in general terms to this in his address, and in after years revealed that he had in mind the reconstruction and extension of death duties—but those could not now be considered. Northcote, therefore decided to retain the tax at 2d. in the pound, a rate so low that he argued that the inequalities of the tax were hardly worthy of mention. He relieved indirect taxation by the total abolition of the sugar duty, a step which the successive reductions had made almost inevitable.[1] Finally, he did something to assist local rates which had been burdened by new obligations imposed by legislation. The Government was to bear an additional part of the cost of police and to contribute to the charge of maintaining pauper lunatics. These concessions, however, were not associated, as Gladstone intended his to be, with any reform of the organs of local government.

The distribution of the surplus in 1874 proved to be the most popular of Northcote's achievements. His promised revision of the whole basis of taxation in 1875 could not be undertaken, for the depression in trade now began to make its influence felt. There was no possibility of doing anything considerable with a surplus of only £417,000. The Budget neither imposed new taxes nor did it make any remissions ; it was estimated that a balance of receipts and issues might be attained in the coming year. The interest of 1875 centres round the proposals for reducing the debt by means of a new form of Sinking Fund. Under the existing arrangements provision was made each year in the estimates for the payment of interest, annuities, and management as National Debt Services, the amount allocated varying with the charges. When there was a realised surplus, i.e., when the total Exchequer receipts exceeded the issues, it was handed over to the National Debt Commissioners to be applied to the purchase and cancellation of Government stock according to the principles of the Old Sinking Fund of 1829. The essence of Northcote's plan was to provide in the estimates each year for a sum, fixed in amount and exceeding that required for interests, annuities and management ; the excess was to be used for redemption of debt. As stock was purchased and cancelled and annuities fell in, a greater proportion of the annual sum would be applicable to this purpose. By

[1] Gladstone's promise of "some great remission in the class of articles of consumption" was privately admitted to mean sugar. Morley's "Gladstone," Vol. II, p. 487. Disraeli wrote privately to Northcote : "The repeal of the sugar duties will satisfy the Free Traders and the democracy." Buckle's "Disraeli," Vol. V, p. 306.

this means, so long as the debt was not increased, the annual sum would effect reduction of the burden at an accelerating rate without any addition to taxation. The principle of this New Sinking Fund was perfectly sound provided that the fixed annual sum came out of taxation and that there was no resort to borrowing. From 1875 the two Sinking Funds—for the New did not supersede the Old—were to work side by side, and it was hoped that their operation would bring about a rapid fall in the capital obligations of the State. These hopes were hardly realised. The Old Sinking Fund lost its effectiveness with the disappearance of the annual surpluses; the New Sinking Fund was not to be in full operation until the end of three years, for, by successive stages, the Debt charge of 1875—£27,215,000—was to be brought up to the £28,000,000, at which it was to stand in order to supply the means to work it. By that time, however, expenditure had outrun the public income and the Chancellor was actually resorting to borrowing

Northcote's difficulties from 1876 to 1880 were due to two sets of causes. The depression in trade and agriculture was so acute that the possibility of a considerable increase in taxation seemed out of the question. At the same time the more active foreign policy which the Conservatives had promised to initiate led to heavy commitments, particularly after the Eastern question had entered upon a critical phase in 1877. In these circumstances the Chancellor found the balance of income and expenditure seriously upset. He put a penny on the income tax in 1876, and another twopence in 1877, but this did not remove the deficit. On the plea that the charges were exceptional and the taxes had for the present lost their elasticity he issued Exchequer bonds in order to spread the expenditure over a number of years. This policy of borrowing has been severely criticised. It has been argued that Northcote ought to have met the expenses of preparation for possible war out of additional taxation. To resort to borrowing before actual hostilities had begun was a bad augury of the method which would be employed to finance the war itself should it come. That war was averted is no justification of the Chancellor's conduct. At one time Great Britain was on the verge of action, which would have involved her in war with Russia. The revolt of the Christian subjects of Turkey in the Balkans raised a difficult issue. Great Britain could co-operate with other Powers in pressing upon the Sultan the necessity for reform, but when Russia decided to go to the assistance of the rebels, the old suspicion of her ultimate motives revived. British interests seemed to demand that the Russian advance towards Constantinople should be stopped, and the fleet was ordered to the entrance of the Dardanelles. Fortunately, an agreement was arrived at, and the subsequent difference about the Treaty of San Stefano—which again aroused war feeling in England—was successfully adjusted. But it is obvious enough that war was narrowly averted. It is therefore useless to pretend that, in spreading out the special charge by temporary borrowing, Northcote was meeting a situation that merely demanded a show of firmness but never threatened actual war. His apologists are on firmer ground when they allege the general distress at home as an excuse for not imposing the whole burden of the war preparations on current taxation. The boom of the early 'seventies was followed by a collapse in trade and industry. Prices and wages fell; unemployment became extensive. The coal, iron and steel industries immediately felt the consequences of the cessation of demand. Short time was introduced in the textiles. Agriculture was suffering from the increase of foreign competition, and had also to face a series of bad harvests at home. As early as 1876 every branch of public income showed a falling off. In the following year Northcote estimated for a contraction in the yield of the taxes. After that increasing expenditure would have required considerable additions to the taxes if it was to be met at the time. The Chancellor refused to take this "heroic" course because "the present time is not a time in which additional taxation would be borne without distress."

The experience of the later 'seventies naturally aroused some misgivings about the free trade system. Alarm was expressed at the excess of imports over exports. The question was asked whether the balance of trade was not unfavourable, and whether it would not remain so as long as Great Britain persisted in her free trade attitude while other countries had protective tariffs. Reciprocity, it was contended, would force other countries to open their markets on equal terms to British goods and ultimately secure free trade all round. The matter was raised in the House of Lords in 1879 by Lord Bateman, but the Prime Minister (who had become a member of the Upper House as Lord Beaconsfield) asserted that " practically speaking, reciprocity, whatever its merits, is dead." The criticism of free trade, however, grew in volume in the 'eighties and assumed new forms. But meanwhile the Conservative Government of 1874 was nearing its term. Troubles in Afghanistan, Egypt, and South Africa had made new claims on the national resources, and the financial position was very unsatisfactory. Northcote's seventh Budget—that of 1880—revealed an estimated expenditure of £82,076,000, and he anticipated a surplus of £184,000. Even to obtain this balance he had to fall back on the New Sinking Fund to provide the means of extinguishing the debt he had recently contracted. The only new source of income he discovered was an improvement in the probate and administration duty, calculated to produce £700,000. The Budget was soon followed by the dissolution of Parliament. As a result of the General Election, Gladstone was recalled and formed an Administration in which he took upon himself the duties of First Lord of the Treasury, and Chancellor of the Exchequer. He introduced a supplementary Budget in June, for the meagre surplus Northcote had estimated for in March was already eliminated by new charges.

Since any immediate reduction in expenditure could not be effected, Gladstone set himself to the task of securing a sufficient increase in revenue to avoid a possible deficit. He had to keep in mind that it might be necessary to make a grant to the Indian Government to meet the heavy costs of the Afghan war, and that the revision of the French

Commercial Treaty—then under consideration[1]—might involve a loss on the wine duties. His Budget was a characteristic production. It included one great fiscal change. Throughout the century the question of the malt tax had been constantly a matter of discussion and agitation. It was admittedly objectionable in many ways, falling as it did on the first stage in production and requiring a good deal of regulation and inspection on the part of the State. Reduction of the charge would not remove these defects and complete abolition meant a loss which the Exchequer could not afford. Gladstone now proposed that the tax should be commuted into one on beer, which would necessitate less interference and reduce the chances of evasion. It would also involve no sacrifice to the Government after the charges incidental to the commutation had been met. The Chancellor made provision for these and other charges, and an estimated surplus of £385,000 by means of additional taxation. Publicans' licenses were increased and a penny was added to the income tax. The latter, Gladstone argued, was justified because it was associated with fiscal reform, " the original purpose and distinction of the tax." A slight revival in trade renewed the elasticity of the revenue, the extra expense of the Transvaal expedition was partly met by the fact that the French Treaty was not concluded, and the upshot was a realised surplus of £933,000.

With such a surplus Gladstone naturally gave precedence to the remission of the extra penny added to the income tax in 1880. His second Budget made adjustments in the spirit duties and revisions of the probate and legacy duties which were estimated to yield over half a million. With continued high expenditure and the promise of recovery of trade hardly maintained, there was no opportunity for dealing with the duties on the succession to property on the scale Gladstone would have liked. On April 24th, 1882, he introduced his thirteenth and last

[1] The French Government gave notice of withdrawal from the Treaty of 1860 in January, 1879. There were protracted negotiations for its renewal, but they ended in failure.

Budget. He had a realised surplus of £350,000, and he estimated that, with practically no changes, he would have a surplus of £315,000 in the coming year. These calculations were upset by the necessity of financing the Egyptian Campaign. A vote of credit for £2,300,000 was asked for, and threepence was imposed on the income tax for the second half of the year in order to discharge it. In December, Gladstone, finding that he could no longer combine the Chancellorship with his other duties, surrendered it to H. C. E. Childers.[1] Since 1853 Gladstone's influence on public finance, whether in office or not, had been the most dominant. He had defined the attitude towards the income tax, which only pressure of circumstances had insensibly modified; the view that its basis should not be tampered with had also ruled out all attempts to remove its inequalities. He had simplified the tariff and thereby completed the free trade system, which had won general acceptance in the middle years of the century. He had always taught the necessity for economy. It must have been with some apprehension for the future that he saw the total public expenditure mount up from the £55,500,000 of 1853 to the £85,000,000 of 1882.

The abnormal increase in expenditure within recent years again directed attention to the possibility of reducing the annual debt charge. It will be remembered that the terminable annuities created from time to time had been so arranged that they would all expire in 1885. This year, therefore, was looked forward to, as 1860 had been, with considerable interest. The Exchequer would be relieved of the payment of some five millions. What was to be done with the surplus which would thus emerge? The danger was that it would be swallowed up in additional expenditure or employed to remit taxation. Childers proposed to use the windfall of 1885 as the means of

[1] Hugh Culling Eardley Childers (1827–1896) had occupied public posts in Victoria as a young man. He returned to England in 1857. In 1865 he became Financial Secretary to the Treasury. Gladstone subsequently appointed him Chancellor of the Duchy (1872) and Secretary of State for War (1880). He was a successful administrator.

making further provision for the reduction of the debt. He carried through his scheme two years before the annuities would fall in. The new Sinking Fund was to stand as originally intended, i.e., £28,000,000 was to be the fixed annual charge for the debt. The amount saved by the termination of the annuities was to be employed to create new annuities. In this way the whole of the £5,000,000 would be applied to the further reduction of the debt, and the annual expenditure would remain as before. Childers attempted to follow up this arrangement by effecting a conversion of 3 per cents. in 1884. Since Gladstone's failure of 1853 no such operation had been seriously contemplated. The holders of 3 per cents. were now offered either 2¾ stock at £102, or 2½ stock at £108 for every hundred. No compulsion was adopted and the scheme fell flat.

When 1885 came it proved a year of heavy commitments. The Government had not been able to escape entanglements which drove up the estimates. In 1884 there was a realised deficit. Relations with Russia again became strained, and a vote of credit of £11,000,000 was asked for. Consequently Childers had to face a deficiency of £15,000,000 in his Budget proposals. His plan was to increase the income tax from fivepence to eightpence, to raise the succession duty, and make additions to the beer and spirits duties. These changes, he estimated, would give him exactly half of the amount he required. For the rest he proposed to suspend for one year the payment of the capital portion of the new annuities and to carry over the balance of the deficiency. When the emergency passed Childers was in a position to modify his Budget proposals, but the Government was defeated on an amendment which dealt with the increase in the beer duty. Gladstone resigned. He was succeeded by Lord Salisbury, who contrived to carry on business in the existing House of Commons for some months. The new Chancellor—Sir Michael Hicks-Beach[1]—felt under an

[1] Michael Edward Hicks Beach (1837–1916) became Viscount St. Aldwyn in 1906.

obligation to drop the proposed additions to the beer and spirits duties, though he did not try to find compensation by raising the tea duty, as he had suggested should be done when criticising Childers' Budget. He also abandoned the suggested changes in the succession duty. Otherwise, he retained the scheme outlined by his predecessor and added to it the temporary suspension of the New Sinking Fund. The year which had witnessed a Budget, an amended Budget, and then an Opposition Budget, was naturally one of financial confusion. In the autumn came the Dissolution, and in the General Election the Conservatives were not confirmed in power. When Parliament assembled they were defeated on an amendment to the Address. Gladstone was therefore called upon to form his third Administration. But 1886 was destined to be a still more troubled year. The Liberal Party was split on the Home Rule issue ; a second Election resulted in the return of an anti-Home Rule majority. Every department of public life was affected by the great political upheaval. The consequences, as far as the Chancellorship of the Exchequer is concerned, are somewhat peculiar. The Budget of 1886 was introduced by the Liberal Chancellor, Sir William Harcourt, and calls for no particular comment. After the General Election Salisbury formed a Ministry with Lord Randolph Churchill at the Exchequer. Churchill was ambitious to restore the financial reputation of his party and wished to enforce strict economy. He found that he could not cut down the demands of the Admiralty and War Office, and suddenly resigned in December. Apparently he had calculated on being asked to reconsider his decision. Salisbury, however, decided to offer the post to George J. Goschen,[1] a Liberal who had seceded on the Irish question. Goschen's acceptance was important in many ways. It created a precedent for a Liberal-Unionist to serve in a Conservative Government ; it also strengthened Salisbury's position by giving him a financier of

[1] George Joachim Goschen (1831–1907) had been Chancellor of the Duchy of Lancaster, President of the Poor Law Board, and First Lord of the Admiralty in Liberal Administrations.

considerable experience in the place of a brilliant, but troublesome, colleague.

The new Government surmounted its early difficulties and ran its course without encountering any serious obstacles. Goschen was responsible for six successive Budgets. As they were all conceived in the same spirit they need not be considered chronologically. He was extremely fortunate, as compared with his immediate predecessors, in the absence of complications abroad. Apart from the new Naval programme, which made heavy demands from 1889 onwards, the fighting services did not embarrass him. At home he had to provide for free education in 1891 and 1892. But, on the whole, he had a fair opportunity to carry out new schemes. By temperament cautious, he was loath to undertake any far-reaching reform, while intricate technical details seemed to have had a positive fascination for him. The consequence was that he touched upon a great number of questions but made no fundamental change in any. His caution was partly due to the doubts he entertained about the taxational system which had resulted from the simplification effected since 1842. It seemed to him that the basis had become too narrow and the remaining taxes on general consumption threatened to be inelastic. Simplicity had been pressed beyond the point of safety, and it was now necessary to increase the number of sources of revenue in order to meet the rise in public expenditure. But, while this view found constant expression in his Budget statements, Goschen did nothing definite in this direction. In fact, his prophecies were belied by the remarkable yield of the indirect taxes, particularly those on the consumption of alcoholic drinks,[1] and consequently he could not substantiate the case for departing from the accepted policy of the last half-century. His apprehension about the future yield of indirect taxes must be coupled with his conservative opinion of the possibilities of direct taxation. He made frequent reference to the unfair incidence of the income

---

[1] In 1892 they amounted to about one-third of the total revenue, i.e., 30 out of 90 millions.

tax, especially on small earned incomes, and admitted that it needed full reconsideration. For his own part, however, he merely reduced the rate from eightpence to sixpence, and did not attempt any differentiation between incomes. In his first Budget he mentioned as tasks for the future, the reform of the death duties and the stamp duties. Four years later he said that a reorganisation of the death duties would demand more time than he could afford, and his changes in the stamp duties were of a minor kind.

Goschen's treatment of the debt was much criticised. In his first Budget he increased the estimated surplus by reducing the charge for the debt service to £26,000,000, thus impairing the efficacy of the new Sinking Fund. In 1889 he made a further reduction of £1,000,000 in the fixed annual charge. The result was not so serious as his critics affected to believe it would be. First, because his cautious estimates gave him substantial annual realised surpluses, which went to reduce the debt under the Old Sinking Fund. Second, because he carried through, in 1888, a conversion of the 3 per cents., which meant a saving of £1,400,000 a year. On the balance, therefore, Goschen was able to claim that he had done much better than his immediate predecessors. He might well be pardoned for pointing to the conversion with pride. It was an extensive operation, carried through with complete success. He offered the holders of the stock the option of redemption or the conversion of their stock into a new 2¾ at par, which was to fall to 2½ in 1903. The moment was opportune, for the funds stood well and money was cheap. It was the first extensive conversion since Goulburn's in 1844. Goschen fully demonstrated that his knowledge of the money market was unrivalled. His reputation as an expert on the problems of local taxation, however, was not enhanced by his treatment of that subject. Legislation had imposed increasing burdens on local authorities which depended for their income on rates mostly levied on property. The ratepayers complained that the existing arrangements penalised them, and asked for some relief. Goschen had prepared a report on the question as long ago as 1871; Gladstone had raised the whole issue in 1874;

and Northcote had made grants for specific purposes in that year. Goschen's first step was to employ part of his surplus in 1887 to create the Local Loans Fund in order to eliminate the confusion caused by making advances out of the Exchequer balances, or out of ordinary State loans. The old system of including these advances and the interest received on them in the annual statement of receipts and issues tended to complicate the accounts. In the following year he introduced a much more important change. All the existing grants-in-aid[1] were to cease, and in their place certain sources of Imperial revenue were to be diverted to local purposes. The newly constituted county councils, for instance, were to have the proceeds of publicans' licences, as well as those of gun, game, dog, and carriage licences. Two years later he made further extensions of this principle. The innovation was hardly free from objections, but Goschen contended that "the mode of giving local assistance by hypothecating certain Imperial revenues" could not be improved upon because it was impossible to find a local tax at once equitable and acceptable.

The growing *rapprochement* between the Conservatives and the Liberal-Unionists in these years had its effect on the reaction against free trade. There seemed some prospect that the former would identify themselves with the doctrines of the supporters of "fair trade." These argued that trade was not fair unless home and foreign producers were on an equal footing with regard to the artificial conditions of production; for instance, a bounty on export paid by one country ought to be neutralised by countries dealing with it, by means of an equivalent import duty on the commodity. Natural differences in the conditions of production were not to be interfered with; to this extent fair traders declared themselves free traders. Joseph Chamberlain, when President of the Board of

---

[1] The annual votes for prosecutions, poor-law medical officers, poor-law school teachers, police, pauper lunatics, disturnpiked and main roads, etc., were discontinued. These grants had been made from time to time from 1834 onwards, *see* pp. 108–9*n*. *supra*.

Trade in Gladstone's Ministry, had strongly resisted the agitation for a countervailing duty on bounty-fed sugar in 1880 and 1881. He was not, therefore, likely to be impressed by the specious arguments of the fair traders. Still, the continued depression of the early 'eighties gave life to their agitation. When Salisbury appointed a Commission to inquire into the causes of the depression—a Commission which had been refused by Gladstone—it was not a matter of surprise that the Minority Report was in favour of fair trade. In 1887 it seemed probable that the rank and file of the Conservative Party would force the policy on their leaders. Co-operation with the Liberal-Unionists precluded this possibility, and the revival of trade suspended the agitation for the time.[1]

[1] It is worthy of note that the crisis of 1890—usually known as the Baring Crisis—was so skilfully handled that it had no adverse effect on trade. Speculation had again threatened a sudden collapse of credit. Baring Brothers had made extensive acceptances, and the Governor of the Bank of England learned that the house was in difficulties. He arranged that the Bank, supported by guarantors, should assume its liabilities. The Bank rate was maintained at 6 per cent. and no necessity arose for suspending the Bank Charter Act. Barings was reconstituted, and in 1894 the guarantors were discharged from further liability. The crisis was thus confined to the City and did not there involve any failures. One reason given for the speculations of 1888–90 was that Goschen's conversion had induced holders of stock to seek more remunerative forms of investment.

(NOTE.—Figures are given to the nearest thousand, and 000's are omitted.)

Year (ending 31st March.)	Exchequer Receipts.	Intercepted for Local Taxation Accounts.	Exchequer Issues.	Surplus (+) or Deficiency (−).	Debt Charge.
	£000	£000	£000	£000	£000
1893	90,395	7,214[1]	90,375	+ 20	25,200[2] (1,752)
1894	91,133	7,164	91,303	− 169	25,200 (1,827)
1895	94,684	7,014	93,918	+ 765	25,000 (1,718)
1896	101,974	7,366	97,764	+ 4,210	25,000 (2,153)
1897	103,950	8,249	101,477	+ 2,473	25,000 (1,454)
1898	106,614	9,402	102,936	+ 3,678	25,000 (1,361)
1899	108,336	9,521	108,150	+ 186	25,000 (1,394)

1 In the second column is given the total of the taxes (Customs, Excise and Estate, etc., Duties) paid to Local Taxation Accounts and not appearing in Exchequer Receipts, although collected by the Imperial Government, *see* p. 234*n*. for details. Mr. Asquith put an end to this system in 1907. The omission of these amounts makes no difference to the Surplus or Deficiency column, but they have to be taken into consideration in comparing the gross revenue of these years with that of others.

2 In the fifth column the Fixed Debt Charge is given with the amount of the New Sinking Fund—which is included in it—in brackets in each year. It was suspended in 1901 and 1902.

(Note.—Figures are given to the nearest thousand and 000's are omitted.)

Year (ending 31st March.)	Exchequer Receipts.	Intercepted for Local Taxation Accounts.	Exchequer Issues.	Surplus (+) or Deficiency (—).	Debt Charge.
	£000	£000	£000	£000	£000
1900	119,840	9,965	133,723	— 13,883	23,217 (20)
1901	130,385	9,740	183,592	— 53,207	19,835
1902	142,998	9,714	195,522	— 52,524	21,686
1903	151,552	9,767	184,484	— 32,932	27,282 (74)
1904	141,546	9,795	146,961	— 5,415	27,000 (1,464)
1905	143,370	9,812	141,956	+ 1,414	27,000 (2,238)
1906	143,978	9,901	140,512	+ 3,466	28,025 (3,449)
1907	144,814	10,222	139,415	+ 5,399	28,500 (5,983)
1908	156,538	—	151,812	+ 4,726	29,500 (8,365)
1909	151,578	—	152,292	— 714	28,000 (7,455)

(NOTE.—Figures are given to the nearest thousand and 000's are omitted.)

Year (ending 31st March.)	Exchequer Receipts.	Intercepted for Local Taxation Accounts.	Exchequer Issues.	Surplus (+) or Deficiency (−).	Debt Charge
	£000	£000	£000	£000	£000
1910	131,696	—	157,945	+ 5,607[1] (1910 and 1911)	21,758 (1,000)
1911	203,851	—	171,996		24,554 (4,112)
1912	185,090	—	178,545	+ 6,545	24,500 (4,448)
1913	188,802	—	188,622	+ 180	24,500 (4,620)
1914	198,243	—	197,493	+ 750	24,500 (5,228)

[1] The Revenue Act of 1911 directed that the income and expenditure of the years 1909–10 and 1910–11 should be aggregated for the purpose of determining the Old Sinking Fund for 1910–11.

CHAPTER VII

ARMAMENTS AND SOCIAL REFORM—1893–1914

I

IN one of his periodical lectures to the House of Commons on economy Sir William Harcourt declared that it was a lost art. " There is," he complained, " a universal demand for more and more expenditure every year, for every conceivable object, all of them excellent objects, but all of them pursued absolutely without regard to their cost." He spoke of Gladstone and himself on another occasion as the last survivors of a vanished creed. Growing expenditure, indeed, was the driving-force of the period. Both Harcourt and Sir Michael Hicks-Beach, who succeeded him, had to accommodate themselves to its demands, though they still professed their allegiance to traditional doctrine. In retrospect, the discussions of the years 1893 to 1903 have a significance which was not so clear to the disputants. On the side of expenditure, while the heaviest charges were due to the building up of a larger Navy, there was a considerable increase under other heads, for the State was forced by the Collectivist tendencies of the time to extend its functions beyond the limits prescribed by the principles of *laissez-faire*. The art of economy, of which Harcourt deplored the loss, was merely part of the Individualist teaching of the middle years of the century. It then seemed the best policy to leave as much money as possible in the pockets of the tax-payer, because it was believed that social well-being was more likely to be promoted if it was allowed to fructify there. The theory of expenditure must obviously rest on that of State function. If it is agreed that public provision for certain contingencies has greater social merits than the free operation of private interests can claim, more money will tend to be taken from the pockets of individuals. This raises important questions on the side of revenue. Taxation had been regarded as a method of supplying the State with the means of discharging well-recognised duties of defence and administration. It had been raised by direct and indirect taxes in a certain proportion of one to the other, which was observed when increases were made or remissions conceded. The supposition was that these taxes fell equally on the different classes of the community. If, however, a social purpose was to be accepted by the Chancellor of the Exchequer, taxation assumed a different aspect. It would not only need to be heavier, but it would have to be so designed that those who had the greater ability to pay would be charged at more than a proportionate rate. This idea is implicit in the discussions of incidence of taxation and of the principle of graduation which aroused considerable interest in the early 'nineties. Taxation might not only supply the wants of the State, but actually become an instrument to redress social inequalities.

The immediate and pressing question was the alarming growth of expenditure. Could it be met without departing from the taxational system which had been built on the foundation of free trade ? Would it be necessary to broaden the basis ? Goschen, if will be remembered, constantly prophesied that the existing taxes would prove inadequate. The same conviction grew on Hicks-Beach, and in 1899 he expressed the opinion that new sources of revenue would soon have to be found. There seemed to be two possibilities. The existing direct taxes might be reconstructed so as to produce a larger yield. This would involve reform of the death duties and of the income tax, and the acceptance of the principle of a graduated as against a proportionate charge. The alternative was a broadening of the basis, which in practice would mean the extension of indirect taxes. Such an extension was virtually impossible without departing from free trade policy. It was also open to the objection that indirect taxes would press more heavily on the general body of consumers than on the wealthy. The problem of incidence was therefore a vital one. It was brought before the public by the Report of the Royal Commission on the Financial Relations between Great Britain and Ireland, which was published in 1896.[1] The majority of the Commissioners agreed that Ireland was, in comparison with Great Britain, over-taxed. In the course of the nineteenth century there had been an approximation to a uniform system of taxation in the United Kingdom. On the face of it this would seem to ensure that the burden would be equal. Ireland, however, was a poorer country. The Commissioners estimated that, while the contribution of Ireland in direct taxes was one-twentieth of the total receipts of the United Kingdom, the yield of the indirect taxes was one-ninth. This is to be explained by the high duties on certain commodities, e.g. tea, tobacco, and spirits, and the fact that the proportion of families with a very low range of incomes is much larger in Ireland than in Great Britain. In other words, indirect taxes falling on articles of general consumption exact a greater contribution from the poor. It is more obvious in Ireland because of the number of the relatively poor; but the same generalisation applies to the lower classes in a wealthier country. Indirect taxation, therefore, seemed to rule out the possibility of adjusting the burden to ability to pay. On the other hand, the intensification of foreign competition in the 'nineties kept alive the agitation for the adoption of a protective tariff. It was pointed out that all other countries were promoting their commercial interests by means of tariffs, bounties, and reciprocal agreements. The agricultural depression was accentuated by the fall in freights and the opening up of new sources of supply. Arable land continued to go out of cultivation. In industry, however, there was a marked revival in the summer of 1895, and the prosperity was well maintained until, and even after, the outbreak of the Boer War four years later. Consequently the agitation for a change in

[1] "Final Report of Her Majesty's Commissioners appointed to Enquire into the Financial Relations between Great Britain and Ireland," 1896. (C. 8262.)

the fiscal system failed to secure any considerable popular support. But there was always the possibility that it would gather strength, particularly as it was becoming more closely associated with the idea of Imperial unity.

Although the country was not called upon to face the alternatives of heavier direct or more diffused indirect taxation until 1903, it had been prepared for the issue, and decisions had already been taken which strengthened opinion in favour of the former. The Budgets of Sir William Harcourt—especially that of 1894—are particularly significant. In 1892 Gladstone formed his fourth Administration supported by a small majority in the House of Commons. The financial situation was not satisfactory. At the end of the current financial year there was only the meagre surplus of £20,000, and several items of revenue seemed to prove that the decline in yield, which Goschen had so often anticipated, was at last a reality. Expenditure was still rising and Harcourt estimated that there would be a deficit of £1,574,000 in the coming year. Additional taxation, he held, was essential. He hinted that he was going to undertake the reconstruction of death duties with the intention of extracting more from that source; but for 1893-4 he proposed to secure the necessary income by putting a penny on the income tax. There was no corresponding addition to indirect taxation. Harcourt held that the defeat of Childers' Budget in 1885—followed by the increase of the income tax by the Conservatives—had made an irreparable breach in the old understanding, and had created a presumption in favour of direct taxes. In practice this meant that the wealthier section of the community would have to pay more than they had in the past. For the moment, however, the fact that the income tax was levied without making a differentiation of incomes or introducing the principle of graduation in the higher reaches to some extent obscured this implication.

The Budget of 1894 put matters in a clearer light. At last the reform of the death duties, which had so often been contemplated, was definitely undertaken. The Chancellor was faced with the task of providing for an expenditure of over £100,000,000, the figure which Lord

Randolph Churchill had seen looming in the future. The charges for the Navy, education and local expenditure accounted for the greater part of the recent increases. There had been a small deficit in the past year, but Harcourt estimated that it would amount to £4,502,000 in 1894–5. He refused to consider the expedient of borrowing. In the first place, he revised the arrangement by which Goschen had spread the charge of outlay under the Imperial Defence Act and the Naval Defence Act over a number of years. He proposed to appropriate the Sinking Funds in order to effect the immediate repayment of the greater part of this sum. This reduced his estimated deficit to £2,379,000. To meet such a deficit he argued that it was necessary to explore the possibilities of "the great staple branches of the revenue." So, secondly, he grappled with the complicated problem of the death duties. The set of taxes comprehended under this general title had grown out of the legislation of two centuries. The point of contact between them was that they were all attempts to take for public purposes some proportion of the property which passed at the death of one person to others. Complications had arisen because the State had recognised differences between the kinds of property—real and personal; had distinguished between the methods by which it passed—whether it was settled or not, or whether the person died intestate or not; and had graded the charge according to the degree of relationship of the beneficiaries to the deceased. Attempts to arrive at some uniformity of practice date as far back as the time of Pitt. He had failed to impose the legacy duty, which he placed on the collateral succession to personal property, on succession to real property. Later he extended the duty to bequests chargeable on real property, but at the same time brought personal property in direct succession within its scope. It will be remembered that Gladstone in 1853 abolished the exemption from the duty enjoyed by the bulk of real property.[1] Lowe, in his abortive Budget proposals of 1871, suggested a number of changes which would have

[1] P. 116 *supra*.

increased the yield of the duties. The " judicious adjustment of existing taxes," which was part of Gladstone's 1874 programme, was intended to cover their reconstruction and extension. But by far the most comprehensive scheme was that worked out by Lord Randolph Churchill in preparation for the Budget which he never introduced.[1] There were four sets of duties, each with its own peculiarities. The probate duty and the account duty were designed to be complementary to one another. The former was charged on personal property, which was valued as a whole before the executor was empowered to administer the estate, and no question of the ultimate destination of it was involved: the latter was merely an attempt to intercept personalty included in a voluntary settlement in order to prevent an evasion of the former. These duties were in a different category from the legacy and succession duties. They were charged on the amount passing to the beneficiaries at rates which depended on their relationship to the deceased. Together they applied to personalty and realty. In the case of realty the duty fell on the capitalised value of the life interest. Churchill had intended to sweep away all these distinctions. He proposed to treat personalty and realty alike, and to abandon the considerations based on consanguinity. The result would have been a single succession duty. This he decided to graduate according to the total benefit received by each individual and not according to the value of the whole estate before distribution. Goschen made several references to the reconstruction of the death duties, but he was far too cautious to commit himself to a drastic scheme. He did, however, make one important innovation in 1889 by adding a new duty to those already enumerated—the estate duty. It was a charge of 1 per cent. on all estates, whether personal or real, above the value of £10,000 when they passed by death. He contended that this was not a recognition of the principle of graduation ; estates under the value should be regarded as enjoying an abatement

[1] For full details of Lord Randolph's scheme *see* " Lord Randolph Churchill," by Winston S. Churchill," Vol. II, c. xv.

similar to that granted to small incomes under the income tax

This summary may serve to elucidate Harcourt's proposals. He did not adopt Churchill's solution of reducing all the duties to one. There were to be two categories. In the first was to be placed a new estate duty to be charged on the total value of all property, whether real or personal, settled or unsettled. It was to take the place of the existing probate, account, and estate duties. The rate was to be graduated from 1 to 8 per cent. in accordance with the value of the estate. In the second category came a duty produced by assimilating the old legacy and succession duties. This was done by adopting the same consanguinity scales and charging the successor to a real estate on the capital value (as in the case of personalty) and not, as formerly, on the value of his life interest. These changes, Harcourt submitted, would substitute two duties for five, and these two would be equal in their incidence on all kinds of property. His plan, it will be seen, differed from Churchill's in two respects. In the first category he retained the principle of valuing the whole estate before distribution as the basis for the graduated charge. Churchill would have imposed the duty on each beneficiary graduated according to the amount received. The criticism was made when the Budget was under discussion, that the beneficiary was penalised because his portion happened to be part of a large estate. The reply to this was that the State had the rlght to the first charge on the property. Obviously, too, the method adopted was simpler and more remunerative to the Exchequer. It was also pointed out that the testator knew that his estate would be subject to the charge, and if he did not wish each legatee to bear his share he could make provision for the whole to fall on the residuary legatee. In the second category Harcourt retained the principle of regulating the graduation according to the degree of consanguinity. Churchill, it has been noticed, would have eliminated this altogether. His argument was that the testator, when he knew that all beneficiaries would pay at the same rate, would normally so dispose of his estate that those nearest of kin would be left rather more than if they were subjected to a lighter charge. The controversy aroused by Harcourt's Budget, however, ranged over a much wider field than that of technicalities of this nature. It was alleged that the State was assuming that it had the right to a man's property on his death, and that his heirs were only granted a proportion through its indulgence. The effect on landed estates would be disastrous. The principle of graduation was altogether vicious. The attempted dispersion of capital would not, in practice, result in social betterment. All these and many other arguments were employed by the Opposition. Harcourt met them with remarkable skill. He piloted his proposals through the House of Commons, and Lord Salisbury, although he disliked them, held that the House of Lords would not be justified in rejecting the Bill.

The new death duties were only to apply to the estates of those who died after they became law. In the current year, therefore, they were not expected to yield more than £1,000,000. Ultimately, it was estimated they would produce between £3,000,000 and £4,000,000 more than those they superseded. So at the moment they did not solve all the Chancellor's difficulties. There was still a possible deficit of £1,379,000 uncovered. He proposed, therefore, to raise the income tax from 7d. to 8d. But he accompanied this by the startling declaration that he was convinced that the principle of graduation was a perfectly sound one, and that only administrative difficulties prevented him from applying it. Such a departure from the traditional attitude towards the income tax is highly significant. For the present he contented himself with a change in the exemptions and abatements to relieve smaller incomes. There was to be a total exemption up to £160; from £160 to £400 there was to be an abatement of £160, and from £400 to £500 of £100. Also in Schedule "A," under which real property was assessed at its gross income, an allowance of one-eighth in respect of lands and of one-sixth in respects of houses was made. These changes meant that the full yield of the extra penny could not be expected. To wipe out the remaining part of the estimated deficit and secure a small surplus Harcourt put an additional 6d. a gallon on spirits and 6d. a barrel on beer.

The Budget of 1894 was successful in its primary purpose of removing the possibility of a heavy deficit. Harcourt had estimated it would yield him a surplus of £291,000; the realised surplus proved to be £765,000. In the following year he remitted the extra duty on spirits, the yield of which had disappointed anticipations, but retained that on beer. He estimated that there would be a surplus of £181,000 in 1895–6. It was Harcourt's last Budget statement. Defeated in the Commons the Government resigned in June, and was succeeded by a coalition of Conservatives and Liberal-Unionists, which now entered upon a long period of power. Sir Michael Hicks-Beach became Chancellor of the Exchequer, and was responsible for a series of seven Budgets. Four of them were peace Budgets, which provided large sums for national defence, and the last three fell within the years of the Boer War. He began with a realised surplus of £4,210,000, a remarkable increase on Harcourt's estimate, which was partly due to the general improvement in trade, and partly to the unexpected productivity of the reorganised death duties. The surplus, however, was not allowed to go to the Old Sinking Fund; it was diverted to capital expenditure on dockyards and other naval works under the provisions of a special Act.[1] Although Harcourt's Budget of 1894 had been roundly denounced, its principles were now accepted. But it was felt that it was necessary to do something to meet the complaints of agriculturists, in view of the continued depression of prices. A substantial part of the estimated surplus for the coming year was set aside for this purpose. Occupiers of agricultural land were to have their rates reduced by half, the deficiency to be made good to the local authorities by grants out of the yield of the death duties.[2] This proposal was naturally attacked as con-

[1] The Naval Works Act, 1896.

[2] The grant comes from that portion of the new Estate Duty which is levied on personalty.

stituting a precedent for giving State assistance to a particular industry. It did amount to a decision to ear-mark for a particular section, relief which the Chancellor could have distributed over the whole community by reducing the amount of direct or indirect taxation. The opposition was so strong that the Agricultural Rates Act, which embodied the proposal, was limited to five years. The arrangement, however, has been continued.

In 1897 Hicks-Beach again found himself in possession of a large surplus—amounting to £2,473,000—and again he appropriated it for special capital expenditure.[1] Although the revenue displayed continued elasticity, expenditure was rising so rapidly that the Chancellor resisted all pleas for remissions. He was apprehensive of what would ensue when the present wave of prosperity had spent itself. The Budget speech, however, was characterised by a review of the material progress which had been effected in the sixty years of the Queen's reign. Its tone and content irritated those who were persistently denouncing what they were pleased to call the shibboleths of free trade. For the moment their protests were drowned in the general chorus of self-congratulation. Satisfaction with the unparalleled achievements of the country no doubt served to stimulate the optimism which resulted in a record revenue of over £116,000,000 in the financial year. There was a realised surplus of £3,678,000.[2] It was impossible to refuse to consider the question of reductions in these circumstances. The concessions made to the taxpayer were carefully balanced. Under the heading of direct taxes new abatements in the income-tax were granted on incomes between £400 and £700.[3] The indirect tax chosen for reduction was the tobacco duty, which was lowered sixpence a pound. For three years there had

---

[1] This time it was devoted to the purposes of the Military Works Act.

[2] £2,500,000 of this was used for the purposes of the Public Buildings Act.

[3] Above £400 and not exceeding £500 the abatement was to be £150
,, £500 ,, ,, £600 ,, ,, £120
,, £600 ,, ,, £700 ,, ,, £70

been abnormal surpluses ; in 1898–9 there was a surplus, but a very modest one.[1] The revenue was still well maintained and exceeded the estimate, but supplementary estimates had made more than a corresponding addition to expenditure. The coming year, it was estimated, would witness an excess of expenditure over revenue of £2,600,000, unless steps were taken to provide against it. Hicks-Beach attempted to justify the heavy outlay, on the Navy in particular, and expressed the hope that the coming Peace Conference would limit the competition in armaments. He also (as has been noticed)[2] suggested that the time was coming when increases in the existing taxes would prove inadequate. But he did not venture to introduce a new tax to meet the probable deficiency. His proposal was to reduce the expenditure to the extent of £2,000,000 by the far from heroic course of taking that amount from the fixed charge for the redemption of the debt. The main argument in favour of invading the New Sinking Fund was that Consols stood at 110, and it was a loss for the Commissioners of the National Debt to purchase them at a premium and in such quantities as to drive them still higher. The remaining £600,000 was covered by minor additions to the stamp duties and a revision of the wine duties. Had 1899–1900 been a normal year, as it was expected to be when the Budget was introduced, the Chancellor would have been open to the reproach that he had resorted to devices to avoid a deficit which errors in the estimates had led him to anticipate. As a matter of fact there would have been no such deficiency. But the whole situation was changed by the outbreak of war in South Africa early in October.

Parliament was summoned for October 17th. Hicks-Beach announced that he had already had in view a surplus of £3,000,000, and consequently it would only be necessary to provide for another £7,000,000 on account of the war. There was, in his opinion, no strong case for extra taxation, because the war would probably not extend beyond the financial year, the income tax was already

---

[1] £186,000. [2] P. 170 *supra*.

at 8d. in the pound, and it was not worth while to disturb trade by imposing indirect taxes. So he asked for power to issue Treasury bills up to the limit of eight millions. This loan was to be regarded as temporary; the Transvaal itself would be required to pay from its wealth towards its liquidation. This optimism, which was not confined to finance, had fatal consequences. In 1900 the Chancellor had to make four separate statements, each of which revealed the growing seriousness of the position. But he failed to recover lost ground. The vote of October had to be supplemented in February by an additional one of £13,000,000. It was clear, therefore, that increased taxation was necessary. He estimated that the deficit of 1899–1900, together with that which would accrue in the coming year on the existing basis of taxation would amount to £60,000,000. To meet this he introduced his Budget so early as March 5th. He proposed to distribute the burden between loans and taxes. The Budget followed the usual course of making increases in direct and indirect taxation, and scrupulously avoided any experiments in new taxes, or what was called "fiscal reform." The income-tax was raised to 1s. in the pound, additions were made to the beer and spirits duties, and also on those charged on tobacco and tea. Altogether these additions were estimated to yield £12,317,000. The remainder—when certain savings in expenditure were effected by suspending the Sinking Fund—was to be met by loans. This involved the renewing of the £8,000,000 of Treasury bills of the previous year and the floating of a special War Loan of £30,000,000.[1] Criticism of the Budget turned on the Chancellor's failure to find new sources of revenue rather than on the difference between the amount raised by loan as compared with that produced by additional taxation. To the charges that his proposals were commonplace he replied that he was content that they should be so, for he did not wish to raise fundamental fiscal issues in facing

[1] Stock, redeemable in ten years and bearing interest of 2¾ per cent. was offered at £98 10s. 0d. per cent. It was heavily over-subscribed.

a temporary emergency. No further changes in taxation were made within the financial year, though, in July and December, Hicks-Beach presented revised estimates of expenditure and obtained additional powers to borrow to the extent of £13,000,000 and £11,000,000 respectively.

The Government appealed to the country in December and was confirmed in power. But the war, which it was returned to conclude, dragged on for over another two years. Financially the outlook became much darker. The hope of a substantial contribution towards the expenses from the Transvaal had to be abandoned; in fact, that country was so wasted by the prolonged fighting that ultimately Great Britain had to advance credit facilities in order to assist it to recover. While the revenue retained its stability expenditure continued to increase. In his Budget statement of April, 1901, Hicks-Beach estimated that it would amount to £187,602,000 in the current year. The taxes, he anticipated, would yield £132,255,000; so he was faced by a deficit of £55,347,000. He pointed out that the war did not account for the total increase: there was a growth in the ordinary annual expenditure. The time had come, therefore, to attempt to broaden the basis of taxation by finding other sources of revenue. The Chancellor made it quite clear that he did not wish to abandon free trade principles, and he definitely refused to consider a tax on imported manufactured goods. He wanted a largely productive tax levied "on some article of universal consumption which is very cheap." He proposed to find this in a revival of the sugar duty at 4s. 2d. per cwt., which would yield £5,100,000.[1] In addition he imposed an export duty on coal at the rate of 1s. a ton, which he expected would produce £2,100,000. For the latter there were precedents, but they carried little weight because the export trade in coal had become by 1901 a totally different business in nature and extent from what it had been in the 'forties of

[1] The duty on sugar, it will be remembered, was repealed by Northcote in 1874. It was free of all charge on and from May 1st, 1874.

the previous century.[1] The duty appealed to Hicks-Beach as neither a direct nor an indirect tax on the ground that it could be passed on to the foreign consumer. This view was contested by colliery proprietors and exporters. They pointed out that it could only be true where there was a monopoly, as, for instance, in the case of Welsh steam coal. Other coal, such as that exported from the Humber and Scotland, had to compete with that of Germany and America in foreign markets, and consequently it would handicap the trade to raise the price to the extent of the duty. Others showed how coal supplied an outward cargo which facilitated the importation of other commodities. In the end the Chancellor met some of the objections by conceding that there should be a rebate on the cheaper kinds of coal. Also, he exempted all coal exported until the end of the year under existing contracts. These concessions meant a reduction of £800,000 in the estimated yield of the duty. To maintain the balance of direct and indirect taxation a further 2d. was added to the income tax. These new taxes and the continued suspension of the Sinking Fund still left a deficit of over £40,000,000. The already large proportion of the unfunded debt forced the Chancellor to raise this in the form of Consols.

On April 14th, 1902, Hicks-Beach introduced his seventh and last Budget. The end of the war now seemed to be in sight. But the state of the finances demanded that further provision should be made to meet expenditure. Although the existing taxes were estimated to produce £147,785,000, that revenue would come short of the requirements of the year by £45,500,000. Consequently he

---

[1] The taxes on the export of coal, which had been imposed in the eighteenth century and increased during the French Wars, were condemned by Parnell in his "Financial Reform," and repealed by Althorp, except with respect to that which was exported in foreign ships. Peel reimposed a duty of 2s. a ton in 1842 on coal exported on British ships, but withdrew it in 1845. Hicks-Beach invoked the authority of Peel. But since he repealed the tax and the export trade was altogether different in his time, this was hardly relevant.

proposed additional taxation, direct and indirect. The former was found in the easy device of adding a penny to the income tax; the latter might also have been secured by raising the rate of the sugar or other duty. But Hicks-Beach thought it was necessary to impose a new tax. He decided in favour of the revival of the registration duty on corn which Lowe had abolished in 1869. It was to take the form of an import duty of 3d. per cwt. on corn and of 5d. on flour and meal. The yield was estimated at £2,650,000. The Chancellor, although he had often deplored the narrow basis of the taxational system, had never given any reason to suppose that he would compromise free trade doctrine. He had, indeed, on more than one occasion professed his unfaltering allegiance to its principles. In advancing this proposal for an import duty on corn he did not anticipate that it would be denounced as protectionist. This was a curious oversight. Possibly the tax would have been accepted without demur at another juncture. But there had been a growing agitation for a return to a protective tariff and the duty seemed to the prime movers in it an indication that the Government was coming round to their views. It also put the free traders on their defence. This tax, possibly not very important in itself,[1] was regarded as a challenge. It was the spark which caused a highly-charged atmosphere to explode. Harcourt denounced the proposal as most objectionable, and Sir Henry Campbell-Bannerman regarded it as a first step towards protection. The suggestion was made—though it was strongly repudiated by the Government—that the corn duty was intended to be the foundation of a policy of Imperial preference. Hicks-Beach, for his part, insisted that the only purpose was to augment the yield of indirect taxes by introducing a new one. When the news arrived at the beginning of June that hostilities had ceased in South Africa, the Chancellor had an oppor-

[1] That the corn duty was no serious infringement of free trade principles may be proved by the fact that Buxton, in his "Finance and Politics," Vol. II, pp. 158–9, questions the wisdom of its repeal by Lowe.

tunity of revising his financial scheme. But he refused to drop the corn duty. Had he foreseen the consequences of its retention there can be no doubt that his decision would have been different.

Lord Salisbury retired from the Ministry in July. Mr. A. J. Balfour became Prime Minister and, among other changes, C. T. Ritchie[1] succeeded Hicks-Beach as Chancellor of the Exchequer. The Budget statement of 1903–4 has a two-fold interest. It glanced back at the cost of the war, and it precipitated the disruption which was threatened in the discussions of the previous year. Ritchie estimated that the total cost of the war amounted to £217,000,000, of which less than one-third had been met out of current revenue. There had consequently been a heavy increase in national indebtedness. The funded debt had been raised by the addition of £92,000,000 in Consols, there was a special War Loan of £30,000,000, and outstanding Exchequer bonds and Treasury bills for £24,000,000 and £13,000,000, respectively. The Chancellor maintained that his predecessor had been remarkably successful in reconciling the interests of the nation and those of the money market in the arrangements he had made. In view of the fact that the trade boom was not checked by the outbreak of war and the ordinary revenue remained well above the pre-war average, it seems obvious that the country could easily have borne a larger proportion of the war cost at the time. The difficulty was to find the means of increasing taxation. Hicks-Beach had been enabled to meet the increasing expenditure before the war by the surprising productiveness of Harcourt's death duties, but

[1] Charles Thomson Ritchie (1838–1906) had first come into prominence in the later 'seventies as an advocate of the countervailing duty to equalise the effect of the bounty paid on the export of Continental sugar. He had consequently come into collision with Joseph Chamberlain, who was strongly opposed, as a Free Trader, to that policy. Subsequently Ritchie had served in Conservative Governments as Financial Secretary to the Admiralty, President of the Local Government Board, President of the Board of Trade, and Home Secretary. He accepted the Chancellorship of the Exchequer with reluctance. It brought him again into conflict with Chamberlain—but now he was the champion of free trade.

he did not explore the possibility of securing more from this source during the war. Nor did he attempt to alter the basis of the income tax; he merely made automatic increases which could hardly go beyond a certain point when they fell equally on all incomes. It has been noticed how he kept within the accepted canons of taxation. His interpretation of the meaning of broadening the basis did not reveal any important new sources of revenue. The first post-war Budget is necessarily affected by outstanding war charges. Ritchie, however, estimated that total expenditure would be £40,000,000 less than in the previous year. The existing war taxation, he anticipated, would give him a surplus of £11,000,000; so he turned to the difficult task of making remissions. He reduced the income tax from 1s. 3d. to 11d. With this he associated the total remission of the corn duty, admitting practically all that the opponents of it had alleged against it in the previous year. Bohind this announcement there was a serious difference of opinion in the Cabinet. Although the duty had been imposed for revenue purposes only, the possibility of retaining it as the basis of a scheme of Imperial preference was suggested by the resolutions of the Colonial Prime Ministers adopted on August 11th, 1902. The Colonial Secretary—Joseph Chamberlain—at a Cabinet meeting in November pressed his colleagues to take this course and he understood that they had agreed to do so. On his return from his South African tour, however, he found that Ritchie definitely refused to embody the tax in the Budget for preferential purposes. Chamberlain lodged a protest, but did not consider that it was incumbent upon him to resign. On May 15th, Mr. Balfour assured a deputation, which asked for the continuation of the duty, that Imperial preference was not yet a practical question. The same day Chamberlain, addressing his constituents at Birmingham, declared himself in favour of preference for the Colonies, and if necessary, retaliation against foreign countries.

A FISCAL & FINANCIAL HISTORY OF ENGLAND

II

Reference has often been made to the reactions against free trade policy, which were apt to gather strength at times of industrial depression. The form they took depended on the conditions of the time. It is also significant of the predominance of free trade opinion that the advocates of both reciprocity and "fair trade" represented themselves as anxious to secure free trade all round. The Tariff Reform movement launched by Chamberlain was moulded by new influences of which the idea of effecting a closer union of the Empire was the most powerful. The taxation of imported foodstuffs was an essential part of any genuine scheme of preference. This Chamberlain frankly acknowledged and set himself to prove that the consequent rise in prices would be slight compared with the other advantages of the scheme. He saw that it was necessary to promise that the increased revenue which the tariff would produce was to be spent on social reforms. But it proved impossible to confine the discussion to the merits of Imperial preference and the possibility of raising by such means the revenue necessary to pay for schemes of social betterment. Chamberlain drifted into wider questions of protection of home industries and retaliation against the methods adopted by other countries. The controversy soon covered the whole field and was conducted with increasing vigour and bitterness. In reply to his opponents' challenge to draw up a draft of the kind of tariff he had in mind Chamberlain proposed in his Glasgow speech 2s. a quarter on foreign wheat and flour and a 5 per cent. duty on meat and dairy produce (excluding bacon), as well as substantial preference on colonial wines. He followed this up by speaking at different industrial centres and paying particular attention to local conditions. It was inevitable that his original programme should be overweighted by continual accretions. His critics demanded that he should correlate his proposals. He had, however, exposed himself to attack at so many points that in the later stages of the campaign the free traders had little difficulty in scoring successes.

The championing of the case for a departure from the established fiscal policy by a prominent member of the Cabinet had a profound effect on the Government itself. Some were prepared to adopt the new policy and others remained convinced free traders. The Prime Minister did not wish to see the party split on the issue and struggled to find a formula which would prevent such a calamity. He thought this might be obtained by a general agreement that the Government was open to conviction on the question and in favour of asserting its freedom of action in its commercial relations with other countries. In the end the negotiations led to the curious result of the simultaneous announcement of the resignations of Chamberlain and the free traders Ritchie, Lord George Hamilton and Lord Balfour of Burleigh, on September 18th. The Duke of Devonshire, who had imperfectly understood the cross-currents in the correspondence between the parties within the Cabinet, resigned a few weeks' later.[1] The Government was thus rid of the chief exponent of the new policy and the firm defenders of the old. It now consisted of persons committed to the general principle of "fiscal reform," but unprepared to make any definite practical proposals. The solution was not altogether a happy one, for Chamberlain's campaign absorbed the attention of the country and the attitude of the Government towards it seemed unsatisfactory to the great majority of the people. One result was that the Budgets of 1904 and 1905—both introduced by the new Chancellor of the Exchequer, Mr. Austen Chamberlain—did not bear on the face of them any mark of the fiscal controversy. They are concerned with the immediate question of balancing revenue and expenditure which was rendered more difficult by the depression in trade. This was no doubt in part due to the consequences of the war on the money market. Although short the depression was acute, and had the effect of upsetting the possibly rather optimistic estimates of Ritchie in the

---

[1] The letters incorporated in Bernard Holland's "Life of the Duke of Devonshire," Vol. II., Chap. xxvii., throw a good deal of light on the Cabinet difficulties.

previous year. Instead of the expected surplus of £316,000 there was an actual deficit of £5,415,000. There was a fall in the yield of the customs greater than the estimated loss on the repeal of the corn duty. Excise and the death duties proved disappointing. Mr. Austen Chamberlain proposed to meet the large deficit by taking £2,800,000 from the Excehquer balances and £1,000,000 from the fund which was formed of the unclaimed dividends on Government stock ;[1] the remainder he hoped would be wiped out by the surplus of the coming year. On the existing basis of taxation, however, he estimated that there would be a deficit of £3,820,000. In order to cover this and restore the balances, additional taxation was necessary. Although the Government was not convinced that the fiscal system was based on sound principles it did not propose to do anything which was contrary to its spirit. A penny was added to the income tax and twopence a pound to the duty on tea. The duties on tobacco were also readjusted in order to increase the yield. Apart from concessions with regard to the tobacco duties, the proposals were adopted. In 1905 the Chancellor was able to announce that the revenue had practically come up to expectations and certain savings in expenditure had given him a realised surplus of £1,414,000, which he intended to devote to the repayment of the temporary advances. The outlook was now brighter. Trade was recovering and there was a fall of £3,500,000 in Naval expenditure, largely due to the fact that suspicions of the designs of Russia and France, which had long dictated an expensive policy, had been dissipated. The subsequent competition in construction with Germany had not yet begun. Mr. Austen Chamberlain estimated that the maintenance of the existing taxes would produce a surplus of £2,972,000. What was he to do with it ? He insisted that the unfunded debt, amounting to the total of £71,633,000, claimed first

1 The Unclaimed Dividend Account consists of unclaimed stock and the dividends which have accrued on it. As the dividends go to augment the capital the Account becomes larger than the liabilities. Gladstone had employed part of the Account in 1866.

attention. Of this £14,000,000 of Exchequer bonds were to fall due in the next December. He was in a position to pay off £4,000.000 of these from funds at his disposal. For the rest, he proposed to substitute new bonds running for ten years, on the understanding that one-tenth of them should be withdrawn and repaid each year. To provide the means to do this he increased the fixed debt charge from £27,000,000 to £28,000,000. This arrangement reduced his surplus to £1,972,000, not enough to justify taking the penny of the previous year off the income tax, but sufficient to remove the additional twopence from the tea duty. He therefore adopted the latter course. It could not be said that he was putting the heavier burden on indirect taxes.

In December the Government resigned. The subsequent General Election was partly fought on the fiscal issue and resulted in the return of an overwhelming free trade majority. Campbell-Bannerman's Ministry was also more definitely committed to a programme of social reform than its predecessor had been. How this was to be financed soon became the dominant political issue, the advocates of tariff reform contending that within the limits of the free trade system sufficient revenue could not be found. The first Budget, introduced by Mr. H. H. Asquith, on April 30th, 1906, was necessarily provisional because the Liberals had not been long in office. He was able to announce that the revival of trade had been reflected in a yield of the taxes which had exceeded the estimate by over £1,500,000. Practically the same amount had been saved in expenditure. Consequently, with the small surplus budgeted for in the last session, he had a total realised surplus of £3,466,000. On the same basis of taxation he estimated that there would be a surplus of £3,074,000 in the coming year. Before disposing of the realised surplus of 1905–6 and the estimated surplus of 1906–7, the Chancellor directed attention to the recent rise in the level of public expenditure and the alarming proportions of the debt. In the previous ten years the population had increased 10 per cent., the national expenditure 39 per cent., and the National Debt

21 per cent. The whole effect of the great reductions in the capital liabilities of the State since 1871 had been wiped out by the Boer war. He insisted that it was necessary to make further and immediate efforts to reduce the unfunded debt, as its existence had an adverse influence on the revival of trade. He proposed, therefore, that the surplus of the past year should go, as in the ordinary course, to the Old Sinking Fund, and that £500,000 of the estimated surplus of 1906–7 should be added to the New Sinking Fund, which would raise it to £9,500,000. The total effect of this provision for redemption of the debt was not so considerable as appeared on the surface. A practice had grown up of meeting capital expenditure by means of special loans for which the department concerned had provided for interest and repayment in its estimates. Mr. Asquith strongly condemned this method and made arrangements by which it would be brought to an end. In the current year, however, indebtedness would be increased under this head to the extent of £6,500,000, while £1,900,000 would go towards the liquidation of such loans. Having placed the debt charge in the forefront and taken the first step in the direction of substantial reduction, the Chancellor turned to possible remissions of taxation. £1,000,000 he devoted to the abolition of the export duty on coal as from November 1st, and the remainder at his disposal to the reduction of the tea duty from 6d. to 5d. For the moment the income tax was to remain at 1s. in the pound, though Mr. Asquith acknowledged that such a high rate raised the questions of differentiation and graduation. A Select Committee under the chairmanship of Sir Charles Dilke was appointed to conduct an enquiry on this subject.

The Budget of 1907–8 laid the foundations of the new financial policy. The auspices seemed good. Under all the important heads of revenue, receipts had exceeded estimates. Death duties alone had yielded £1,200,000 more than was expected. Economies had also been effected, including a saving of nearly £2,500,000 on the Army and Navy. The realised surplus turned out to be £5,399,000. In the coming year Mr. Asquith anticipated a revenue of £144,190,000 and an expenditure of £140,757,000, leaving an estimated surplus of £3,433,000.[1] He declared that his proposals would be governed by three general principles. In the first place, he reiterated his warning against allowing the outstanding national liabilities to remain at a high figure and insisted that a substantial effort ought to be made to reduce the debt. Secondly, he considered it was full time to invade the "still unconquered field of social reform." Thirdly, he laid it down that the necessary money would have to be found within the free trade system. The practical conclusion was that he could not afford to ascribe any part of his estimated surplus to the reduction of taxation. Indirect taxes were to remain untouched and the revisions of direct taxes—important as they were—were not to result in any change in their total yield. The Select Committee on the income tax had reported in November, 1906, that both graduation and differentiation were in certain forms practicable. Graduation, however, presented some difficulties which impressed the Committee. In theory a progressive tax rising so much per cent. as the amount of total income becomes larger might seem simple. But it presented administrative problems of which the most formidable was the fact that two-thirds of the tax was stopped at the source. The Committee would not contemplate the abandonment of a method which they regarded as "mainly responsible for the present development of the tax and the ease with which it is collected." Alternatives were proposed and accepted, but the Com-

[1] It will be remembered that Goschen had, in 1888, diverted certain taxes to augment local rates. These did not appear in the annual Imperial balance sheet, although they were collected by the State. Mr. Asquith condemned this method and arranged in this year that the sums should first be paid into the Exchequer and the Local Authorities should receive an equivalent from the Consolidated Fund. The consequence was that the total revenue *seemed* considerably larger, e.g., for 1907-8 the figures given above would need to be corrected to £154,235,000 and £150,802,000: the surplus, of course, remains the same. In subsequent issues of the "Statistical Abstract" the figures of the years prior to 1907-8 were revised so as to include the amounts paid to Local Taxation Accounts.

mittee did not arrive at the same degree of unanimity on graduation as on differentiation.[1] Mr. Asquith recognised this in the scheme he now put forward. He argued that it would be imprudent to attempt to apply the two principles at the same time. For the present, he proposed to distinguish between different kinds of incomes, but not to complicate this by imposing a progressive tax according to the amount of income. A distinction was to be drawn between earned and unearned income and the former was to be charged at a lower rate than the latter. While the general rate was to remain at 1s. in the pound, persons with an income of not more than £2,000 could claim that any part of it was earned; the rate on earned was to be 9d. The existing allowances up to £700 were to be retained, but it was provided that they could only be deducted from earned income. The Chancellor claimed that these changes gave relief to those who bore an undue share of the tax and made it much more suited to be a permanent part of the fiscal machinery. At last Gladstone's objection against tampering with the basis was set aside and the permanent nature of the tax frankly acknowledged.

The ultimate loss involved in the acceptance of the principle of differentiation was estimated at £1,250,000. Mr. Asquith, in accordance with his aim to keep up the revenue to its present standard, had to find compensation. This he proposed to do by revising the rates of the death duties. Estates under £150,000 were not affected by the changes. After that figure the duties were raised, reaching 10 per cent. at £1,000,000 in place of the previous 7½ per cent. Estates valued at more than £1,000,000 were to pay an extra percentage on the amount by which they exceeded

1 "Report from the Select Committee on Income Tax." The problem of differentiation, i.e., of distinguishing between the nature of different kinds of income had long been discussed, p. 112 *supra*. Graduation, i.e., progressive taxation based on the amount of income seemed a more revolutionary proposal. The abatements allowed to incomes under £700, as the Committee pointed out, really constituted a graduation in favour of small incomes. The question was whether the principle could be applied to the whole range of incomes.

that figure. Ultimately the increased yield was expected exactly to balance the loss on the income tax. The burden was thus transferred from the shoulders of the payers of income-tax below a certain figure to those of the successors to estates above a certain value. The primary object was to find additional revenue, but the relation between the death duties and the income tax had long been recognised. They had already effected a differentiation in the latter. Large fortunes might escape with what was, relatively to small fortunes, a light tax during the life of their possessors, but at death they had to meet a heavier charge. Similarly, while smaller incomes paid at the same rate as large ones, the latter ultimately came within the scope of the death duties. Mr. Asquith, however, added to the differentiation effected by the complementary nature of the two taxes, (1) by introducing the principle directly into the income tax, and (2) by increasing the death duties. He thereby took a very important step in the strengthening of direct as against indirect taxation.

The first great measure of social reform which the Government intended to undertake was the granting of Old Age Pensions. To prepare for it Mr. Asquith proposed to forego the remission of taxation to the extent of £1,500,000, which his estimated surplus would have enabled him to concede when all the temporary charges of the alterations he was making had been covered. His plan was to add the sum to the Sinking Fund for the year: in the future, however, it was to go towards the financing of Old Age Pensions. The Budget of 1907 was therefore a preparation for that of 1908. Campbell-Bannerman's state of health forced him to resign in April, 1908, and Mr. Asquith became Prime Minister, Mr. David Lloyd George succeeding to the Chancellorship of the Exchequer. It was arranged, however, that the Prime Minister should introduce the Budget which he had prepared. The revenue during the past year had shown unexpected elasticity under all the main heads. The income tax was the greatest surprise, for it produced £1,880,000 more than the estimate. The total realised surplus was £4,726,000. Mr. Asquith was able to assure the House that the changes in the income tax had created no administrative difficulties. A plan which had been thought unworkable for sixty years had proved "not only practicable, but smooth and easy in its operation." In the coming year the existing taxes were estimated to yield a surplus of £4,901,000. He proposed, therefore, to make a beginning with Old Age Pensions. The Government scheme, which was non-contributory, was to come into operation on January 1st, 1909, and was expected to cost £1,200,000 in the current financial year, and about £6,000,000 a year afterwards. Instead of keeping the balance of his estimated surplus to meet the future charge of Old Age Pensions—which he might have been expected to do in accordance with his own example of last session—he reduced the sugar duty from 4s. 2d. to 1s. 10d. per cwt. at an estimated cost to the revenue of £3,400,000. To the argument of the Opposition that this sum should have been provisionally devoted to the reduction of the debt, Mr. Asquith was able to point to what he had achieved in in the last three years. Altogether he had provided £46,700,000 for repayment of debt, and he did not think he was justified in maintaining taxation in order to continue reducing it at this rate. The reduction of the sugar duty, it was also alleged, further changed the proportion of direct and indirect taxes at a moment when a heavy burden was placed on the revenue in favour of the poor. But to this redress of inequalities of income by means of the heavier taxation of the wealthy, a considerable body of opinion in the House found no objection.

After reducing the sugar duty Mr. Asquith estimated that there would be a surplus of £241,000. But a temporary depression in trade reacted unfavourably on the yield of the taxes, and it fell short of what was expected by over £1,500,000. When Parliament assembled the King's speech called attention to the fact that increased Naval Estimates and the charge of Old Age Pensions would involve heavy expenditure in the coming year. With a deficit on the basis of the existing taxes, and prospective additional charges, the potentialities of free trade finance were sharply challenged by the advocates of tariff reform.

Mr. Lloyd George might have vindicated the former by relying entirely on increases in the income tax and death duties, with a corresponding revision of indirect taxes. In other words, he had to his hand the means of meeting the emergency without departing from principles which had, since Harcourt's 1894 Budget, won general recognition. As a matter of fact, as far as immediate revenue was concerned, this is what he did. But he chose to raise new issues. The Budget was really twofold. The one part, which was on the lines indicated, was calculated to provide him with what was necessary in the coming year, and, although it made considerable changes in the income tax and death duties, the circumstances were such that it could hardly have been strongly opposed. The other part was highly contentious. The Chancellor wished to institute new taxes, which were at first not only unproductive but even involved expenditure, in order to lay the foundations of an expansive revenue to meet the future claims of social reform. This was a unique proposal. It opened up two questions, namely, whether the Chancellor was justified in contemplating the supposed requirements of an undefined period in making provision for the following year, and whether (if he was justified in doing so) this was the right time to attempt to graft new taxes, prospectively productive, on to the trunk which had to bear the strain of the present pressure. Purists had often contended that the Chancellor ought to confine his attention to the year for which he was budgeting. Strong arguments, however, could be adduced on the other side. Peel had a number of years in view when he revived the income tax, and Gladstone's Budget of 1853 was framed in anticipation of the position in 1860. More recently, Mr. Asquith had, in 1907, earmarked money for subsequent use. Hard and fast rules have often to be set aside in practice. It was really a matter of expediency. Was Mr. Lloyd George well advised in attempting to grapple with the problems of a succession of years—for he seems to have thought that it would not have been necessary to impose fresh taxation for some time to come—and thereby overburdening the Budget of 1909–1910, when he was faced by so many immediate charges? If it was desirable to introduce new taxes not at once productive—and it is impossible to maintain that the Chancellor is precluded from imposing such taxes—ought he not to have waited for a year or so?

Mr. Lloyd George described his Budget as a war Budget. It was intended to raise money to wage implacable warfare against poverty. He conducted his campaign in this spirit. The result was the most prolonged and bitter contest which had ever been experienced in the discussion of a year's financial proposals. The Budget was presented on April 29th, 1909, and it did not receive the Royal assent until the anniversary of that day. Meanwhile there had been an appeal to the country, and considerable dislocation had been caused because the Treasury had no authority to collect the taxes. It is difficult now to appreciate the passions which were aroused in the conflict, the free use of the word "revolutionary" on the one side, and the enthusiasm displayed by the other. Mr. Lloyd George undoubtedly had to face a difficult problem when he reviewed the financial possibilities of 1909–10. The existing taxes would yield him, it was estimated, a revenue of £148,390,000, while the expenditure would be £164,152,000. He had therefore to meet a prospective deficit of £15,762,000. His first step was to adjust the estimated expenditure by reducing the fixed charge for the debt from £28,000,000 to £25,000,000.[1] To make up the balance he relied, as has been pointed out, on increases in the staple taxes. (1) Important changes were introduced in the income tax, which the Chancellor described as "the sheet anchor of our financial system." He raised the general rate to 1s. 2d. in the pound; but persons whose total income did not exceed £3,000 were to be charged at the old rate of 9d. on earned income, if the total income was not more than £2,000, and 1s. between £2,000 and £3,000. A new abatement was also added of £10 for each child for those whose incomes were under £500. But the great

[1] It was subsequently reduced by another £500,000 to £24,500,000. This would leave £6,380,000 for the New Sinking Fund. As a matter of fact, only £3,531,419 was allotted in the year.

innovation under this head was the acceptance of the principle of graduation in the higher reaches. Mr. Lloyd George agreed with the Committee of 1906 that a complete system of graduation would involve the abandonment of the method of stoppage at the source, and therefore was not desirable. So he adopted their suggestion of a super-tax on incomes over £5,000, to be based on personal declaration. Such incomes were to pay an additional 6d. in the pound upon the amount by which they exceeded £3,000. When the machinery was in full working order he estimated that the super-tax would produce £2,300,000. These proposals met with little direct opposition. (2) The death duties were made much heavier. From estates of £5,000 and above, a new and steeper scale of duties was exacted, ranging from 4 to 14 per cent. (instead of from 3 to 10 per cent.), as the value of the estates rose from £5,000 to £800,000. The revision was expected to yield £2,850,000. (3) Various increases were made in the stamp duties, estimated to produce an additional £650,000. (4) With regard to indirect taxation, tobacco and spirit duties were raised, with a view to bringing in a further £3,500,000.

The main contest, however, raged round the "land taxes." Mr. Lloyd George proposed to take for national purposes a proportion of the increase in the value of land when it could be shown to be due to the growth and activities of the community. This involved a complete valuation of the land in order to provide the basis for assessing the "unearned increment" as from April 30th, 1909. There were four new duties introduced. A tax of 20 per cent. was to be imposed on increases in the site value of land after the fixed date,[1] to be paid whenever the land

[1] J. S. Mill had pointed out in his "Principles of Political Economy" that the ordinary progress of society tends to augment the income of landlords, and he advocated the appropriation of a portion of this "unearned increment" by the State. ("Principles," Book V., Chap. ii, 5). In the 'eighties the influence exercised by Henry Georges "Progress and Poverty" strengthened the conviction of Radical reformers that something ought to be done. The advocates of the Single Tax and of the taxation of land values

passed from hand to hand, either by sale or on account of death. On the reversion of a lease, the lessor was to pay 10 per cent. on the benefit he received. An annual tax of ½d. in the pound on the site value of undeveloped land was to be charged. This was intended at first to apply to ungotten minerals, a proposal which was withdrawn in favour of a duty of 1s. in the pound on mining royalties. During the Committee stage attention was concentrated on this aspect of the Budget, but, although the original proposals suffered a good deal of amendment, the main principles were established. When the controversy was transferred to the Lords it reached a new stage, for it became increasingly clear that they would take the fateful step of rejecting the Budget. The Government accordingly appealed to the country and was returned, but with a greatly reduced majority. The Budget proposals were incorporated in the Finance (1909–10) Bill, and duly found their way to the Statute Book.[1]

One consequence of the rejection of the Budget was that it was impossible to state the annual accounts in the usual way. In the circumstances it is remarkable how much revenue was actually collected. Customs and excise duties were largely paid under an arrangement that

---

were in agreement on the point that causes of a natural or public nature increased the value of land. Henry George would have ascribed the whole of the "economic" rent to State purposes, thus making it possible to dispense with all other taxes. Mill had merely contended that a valuation should be undertaken and a tax placed on *future* increases in value. The taxation of land values has been in operation for some years in Australia and New Zealand, and the municipalities of Western Canada employ it for local purposes.

[1] The Land Value Duties never produced more than £715,000 (in 1914): in some years they fell far below that amount. In his Budget statement of 1919 Mr. Chamberlain announced that not only had the yield been disappointing but, for a variety of reasons, the duties had become unworkable. It was therefore necessary either to amend or repeal them. He had agreed with Mr. Lloyd George to refer the question to a Select Committee. The upshot was that in 1920 the Government, of which the author of the duties was the head, abandoned them, with the exception of the duty on mining royalties.

part would be refunded if the Budget was ultimately rejected. Death duties were accepted at the old or new rate, subject to later revision. Income tax was deducted at the source on the same condition. Still, when the Chancellor summed up the result, he had to announce a deficit of over £26,000,000, which was due to the fact that payments were in arrears. The difficulty had been tided over by borrowing under the provisions of the Treasury (Temporary Borrowing) Act. Mr. Lloyd George introduced his second Budget two months after the passing of his first. In it he did not propose any additions to the new taxes, nor did he make any reductions. He had by that time received the greater part of the arrears of the last year, and the deficit had been wiped out. Assuming that there would be a year of good trade, the Chancellor estimated for a total revenue of £199,791,000, which would give him a surplus of £309,000, after he had provided for the removal of the pauper disqualification which had so far barred claims for old age pensions. On the side of expenditure he mentioned the charges to be met for labour exchanges, education and development grants; he also indicated that in the next year he would take up the question of national insurance against sickness and unemployment. In the meantime the constitutional issues, which had been raised by the action of the Lords in 1909, were attracting more attention than finance. The Government eventually decided to dissolve Parliament and make a second appeal to the country. As the Finance Bill had not yet passed through all its stages Mr. Asquith announced that only the essential portions would be taken. At the General Election the Government obtained a further lease of power, and the remaining part of the Budget was carried through early in 1911.

In his third Budget statement Mr. Lloyd George was in a position to review the results of the abnormal conditions of the previous two sessions. Taking them together he was able to show a realised surplus of £5,607,000.[1] He had

[1] This did not all go to the Old Sinking Fund. £1,500,000 was set aside for the building of sanatoria and a similar sum was ascribed

been justified in anticipating a good year in 1910–11, the Exchequer receipts having exceeded the estimate by £3,469,000. Apart from some small changes in the cocoa duty and liquor licence duty—involving an estimated loss of £95,000 in all—no changes were made in 1911. The Chancellor expected a surplus of £337,000. During the session the Chancellor was again the central figure in a heated controversy. He had introduced his National Insurance Bill on May 4th. It was a measure on a compulsory contributory basis, providing sick pay and medical aid, together with an unemployment benefit scheme for a defined group of trades. As in Germany, where such a scheme was in operation, a State contribution was granted. Such obligations, however, seemed well within the possibilities of the new finance. In 1912 Mr. Lloyd George was able to announce the largest realised surplus on record, namely, that of £6,545,000. The greater part of the excess of revenue over estimates was due to the heavy yield of the customs, itself an indication of the general prosperity of the year. Expenditure had been increasing at an average of over £6,000,000 a year since 1909—one-half of it being due to the naval programme, and the other to social reform projects—and yet the revenue provided a handsome balance. Some alarm was expressed when Mr. Lloyd George suggested that the surplus should be held in temporary suspense and not devoted to the redemption of the debt. He eventually met the strong protests against this course by handing over £5,000,000 of it to the Old Sinking Fund. The remainder was to meet the special charges of the Navy and the development of Uganda.

There were again no changes in taxation in 1913. The past year had justified optimistic expectations. The Chancellor boasted that overseas trade had reached a higher point than ever before, and unemployment at home was almost eliminated. The great coal strike had resulted in a temporary dislocation, but the loss had soon been made

---

to the Development Fund. £250,000 was lent for public works in Uganda. £2,357,000 remained for the Sinking Fund. The Development Fund was established under an Act of 1909.

up. His realised surplus, however, was not to be compared with that of the previous year. It was merely £180,000. In the coming year he estimated that the expenditure would amount to £195,640,000, while the income, allowing for the increased yield of the taxes, would not be more than £194,825,000. To secure a balance he proposed to take £1,000,000 of the surplus of 1911–12, which he had retained in hand to meet outlays on the Navy and Uganda but had not needed to spend. This, he anticipated, would give him a surplus of £185,000. As a matter of fact he realised £750,000. But expenditure had at last caught up with revenue, and in his Budget of 1914 he had again to face the question of imposing additional taxation. His estimates for 1914–5—expenditure, £210,455,000, and revenue, on the basis of existing taxes, £200,655,000—presented him with a prospective deficiency of £9,800,000. The Budget of 1914 followed the precedents of 1909. The additional money was to be found by changes in the income tax and death duties. The tax on earned income was to remain at 9d. up to £1,000, then it was to be raised to 10½d. up to £1,500, 1s. up to £2,000, and 1s. 2d. up to the limit of £2,500. The unearned rate was raised to 1s. 3d., and the super-tax was also stiffened. Under death duties the scale was revised on estates above £60,000. It was surmised that Mr. Lloyd George was budgeting for a large surplus in the following year, and that possibly he had in mind not only new schemes for expenditure, but also the remission of indirect taxation. What would have been the final result of the new finance can only be conjectured. Many were of opinion that the limit of tolerable taxation had been almost reached, and that retrenchment in expenditure would soon become inevitable. Armaments and social reform had together exerted an enormous influence on the national finances. The advent of the £200,000,000 Budget seemed a portent. But events were at hand which were to make a Budget of that dimensions seem to belong to the distant past and the still more remote future.[1]

[1] In the Estimates of Expenditure for 1920–1 the item "Interest, etc., on War Debt" alone amounts to £320,500,000.

(NOTE.—Figures are given to the nearest thousand, and 000's are omitted.)

Year (ending 31st March.	Exchequer Receipts.	Exchequer Issues.	Deficiency.	Debt Charge.[1]	
	£000	£000	£000	£000	£000
1915	226,694	560,474	333,780	20,977	2,171
1916	336,767	1,559,158	1,222,391	20,338	39,911
1917	573,428	2,198,113	1,624,685	19,782	107,467
1918	707,235	2,696,221	1,988,986	19,828	170,023
1919	889,021	2,579,301	1,690,280	23,638	246,327

1 Under " Debt Charge " the fixed charge is distinguished from the charge for interest, etc., on the War Debt.

CHAPTER VIII

WAR FINANCE—1914–1918

THE fact that public finance functions within a complex system and is affected by disturbances which tend to throw it into dislocation has been fully demonstrated by the review of the history of the nineteenth century. General prosperity has been attended by great elasticity in the yield of the taxes and depression of trade has always involved the Chancellor of the Exchequer in difficulties. But, in addition to the alternate rise and fall, there have been critical moments when exceptional measures have been necessary in order to prevent a collapse of the whole credit economy. Of these crises those of 1847, 1857 and 1866 have been noticed. On these occasions the Government empowered the Bank of England to assist the commercial world to meet its obligations by advancing money, in the form of notes, on all sound bills presented for discount. The mere knowledge that such facilities were available proved sufficient in two of the instances to allay panic; only once had it been necessary to exceed the legal limit in issuing bank notes.[1] Past experience had indeed so perfected the skill of the bankers in dealing with emergencies that in 1890 a serious situation was successfully handled without resort to the device of the suspension of the Bank Charter Act.[2] One natural consequence of the fuller understanding of the working of the credit system was that it became more elaborate; for confidence is the basis of all financial operations. The preservation of peace, however, was the underlying assumption on which the whole fabric rested. When peace was endangered it began

[1] Pp. 106, 128 and 141 *supra*. [2] P. 165*n*., *supra*.

to totter, and when war between the Great Powers seemed imminent, it came down with a crash.

The emergency measures of August, 1914, can only be noticed in briefest outline. A fatal train of events was set in motion by the dispatch of the Austrian ultimatum to Serbia on July 24th. Continental Bourses experienced a panic and one after another they closed down. The London Stock Exchange was therefore flooded with selling orders from abroad. Prices fell rapidly and were in danger of a complete collapse. On July 31st—the day before the German ultimatum to Russia—the Stock Exchange closed, a step unprecedented in its history. This had an immediate effect on the banks. They were being pressed by depositors who wanted cash. But they now had no means of selling the securities which they held against their liabilities. Through no fault of their own they found themselves in the position which it had always been their policy to avoid; their assets were no longer fluid. They could neither sell their own investments nor could they dispose of the stocks and bonds which they held as collateral security against loans. A run on the banks might develop at any moment with serious consequences. To meet it they had only their cash in hand, their balances at the Bank of England and their loans at call or short notice. Some of them showed a disinclination to pay out what gold they had, and handed Bank of England notes to their customers. This had the effect of suggesting that it was advisable to hoard gold, and of sending the recipients of notes to the Bank of England itself for cash. The calling in of loans at short notice from the bill-brokers, to whom they are usually made, also drove them to the Bank of England for assistance. Consequently the pressure on the central institution became increasingly heavy The Bank rate went up from 4 to 8 per cent. on July 31st, and the following day it was raised to 10 per cent. The reserve fell below £10,000,000.

The extent of the collapse, however, can only be realised when its effect on international trade is examined. A highly complex system had been evolved for facilitating payments. It was centred in the London money market.

In fact, the bill on London was the chief medium of international exchange. The seller of goods in one part of the world did not normally wait until they had been delivered and paid for by the buyer in another part. The buyer's promise to pay at the end of three months or so was converted into present money by the mechanism of the bill of exchange. He opened a credit with an accepting house in London in favour of the seller, the effect of which was that the acceptors assumed responsibility for the payment of the amount. The bill drawn by the seller and duly " accepted " in London became a first-class credit instrument and could be presented to a bank for discount, that is, a bank would advance money on it because the ability of the acceptors to meet it on maturity was beyond doubt. Obviously, however, the accepting house would depend on the buyer remitting the money before that date. At ordinary times the system worked smoothly, and bills of exchange were looked upon as excellent investments, because they usually represented goods on their way to market and they were not long outstanding. It was estimated that prior to the crisis of 1914 there were bills of exchange for over £300,000,000 due to mature in London within the next few months. Millions fell in daily. But the danger of war completely dislocated the machinery. The foreign exchanges broke down, and it was impossible for the foreign customers to remit funds to the London accepting houses. They were therefore thrown back on their own resources, which were not sufficient to enable them to remain solvent.

It was not merely a question of the losses which the accepting houses would have to face because the vast sums for which they were responsible were not forthcoming from abroad. The machinery of international trade had broken down, and it was of the utmost importance to repair and set it in motion again. How was this to be done ? The first step taken by the Government was to issue a Proclamation which allowed accepting houses to re-accept bills, originally accepted before August 4th, as they fell due and to postpone payment for a month. This was part of the *moratorium*.[1] It saved the accepting houses for the moment, but offered no ultimate relief unless the remittances from abroad were paid within the time. The fact that one country after another was drawn into the war ruled out this possibility. Nor did it give any assistance to the banks and discount houses, for they depended on the acceptors meeting their bills on maturity. Business was therefore at a standstill. This problem was met on August 12th by the Treasury arrangement with the Bank of England, by which the Bank offered to discount bills accepted before August 4th, the State assuming the responsibility for any ultimate loss. Any bank or discount house could thus sell the bills it held, if accepted before August 4th and otherwise satisfactory, and be free from all future responsibility. The effect was to give the banks large credits at the Bank of England by rendering their assets in the form of bills fluid once more. They were now in a position to discount new bills and advance money for other purposes. The liability of the acceptors still remained and consequently they did not undertake new business. To remove this difficulty the Government decided to empower the Bank of England to advance money to the accepting houses to enable them to pay all bills they had accepted before August 4th. The Bank engaged not to seek repayment of the loan until twelve months after the conclusion of the war. Relieved of their obligations for pre-war bills for a definite period, the accepting houses were in a position to resume their activities as far as conditions would allow.

It will be recalled that the crisis in August occurred on the eve of the holidays. Many who formed the queue at the Bank of England on July 31st and August 1st wanted to change bank-notes into gold because the latter would be

[1] A *moratorium*, which is a legal authorisation to postpone the payment of debts, can hardly be partial without involving hardship. On August 6th, therefore, a Proclamation was issued which made the *moratorium* much more comprehensive. Originally intended to run until September 4th, it was continued until November. Before that time the Courts (Emergency Powers) Act of August 31st had provided for the protection of debtors in hard cases.

more convenient when away from home. The approach of Bank holiday—Monday, August 3rd—seemed an embarrassment. It was really a blessing in disguise. The banks remained closed for three additional days, and steps were taken to deal with the emergency. An adequate currency was the first necessity. Precedent would have required that the Bank Charter Act should be suspended in order that bank notes in sufficient number to meet requirements might be issued. This course, however, was not adopted.[1] The Treasury itself supplied the requisite paper money in the form of one pound and ten shilling notes, under the provisions of the Currency and Bank Notes Act of August 6th. The currency notes were made legal tender for any amount, and no limit was set to the issue. Technically, they were convertible into gold, for a clause in the Act provided that the holder of a currency note should be entitled to obtain, on demand, payment in gold at the Bank of England. In practice this apparent safeguard against an over-issue came to mean very little. The so-called "emergency" currency remained as a reminder of the financial crisis which heralded the war: it played an important part in the financing of it, and is an element in the difficulties it has bequeathed. What would have happened had the Bank of England supplied the notes required it is impossible to say. The Currency and Bank Notes Act did include a clause which indemnified the Bank of England if it issued notes in excess of the legal limit. But the ample provision of currency notes did not make this necessary. They were issued to the bankers up to 20 per cent. of their liabilities on deposit and current accounts. The Treasury's security was a floating charge upon the bank's assets, and the notes were to bear interest at the current Bank rate.

The re-establishment of the credit system was an essential preliminary to the prosecution of the war. By September the Banks were provided with currency to meet their requirements and their assets were again fluid. The assistance given to the accepting houses, together with the arrangements made for shipping insurance, had promoted

[1] There seems to have been a temporary over-issue on August 7th and 8th, but it was corrected by 10th.

the resumption of international trade. Meanwhile the Government had to secure immediate means to cover the expenses of the early days of the war. A vote of credit for £100,000,000 on August 6th enabled the Treasury to take what steps it thought necessary without submitting any details of expenditure to the House of Commons. This was in accordance with the recognised procedure of the House in the case of an unforeseen national emergency; but the vote was enormously larger than on any previous occasion. The method of giving the Treasury authority for expenditure by means of votes of credit was retained throughout the war, partly because the publication of estimates and supplementary estimates would have given some indication to the enemy of the sums spent on various services, and partly because it was impossible to foretell the costs with any degree of certainty. After the first vote of credit, however, the practice arose of giving some idea of the total cost by attempting to express it in terms of the cost per day, thereby informing the House how long the vote of credit under consideration might be expected to last. The Government was also given wide powers in deciding how it would raise the money it was from time to time authorised to spend. At first it mainly relied on Treasury bills, which were to run for six months. The early issues were over-subscribed by the banks at a comparatively low rate of interest. The explanation of this was that the banks had, owing to the assistance the State had given them in realising their assets, very large balances and Treasury bills offered the most attractive investment at the moment. It soon became essential, however, to arrange for a long-dated loan. The first War Loan was opened for public subscription in November. It was issued at 95 bearing 3½ per cent. interest and repayable in 1928 or, at the option of the Government, in 1925. The net yield was £331,798,000. On November 15th the Government asked for a second vote of credit for £225,000,000.[1]

The first attempt to answer the difficult question of how much of the expenses of the war was to be met by taxation

---

1 A third Vote of Credit for £37,000,000 was granted on March 1st, 1915, making in all £362,000,000 in the financial year.

was the special Budget introduced by Mr. Lloyd George on November 16th. He proposed that the Budget of the previous May should remain intact and that increases should be made within the scheme then laid down, that is, he did not try to discover any new taxes. His declared policy was to raise as much as possible by means of taxes without doing damage to productive industries. The public was certainly prepared for heavy taxation, and the Budget proposals seemed to err on the side of moderation. The income tax was doubled for the last four months of the financial year. Spreading the increase over the whole year this raised the rate on earned income to 1s., and on unearned incomes to 1s. 8d. The indirect taxes chosen for increase were those on beer and tea ; the tax on beer was raised to 17s. 3d. per standard barrel, and 3d. a lb. was added to tea. The estimated result of these changes was an additional yield of £12,500,000 from the income tax (including the super-tax), and of £3,000,000 from beer and tea. If the estimated tax income in the two Budgets of 1914 is compared it will be seen that the outbreak of war had necessitated a revision of the figures for Customs and Excise, and that the additions to beer and tea did not cover the expected shrinkage in their yield. The total estimated produce of taxes was only £175,866,000. To this must be added the non-tax revenue of £35,430,000, making a total revenue of £211,296,000, which was not a substantial increase on the pre-war basis.[1] The Chancellor's task was extremely difficult because it was too soon to assess the full significance of the change from peace to war. How long the war would last, what it was likely to cost, how national production would be affected, and many other questions contributed to produce an unprecedented element of uncertainty. In the circumstances it is hardly remarkable that he contented himself with strengthening the May Budget, which had been regarded as one that imposed very heavy burdens on the community. It is remarkable, however, that Mr. Lloyd George's second

[1] The realised revenue for 1914–15 proved that the estimate was conservative. It amounted to £226,694,000.

war Budget did not reveal a fuller appreciation of the situation. It was presented on May 4th, 1915. The review of the yield of the taxes was highly satisfactory, all of them having produced more than had been expected. Without any alteration it was estimated that the revenue, tax and non-tax, would amount to £270,332,000 in 1915–16. The Chancellor therefore did not propose to make any changes but to allow those of the previous November to stand. In view of the rapidly increasing cost of the war and the great sums which were being raised by borrowing, Mr. Lloyd George missed an opportunity. Experience had often demonstrated that it was of first importance to impose adequate war taxes as early as possible. The temper of the people was such that considerable sacrifices would then have been borne without complaint.

Up to March 31st, 1915, the net borrowing was almost double the total revenue, and there was every prospect that in the coming financial year the proportion of borrowing to revenue would be much larger. Was this a satisfactory outlook? The precedents of the financing of the later stages of the French wars of a century ago, and of the Crimean War were quoted in favour of raising more by means of taxation. An analysis of the consequences of the transition from peace to war would have served to confirm the wisdom of this course. War means that public finance is called upon to play the predominant part in national economy. The State has its functions enormously enlarged, and the result of the contest on which it is embarked is so vital to all other interests that they are necessarily subordinated to the requirements of the war. There is such a demand for the commodities and services essential for the conduct of the war that the whole face of industry is changed. To exercise and strengthen this demand the State needs to acquire great spending power. But it is important to notice that the real demand is for commodities and services. There are ways and means of creating money, and there are devices for saddling posterity with repayments of debts, but they do not increase the total of goods available at the moment. In other words, if the State is to get what it requires, current production must be largely directed to supply what it wants. This can only be effected if the demands of individuals are curtailed. If they remain in possession of purchasing power to the same extent as in normal times and choose to exercise it, the demand for commodities will obviously outrun the supply. The general level of prices will rise, and social consequences will follow which tend to produce friction between different sections of the community. A proper adjustment of purchasing power is therefore necessary. The State can acquire a greater control over current production if individuals transfer part of their purchasing power to it. This they may be induced to do by lending their money, or forced to do by the imposition of taxation. By these methods the whole of current production might conceivably be transferred to the State after provision has been made for the maintenance of the efficiency of the producers and the necessary plant. As far as the immediate effect is concerned it is immaterial whether the State secures its control over commodities and services by means of taxation or loan. The difference is that, in the former case, it assumes no obligation, while, in the latter, it recognises a claim on future production. It may be admitted that in practice it is necessary to employ the two methods. The question then arises whether any proportion between taxation and borrowing ought to be observed. A fixed ratio, however, is out of the question. The Chancellor of the Exchequer must be guided by practical considerations and not bound by a mere formula.

What these practical considerations are may be discovered by examining the merits of taxation and borrowing in time of war. Both are means of diverting part of the productive capacity of the community to public purposes. Taxation has the psychological effect of impressing on the people the reality of the burden which they have to carry. It also compels them to limit their demands on current production, which enforces the necessary economies. Borrowed money, on the other hand, is lightly spent. An impression of prosperity is created and public lavishness stimulates private expenditure. At every step the resources of the future are more deeply mortgaged. After the war the burden of taxation has to be maintained in order to meet the charges of the heavy debt which has been contracted. Extensive borrowing, however, leads to other serious complications. So far it has been assumed that the State borrows from the current savings of the people, that is, money which might be taken by taxation, if it was thought advisable. It is also possible to sell existing securities abroad and to raise a foreign loan. Both these courses were taken later, with important results. The sale of securities abroad either means that the interest would have to be remitted from this country in future, or that the receipt of interest from abroad would be foregone, according to the nature of the security. A foreign loan, while it may be a temporary convenience, is ultimately a heavy handicap. But the real danger of too great dependence on borrowing is that undue resort is made to temporary borrowing from the banks on a purely credit basis. The money involved in this transaction has no real existence. The Government wishes to pay for commodities and services. It contracts with a bank to credit the amount to the individuals to whom it is due, and the Government pays interest on the advance. If such advance is employed for productive purposes the temporary effect of the increase in deposits—which is the result of the transaction—is in the end eliminated by the sale of the articles produced, and purchasing power is again contracted. During war, however, the commodities and services are unproductively consumed, and the loans remain outstanding. The purchasing power is therefore not contracted and a condition of inflation arises, that is, the purchasing power has been increased relative to the amount of goods which are to be purchased. This is a condition associated with high prices. With a paper currency to which no limit applied in practice the whole process was fatally easy. Excessive borrowing, in fact, results in an objectionable form of taxation, for the rise in prices is equivalent to a tax on general consumption. Consequently there was all the more reason to attempt to restrict borrowing. The possibilities of overt taxation ought to have been fully explored as a check on, even if it could not be regarded as a safeguard against, these evils

In June, 1915, Mr. Lloyd George became Minister of Munitions, and Mr. Reginald McKenna succeeded to the Chancellorship. It soon became obvious that the increase in expenditure demanded a revision of the Budget. In asking for a vote of credit for £250,000,000 the Prime Minister announced on June 15th that the estimated cost of the war had reached £3,000,000 a day. This figure was passed in the autumn, and an average of £5,000,000 a day was within sight. In these circumstances Mr McKenna introduced a new Budget on September 21st. It was a belated, but courageous, attempt to impose adequate war taxation on the country. The revised estimated expenditure of the year came to a total of £1,590,000,000, while the revenue, on the existing basis of taxation, was expected to yield £272,110,000. Mr. McKenna's task was to find sources of revenue which would enlarge the latter amount. (1) He increased the income tax, adding 40 per cent. to the rate, and also applying a new scale to the super-tax. The exemption level was reduced to £130, and the abatement was lowered to £120. (2) The tea duty was raised from 8d. to 1s. a lb., and the sugar duty from 1s. 10d. to 9s. 4d. a cwt. The duties on cocoa, coffee and tobacco were increased 50 per cent. The motor spirit and patent medicine duties were doubled. (3) Import duties at the rate of 33⅓ per cent. *ad valorem* were imposed on motor-cars, motor-cycles, clocks, watches, etc., and (4) a duty of 50 per cent. was placed on excess profits. The first two of these divisions come within the traditional system and represent the apportionment of the charges between direct and indirect taxes. It was, however, impossible to maintain any ratio between the yield of these two main types of taxes. War experience was to prove that the countries which relied heavily on indirect taxes found them a disappointment. They served to limit consumption—a desirable end in some cases—but they did not thereby assist to augment public income. It is a proof of the superiority of direct taxes, from this point of view, that while the yield of the Customs and the Excise was

£10,000,000 more than that of the income-tax in 1914–15, it was £8,000,000 less in 1915–16, in spite of the substantial increases made by Mr. McKenna. The last two divisions enumerated above include the innovations of the Budget. The first was put forward as a means of restricting the importation of the articles mentioned because some limitation of imports was desirable. There was no intention of protecting the home manufacture, though naturally some objection was raised to the principle of these duties. But the Excess Profits Duty proved to be the strongest point of the Budget. It was really of the nature of a special income tax. Any trade or business in which the profits exceeded the pre-war standard—which normally meant those of any two of the three pre-war years—had to pay 50 per cent. of the excess. The undoubted flaws in the tax were immediately exposed. But the Treasury found it unexpectedly remunerative and naturally wished to retain it; while the public felt that, if no means could be adopted to prevent the earning of high profits, the State ought at least to appropriate a share of them.

Mr. McKenna's Budget was estimated to produce £107,000,000 of additional revenue within the year, which would mean a total of £305,000,000 in 1915–16. It actually realised £336,767,000, an increase of over £100,000,000 on the previous year. In introducing his second Budget,[1] however, he proposed to go beyond the £500,000,000 figure because the rate of expenditure was still rising steeply. The graduation of the income-tax was amended so that earned incomes over £2,500 and unearned incomes over £2,000 reached the maximum charge of 5s. in the pound. The Excess Profits Duty was raised to 60 per cent. These changes were expected to produce an additional £54,000,000, or three-fourths of the increased taxation now imposed. The remaining quarter was to be raised, (1) by increases in the sugar, cocoa, coffee, etc., duties, and (2) by new taxes on matches, mineral waters and entertainments. A £500,000,000 Budget seemed a daring proposal. As a matter of fact the estimates were

[1] On April 4th, 1916.

greatly exceeded. The realised revenue was £573,427,000 a result largely due to the fact that the Excess Profits Duty produced £53,000,000 more than was anticipated. In the meanwhile the second War Loan had been issued in the summer of 1916. It was more complicated in its provisions than the first, because arrangements were made for the conversion of old loans into the new one. The loan was issued at par bearing 4½ per cent. interest, and was redeemable in 1945 with an option of repayment in 1925. Various terms of conversion were offered to the holders of consols, annuities and the first loan. Consequently the actual amount which would be received in subscriptions could only be estimated. It was expected that £600,000,000 of new money would be forthcoming, a result which was practically attained.[1] The Bank of England was the Government's chief agent in disposing of the loan, but the needs of small investors were met by selling bonds for £5 and £25 through the Post Office, and these subscriptions were facilitated by the offer of scrip vouchers for 5s., 10s., and £1, which might be used in making purchases.

With the change of Government in December, 1916, Mr. A. Bonar Law became Chancellor of the Exchequer. He introduced the fifth war Budget on May 2nd, 1917. No new taxes were proposed, but additions were made in three existing taxes: the Excess Profits Duty was raised to 80 per cent. and changes were made in the tobacco duty and entertainments tax with a view to increasing their yield. It was estimated that the three taxes would produce an additional £27,500,000, but much more was expected from the elasticity of the existing taxes. The Chancellor anticipated that the total tax revenue in 1917-18 would amount to £569,700,000, which, together with a non-tax income of £68,900,000, would give him a revenue of £638,600,000. Large as this figure was it was entirely dwarfed by the estimates of expenditure. They amounted to £2,290,000,000, that is, £1,651,400,000 had to be raised by the various forms of borrowing. In the circumstances

[1] The net yield was £592,346,000.

a Budget which virtually marked time seemed quite inadequate. It was characterised as a retrograde step in the war financial policy and a movement was set on foot in the House of Commons to review national expenditure. Taxation, it was urged, could be more easily borne during war than after the return to peace. Borrowing would make the debt charge so heavy that it would be necessary to maintain the same scale of taxation after as during the war, unless the ratio of borrowing to taxation was lowered by increasing the yield of the latter while the war was in progress. The method of finance aggravated the condition of inflation. And apart from the immediate effect in raising prices, this meant that the Government was borrowing in depreciated currency and assuming the obligation of paying the interest in good money, if and when the standard was restored. These considerations, however, were not allowed to carry much weight in the remaining months of the war.

The system of borrowing went through a number of phases in the course of the war. At first, as has been noticed, money was secured by means of Treasury bills of a temporary kind, Enormous sums falling due at short intervals soon created a pressure which had to be relieved, partly by the issue of Treasury bonds running for three to five years and partly by the flotation of large war loans which postponed repayment for a longer period. Of these long-dated loans those of 1914 and 1915 have already been recorded. By the end of 1916 outstanding Treasury bills alone amounted to £1,115,815,000 and the time had arrived for a further attempt to reduce the amount of unfunded debt. Early in January it was announced that the sale of Treasury bills and Exchequer bonds would be suspended. On January 11th the terms of the third war loan were outlined by Mr. Bonar Law. It was to be issued in two forms (1) a 5 per cent. loan, subject to income tax, and repayable in 1947 or, at option of the Government, in 1829, and (2) a 4 per cent. loan, free of income tax, and repayable in 1942, or 1929 as in the former case. The 5 per cent. stock and bonds were issued at 95 and the 4 per cent. at par. A widespread publicity campaign was undertaken to popularise the loan. The banks offered to advance money to would-be subscribers. The Press also lent the strongest support to the Government's appeal during the period of subscription. On February 26th the Chancellor announced to the House of Commons that his anticipations had been exceeded and the total amount applied for had been more than £1,000,000,000. He computed that there had been 5,289,000 subscribers. The success which attended the efforts to attract large numbers of subscribers made it possible for the Government to consider a change in policy. In September it adopted the suggestion of continuous borrowing, that is, instead of fixing subscription periods for specific loans, it offered National War Bonds. These could be bought at any time and no limit was set to the issue. The Chancellor estimated that the minimum amount required week by week was £20,000,000. This method had the double advantage of drawing on the savings of the people towards Government expenditure and of avoiding calling for heavy advances from the banks, a procedure which was inevitable in raising a large loan within a limited subscription period. The National War Bonds ran through four series between October, 1917, and May, 1919, when the sale of the last series was suspended because it was proposed to issue the fourth, or Victory, loan in the following month. During the last year of the war the National War Bonds secured a steady weekly subscription. But their yield was augmented by loans negotiated abroad. It has already been pointed out that external loans have a distinctive character of their own. Subscriptions to an internal loan must come either from current production or from bank advances. In the first case, they turn part of the available surplus into a particular channel with important consequences on future production and distribution. To the extent that the loan represents credit created by the banks it contributes towards inflation. An external loan, on the other hand, affords the means for increasing the supply of commodities and services which may be secured from abroad. The only possible market for a considerable loan was in the United States. As early as 1915 a joint

Anglo-French loan had been negotiated with an American syndicate on terms very favourable to the lenders. The main purpose was to strengthen the exchanges by securing a credit in America against future purchases there. This policy was continued on a rather different basis. Great Britain, as is well known, derived a large income before the war from foreign investments. Necessity was driving her as the war proceeded to buy increasing quantities of food and war supplies in the United States. The unfavourable balance of trade caused by this could be redressed by borrowing in the United States and the foreign investments were excellent collateral security to assist in such an operation. The Government, therefore, took steps to acquire the foreign investments—which were, of course, in private hands—by buying them outright or borrowing them on certain conditions. It even requisitioned specified securities under the Defence of the Realm Regulations. A series of loans were raised in the United States by this method before that country joined in the war and collateral security was no longer necessary.[1]

Mr. Bonar Law opened the sixth and last war Budget on April 22nd, 1918. He was able to announce an excess of receipts over estimates under every head of taxation. The total revenue had yielded £68,000,000 more than he had estimated for in the previous year. An examination of the figures reveals the fact that the Excess Profits Duty was pressing up to the level of the income tax. Out of a total tax revenue of £613,040,000, it accounted for £220,214,000. It was regarded as essentially a temporary war tax; but it was obvious that its repeal at the end of the war would be a considerable sacrifice, for there would be heavy burdens which would have to be met out of taxation. The total receipts—tax and non-tax—came to more than £700,000,000 and some spoke of them as three

[1] "The association with the United States of America as a co-belligerent. . . . relieved the British Treasury of all pressing necessity as regards supplies from North America, and to this extent the most important problem of external finance, which existed during the earlier period of the war, practically ceased to exist."—Report of War Cabinet, 1918, p. 320.

and a half times more than those of the highest pre-war Budget. The comparison, however, was fallacious. There had been a change in the general level of prices which made it extremely misleading. Turning to the expenditure side, it will be found that the excess over estimates was no less than £405,800,000. When every allowance had been made for recoverable items—loans to the Dominions and Allies as well as the probable result of the sale of war stores—it was obvious that the rate of war expenditure was creating a post-war financial problem of unprecedented dimensions. But the demand for economy in expenditure, although it was strengthened by the work of the Committee on National Expenditure, could have little practical effect as long as the war continued. The Budget provided for an estimated expenditure in 1918–19 of £2,972,197,000 or £275,000,000 more than the actual expenditure of the previous year. In the face of the increasing costs of the war per day the Chancellor proposed additional taxation. The standard rate of the income tax was to be raised to 6s. in the pound and the super-tax limit was to be lowered to £2,500. The duties on spirits, beer, tobacco, sugar and matches were to be increased. Various changes were also made in postal rates. It was estimated that these additions would yield £67,800,000 in 1918–19. A proposed new tax on luxuries was discussed but was ultimately abandoned on the ground that the idea was not practicable. Mr. Bonar Law's actual Budget proposals, however, passed through the House with hardly any amendment. The armistice on November 11th suspended hostilities in the main theatre of war.[1]

The fiscal and financial problems of the nineteenth century took form during the long war with France ; those of the twentieth century have been set by the Great War

[1] The total revenue of 1918–19 reached the £889,021,000, exceeding the estimates by £46,971,000. Of the tax revenue of £622,058,000 the income tax produced £291,186 000 and the Excess Profits Duty followed it closely with £285,028,000.

of 1914–18. Here, it might be supposed, is a striking historical parallel from the examination of which some clue to future developments could be discovered. But the circumstances of two different periods, however similar in broad outlines, present such discrepancies in details that the candid enquirer will refuse to draw definite inferences. To attempt to find in history a formula which will solve any specific problem or indicate the course of future events is to misunderstand the nature of that study. The appeal to history does not give unequivocal guidance in practical affairs. This is not to say that a knowledge of history is not necessary. It is essential. The real value of an historical survey, however, is not that it yields the key to the future but that it tends to create the type of mind which knows what it is looking for. Without some acquaintance with what has happened in the past it is impossible intelligently to formulate the questions to be asked of the future. But—to return to the parallel suggested—more is to be learnt from contrasts than from comparisons. It has been shown that the country entered upon the war in 1793 with a presumption in favour of indirect taxation and that the considerable use of this method made a tariff, already sufficiently complicated, so unwieldy that its simplification was the chief fiscal achievement of the following half century. The resort to the income tax was for the period of the war only. During the later stages of the struggle it was remarkably successful in adjusting the burden between taxation and borrowing, and therefore in lessening the indebtedness which posterity had to bear. During the late war the example of the proportion of the cost which was borne by taxation in the earlier war was constantly appealed to in support of heavier taxation. It was alleged that nearly half of the charge was covered by taxation. If the whole period of the war is taken this is certainly a considerable exaggeration, but from 1806 to 1815 the taxational effort was notable. The post-war problems were accentuated by the repeal of the income tax, which precluded the possibility of immediate reform of indirect taxation. The debt, together with the Sinking Fund, was such a heavy item in public expenditure that attention was concentrated on it and the fact that fund-holders derived so much from their investments was constantly pointed out. But the unfunded debt was relatively small and the complications of heavy foreign loans were not present. It is true that the currency was in an unsatisfactory condition, but the over-issue of notes seems almost negligible when compared with modern conditions. To appreciate the real contrast between the two periods a wider view must be taken. The earlier war was fought between States which were not vitally dependent upon one another. It was not then entirely absurd for writers to contend (as some did) that this country could dispense with its foreign trade. An international economic unity had not been created. But the great achievement of the nineteenth century was the foundation of such a unity, within which large industrial communities grew up dependent on a complicated system of international exchange. It follows, therefore, that a century ago the nations could not do so much damage to one another as they were able to do in the late war. This means also that recovery was then altogether a simpler process than it is now. Continental States were then still largely agricultural. Great Britain was only becoming industrialised, a fact which no doubt contributed very materially to her recovery.

The present post-war problems are all ultimately dominated by the fact that a complex economic society has received a heavy and possibly fatal blow. It is impossible for the industrialised communities to work out their salvation independently. They have to be inter-related or they die of inanition. A hundred years ago the States had to face internal economic problems ; now they have to grapple with international ones. Superficially, of course, there are similarities. There is a crushing war debt. There is heavy taxation. There is a deranged currency. Of these a few words may be said. It is obvious that they are all intimately connected with one another. The debt charge represents an item in annual expenditure which cannot be reduced by economy. It, together with war pensions, makes heavy taxation inevitable. As prices fall the burden will become proportionately heavier. The bulk of the loans were contracted when money was worth less than it is likely to be in the post-war period. Consequently the debtor will have to pay the creditor a premium or, in other words, the taxpayer will have to pay to the fundholder an increasingly heavy tribute. If the debt charge remains constant every step towards monetary deflation will make it more onerous. The reduction of public indebtedness therefore stands out as the most pressing problem in post-war finance. First, it is generally agreed that it is desirable to strengthen the general financial position by dealing with the large floating debt. Second, there are strong reasons in favour of discharging as soon as possible the part of the debt raised abroad. Third, the internal debt is sometimes regarded with more complacency. It is pointed out that the debtor and creditor are really the same person; in his capacity as taxpayer he pays himself as fundholder. The total national income is not affected by this operation. But this is to overlook the fact that the payments do affect the distribution of the national income and therefore must exercise a considerable influence on production.

The orthodox ways of dealing with a heavy annual debt charge are to take the earliest opportunity of effecting a conversion in the rate of interest and to provide out of taxation for the repayment of capital by means of a sinking fund. The first must depend on the terms on which the loan was raised and also on whether the circumstances are favourable when the State has the option of effecting a conversion. Unless the stock is at par and provision can be made to pay off dissentients the operation cannot be profitably or equitably carried through. It will be remembered that the State can exercise an option with regard to part of the war loan in 1927, but whether conditions will be in favour of it remains to be seen. A sinking fund depends on a surplus of income over expenditure. With a debt of the present dimensions a substantial sinking fund would involve a considerable addition to an already high rate of taxation. No immediate relief therefore can be looked for in these directions. There is, however, a strong case for not postponing the question. It would to some extent undo the errors of war finance if a levy could be imposed on war-made wealth and a considerable reduction in the debt effected while the currency is still depreciated. The administrative problems of valuation would be formidable but not insuperable If this step is not taken within a limited period the advocates of a general levy on capital, which is in many ways to be preferred to the special levy on war-made wealth, will hold the field. Probably they are working with the grain of the post-war society which is slowly being built up. The burden of indebtedness will become more obvious when public finance returns to a more normal condition. A restoration of the currency will accentuate it. The pressure of the claims of social reform, which cannot be successfully resisted in a modern State, will also mean that it will be impossible so to frame future Budgets that economy on public services is set off against the charge of the debt. The international situation, with the vast system of inter-Allied indebtedness as well as the obligations imposed on Germany, must long remain one of uncertainty.

APPENDIXES

A.—Notes on Books.

B.—i. Total Exchequer Receipts and Issues, 1913–14. (The year is chosen because it was the last normal peace year.)

ii. The yield of the Staple Taxes, i.e., of Customs and Excise, 1815 to 1842, of Customs, Excise, and Income Tax, 1843 to 1894, of Customs, Excise, Income Tax and Estate, etc., Duties, 1895 to 1915, and of Customs, Excise, Income Tax, Estate, etc., Duties and Excess Profits Duty, 1916 to 1919.

iii. Population of England, Wales, Scotland and Ireland at each census from 1811 to 1911.

APPENDIX A.

Notes on Books.

An excellent introduction to public finance will be found in Henry Higgs' "Primer of National Finance," mentioned in the note to p. 1 *supra*. The same author's "National Economy," which deals with the administrative side, and his "Financial System of the United Kingdom," which explains procedure, will also prove valuable. C. F. Bastable's "Public Finance" is a comprehensive treatise on the subject. On the historical side Stephen Dowell's "History of Taxation and Taxes in England" (4 vols.; published in 1885) is useful for reference. It takes taxation as a whole chronologically in the first two volumes and gives the history of particular taxes in the last two volumes. "The Economic Annals of the Nineteenth Century," compiled by William Smart (Vol. I, 1801–1820, and Vol. II, 1821–1830) is a convenient analysis of "Hansard," together with many references to other contemporary sources. It is always particularly full in the treatment of financial questions. "Commerce and Industry," (1919), edited by William Page, proceeds on the same plan of using Parliamentary Debates as the basis. It is much less discursive than the "Economic Annals," and covers the whole period from 1815 to 1914. The sections which deal with the important Budgets are among the most satisfactory, probably because the subject suffers less than others from being set out as it was discussed in Parliament. A second volume gathers together in a convenient form an extensive collection of statistical tables. "Finance and Politics: An Historical Study, 1783–1885," by Sydney (now Lord) Buxton, in two volumes (published in 1888) is an interesting attempt to combine a treatment of finance with a narrative of political developments. It is admittedly discursive and uneven; but it is always readable and suggestive. "British Budgets," by Sir Bernard Mallet (1913) covers the period from 1887 to 1913. It is a lucid and concise interpretation of the tendencies of the period, and is furnished with a useful analysis of the Budgets. E. R. A. Seligman's "The Income Tax" (1911) devotes a long section to the history of the income tax in England, paying particular attention to contemporary discussions. G. Armitage-Smith's "The Free Trade Movement and its Results" (1903) is a good guide to the history of tariff policy. For the history and problems of local taxation the reader may be referred to "National and Local Finance" (1910), by J. Watson-Grice, "History of Local Rates in England," (second edition, 1912), by Edwin Cannan, and "Grants in Aid" (new edition, 1920), by Sidney Webb.

I.—Introductory.

The best recent discussion of the taxational theories of the eighteenth century is the late William Kennedy's "English Taxation, 1640–1799," published in 1913. He contests the view that Adam Smith, in the "Wealth of Nations," "brought to the world a new revelation of the principles of taxation." In his opinion (pp. 141–2), "He (Smith) gave a wide intellectual sanction to a set of opinions already very influential. Apart from Pitt's commercial treaty of 1786 and Peel's and Gladstone's reform of the tariff between 1842 and 1860, no important change in English tax policy is connected with Adam Smith's influence; on the contrary, all the large changes since his day, such as the imposition of the income tax in 1799, have been made independently, or in spite of, the influence of his ideas."[1] Pitt's financial policy is

[1] J. Holland Rose in "William Pitt and the National Revival," pp. 183–4, contends that the influence of Adam Smith on Pitt has been exaggerated. He adds that, "it seems certain that the later editions of the 'Wealth of Nations' were modified so as to bring them into line with some of Pitt's enactments." A footnote acknowledges the indebtedness of the author to Archdeacon Cunningham for "this interesting fact." I have failed to discover any ground for the statement. Pitt began his fiscal reforms in 1784. Between that date and the death of Adam Smith (1790) two editions of the "Wealth of Nations" appeared—those of 1786 and 1789—and they are both practically identical with the third edition, which was published in 1784, and could not have been influenced by Pitt's proposals.

noticed, though not so fully as other aspects of his career, in Holland Rose's " Pitt and the National Revival " and " Pitt and the Great War." A somewhat unfavourable view of his relations with the Bank of England is taken in A. Andréadès' " History of the Bank of England," where the main criticisms of his war finance are summarised. For the latest discussion of the causes which led to the restriction of cash payments R. G. Hawtrey's " Currency and Credit " (1919) should be consulted. W. R. Bisschop's " The Rise of the London Money Market, 1640–1826 " (1910) traces the consequences of the monopoly of the Bank of England and throws a good deal of light on the operations of " country banks." Robert Hamilton's " Inquiry Concerning the Rise and Progress of the National Debt " is still well worth attention (p. 17*n. supra*).

II.—The Aftermath of War. 1815–1822.

The relevant chapters of Smart's " Economic Annals " supply much useful material. They should be read in conjunction with the second chapter of Page's " Commerce and Industry." Buxton passes briefly over these years. J. H. Clapham dealt with some aspects of this period in his Presidential address to the Economic Section of the British Association in 1920 (*see* the December number of the *Economic Journal*). There is an article on " Trade after the Napoleonic War," by J. S. Nicholson, in the *Scottish Historical Review* for July, 1917, which is reprinted in his " War Finance." Thomas Tooke's " History of Prices " would well repay study. The first two volumes appeared in 1838, but his " Thoughts and Details on the High and Low Prices of the last Thirty Years " (1823) anticipated his main conclusions. The less well-known essay by Joseph Lowe on the " Present State of England in regard to Agriculture, Trade, and Finance " (1822) is an able performance. He deals with the financial consequences of the war and examines the effects of the transition to peace. His remarks on the relative taxable capacity of England and France, his estimate of the total national income and his conception of index numbers are all worthy of attention. The resumption of cash payments is discussed in E. Cannan's " Paper Pound."

3.—A Transitional Period. 1823–1841.

Huskisson's reforms are noticed in detail in Smart's second volume of " Economic Annals." Dowell summarises the changes in taxes. The most comprehensive guide to the fiscal problems of the period is Sir Henry Parnell's treatise " On Financial Reform." The first edition was published in 1830 and was followed by a second in the same year. A third came out in 1831, and an enlarged and revised edition in 1832. Parnell indicated quite clearly the lines along which reform was destined to run. His work should be supplemented by the study of the " Report from the Select Committee appointed to inquire into the Duties levied on imports into the United Kingdom and how far these Duties are for protection to similar articles, the produce or manufacture of this country, or of the British Possessions abroad, or whether the Duties are for the purpose of Revenue alone " (1840). Parnell was a member of the Committee and Joseph Hume took a prominent part in the inquiry. It reported that " the Tariff of the United Kingdom presents neither congruity nor unity of purpose." The evidence of J. Deacon Hume and G. R. Porter is significant, as it expresses official opinion at the Board of Trade. Hume declared, " I conceive myself, if I were compelled to choose, that food is the last thing upon which I would attempt to place any protection "—Minutes of Evidence, p. 97. When G. R. Porter was asked whether he thought that the probable effect of the removal of protective duties would be to promote commerce and improve the condition of the people he answered " I have no doubt that it would do so in this country to a degree of which the world has hitherto seen no example (*ibid.* pp. 194–5).

4.—Fiscal and Financial Reform. 1842–52.

Sir Stafford Northcote's " Twenty Years of Financial Policy " (1862) is the earliest and still the most suggestive general commentary on the changes which took place between 1842 and 1861. J. R. McCulloch's " Treatise on the Principles and Practical Influence of Taxation and the Funding System " (1845) provides a comprehensive review of taxes and taxational policy. The " Fall of Protection " (1840–1850), by Bernard Holland (1913), retells the story with vigour and charm. The personal element plays such a large part in the critical years, that the standard biographies should be consulted—Morley's " Gladstone " and " Cobden," Monypenny's " Disraeli," and Disraeli's own " Life of Lord George Bentinck." C. S. Parker's " Sir Robert Peel from His Private Papers," 3 vols. (1899) is very valuable. J. R. Thursfield's " Peel " (English Statesmen Series) is an excellent summary of his career. There are some interesting comments on the free trade movement in Alfred Marshall's " Industry and Trade " (1919), especially in Appendix " E," pp. 733–750. Discussion of the merits of the Bank Charter Act has never ceased since it was placed on the Statute Book, e.g. the late Sir Edward Holden criticised it adversely in 1919. The Committee on Currency and Foreign Exchanges (Cd. 9182) practically recommended a return to its principles in 1918.

5.—The Completion of Free Trade. 1853–66.

Gladstone's " Financial Statements " (1863) contains the 1853, 1860, and three subsequent Budget speeches. The speech of 1853 should be made the basis of any study of the period covered by this chapter. Buxton's "Finance and Politics" now becomes much fuller; it carries on the story after the conclusion of Northcote's survey. J. A. Hobson re-examines the negotiations which preceded the Anglo-French Treaty in his "Richard Cobden: The International Man" (1918). C. J. Fuchs, in his "Trade Policy of Great Britain and Her Colonies since 1860" (English translation, 1905), traces the consequences of the Treaty in building up a complicated system of commercial treaties.

6.—Strains and Stresses. 1866–92.

Sir Robert Giffen's "Essays in Finance" will be found useful for the earlier part of this period. In the First Series appears the essay on "Mr. Gladstone's Work in Finance," written in 1868. "The Liquidations of 1873–76" and "The Fall of Prices of Commodities in Recent Years" also throw light on problems of these years. Buxton is particularly good in dealing with Gladstone's Budgets, and his "Finance and Politics" may be supplemented by his "Mr. Gladstone as Chancellor of the Exchequer." Morley's "Gladstone" is indispensable, because of the access to special material which the author enjoyed. Mallet's "British Budgets" summarises Goschen's work at the Exchequer. Winston S. Churchill's "Lord Randolph Churchill" should be consulted.

7.—Armaments and Social Reform. 1893–1914.

For these years Mallet's "British Budgets" is an invaluable guide. The tariff controversy, precipitated by Chamberlain, was responsible for the appearance of numerous books and pamphlets, mostly of ephemeral interest. Of more permanent value are W. Cunningham's "Rise and Decline of the Free Trade Movement" (1905), W. J. Ashley's "Tariff Problem" (1904), and W. Smart's "Return to Protection" (1906). "Customs' Tariffs of the United Kingdom from 1800 to 1897," Cd. 8706 (1897), supplies abundant material for an historical retrospect of the British tariff.

8.—War Finance. 1914–18.

A convenient summary is provided by F. L. McVey's "Financial History of Great Britain, 1914–18" (1918). It is admittedly provisional; but there are several slips which might have been avoided with a little more care in compilation. F. W. Hirst published in 1915 his "Political Economy of War", which attempts to set out the economic consequences of past wars. "The Economics of War and Conquest" (1915), by J. H. Jones, should also be consulted. The series of reports and inquiries edited by A. W.

Kirkaldy for the Economic Section of the British Association, under the title of " Credit, Industry, and the War," and " Industry and Finance," contain summaries of the public finance of each year. Hartley Withers's " War and Lombard Street " (1915) describes the crisis of August, 1914, and how it was met. Some comments on the conduct of war finance will be found in the same author's " War-Time Financial Problems " (1919). There are valuable articles in the " Economic Journal " and " The Round Table." R. G. Hawtrey's " Currency and Credit " (1919) is highly suggestive. J. S. Nicholson (1917) has collected his war-time essays in his " War Finance," and has also published a short course of lectures on inflation under that title. Some of the problems of the future are discussed in J. A. Hobson's " Taxation in the New State " (1919). Pethick Lawrence, in his " Levy on Capital," advocates that scheme. It is discussed in a number of articles in the " Economic Journal " for 1918. A. C. Pigou devotes a chapter of his " Economics of Welfare " (1920) to the question, and has also published a short statement of the case in " A Capital Levy and a Levy on War Wealth " (1920).

TOTAL EXCHEQUER RECEIPTS

RECEIPTS

	£
Customs - - - - - - - - - -	35,450,000
Excise - - - - - - - - - -	39,590,000
Estate, etc., Duties - - - - - -	27,359,000
Stamps - - - - - - - - - -	9,966,000
Land Tax - - - - - - - - -	700,000
House Duty - - - - - - - - -	2,000,000
Property and Income Tax - - - - -	47,249,000
Land Value Duties - - - - - - - -	715,000
Total Tax Revenue - - - - - - -	163,029,000
Postal Service - - - - - - - -	21,190,000
Telegraph Service - - - - - - - -	3,080,000
Telephone Service - - - - - - - -	6,530,000
Crown Lands (net receipts) - - - - - -	530,000
Receipts from Suez Canal Shares and Sundry Loans	1,579,972
Miscellaneous - - - - - - - - -	2,303,925
Total Non-Tax Revenue - - - - - -	35,213,897
Total Revenue - - - - - - -	198,242,897

Surplus,

APPENDIX

AND ISSUES, 1913–14.

Issues

		£
Consolidated Fund Services:		
Fixed Charge for the National Debt		24,500,000
Road Improvement Fund		1,394,951
Payments to Local Taxation Accounts		9,734,128
Other Consolidated Fund Services		1,693,890
Total Consolidated Fund Services		37,322,969
Supply Services:		
Army		28,346,000
Navy		48,833,000
Civil Services:	£	
1. Public Works and Buildings	3,338,000	
2. Salaries and Expenses of Civil Departments	4,287,000	
3. Law and Justice	4,491,000	
4. Education, Science and Art	19,450,000	
5. Foreign and Colonial Services	1,523,000	
6. Non-effective and Charitable Services	824,000	
7. Miscellaneous	322,000	
8. Isurance and Labour Exchanges (including Old Age Pensions)	19,666,000	
Total Civil Services		53,901,000
Customs and Excise		2,431,000
Inland Revenue		2,052,000
Post Office Services		24,607,000
Total Supply Services		160,170,000
Total Expenditure		197,492,969

£749,928.

A FISCAL & FINANCIAL HISTORY OF ENGLAND

THE YIELD OF THE STAPLE TAXES, 1815–1918.

(Note.—Figures are given to the nearest thousand, and 000's are omitted.)

Year (ending January 5th).	Customs. £000	Excise. £000
1816	10,522	26,538
1817	9,716	24,566
1818	11,258	21,483
1819	11,639	24,742
1820	10,871	24,895
1821	9,837	27,930
1822	10,583	28,183
1823	10,664	27,283
1824	11,499	25,343
1825	11,328	26,768
1826	16,542	21,004
1827	17,281	19,172
1828	17,894	18,439
1829	17,235	20,760
1830	17,212	19,540
1831	17,540	18,644
1832	16,516	16,303
1833	16,975	16,611
1834	16,209	16,544
1835	18,403	14,892
1836	20,367	13,249
1837	21,488	14,554
1838	20,539	13,419
1839	20,846	13,632
1840	21,584	13,510

The other taxes, of which the chief were : the Land Tax, the Assessed Taxes, and the Stamp Duties, produced between ten and twelve millons a year on an average, from 1816 to 1842. Customs and Excise, it will be seen, yielded together between thirty and thirty-six millions on an average in the same period, i.e., they produced two-thirds of the tax revenue. For details of the additions to, and reductions from, the rates of Customs and Excise Duties during the years 1800–1853, reference may be made to " Accounts and Papers," 511, of 1857–1858.

THE YIELD OF THE STAPLE TAXES, 1815-1918—*contd.*

Year (ending January 5th).	Customs. £000	Excise. £000	Income Tax. £000	
1841	21,784	13,752	—	
1842	21,899	13,679	—	
1843	21,025	12,518	571	
1844	21,033	12,878	5,249	
1845	22,505	13,308	5,192	
1846	20,197	13,586	5,026	
1847	20,569	13,988	5,395	
1848	20,024	12,884	5,451	
1849	20,999	14,154	5,347	
1850	20,637	13,985	5,408	
1851	20,442	14,316	5,383	
1852	20,615	14,442	5,305	
1853	20,552	14,835	5,510	
1854	27,638	18,877	8,270	
1855 [1]	21,630	16,696	10,643	The other taxes, of which the most important were the Stamp Duties, produced between ten and twelve millions.
1856	23,242	17,117	15,071	
1857	23,532	18,165	16,090	
1858	23,109	17,825	11,586	
1859	24,118	17,902	6,684	
1860	24,461	20,361	9,596	
1861	23,306	19,435	10,924	
1862	23,674	18,332	10,365	
1863	24,034	17,155	10,567	
1864	23,232	18,207	9,084	
1865	22,752	19,558	7,958	
1866	21,276	19,788	6,390	
1867	22,303	20,670	5,700	
1868	22,650	20,162	6,177	
1869	22,424	20,462	8,618	
1870	21,477	21,737	10,044	
1871	20,135	22,760	6,350	

[1] The amounts are net up to 1855, and thereafter gross, i.e., including the costs of collection.

THE YIELD OF THE STAPLE TAXES, 1815-1918—*contd.*

Year (ending March 31st).	Customs. £000	Excise. £000	Income Tax. £000	
1872	20,355	23,326	9,084	
1873	21,033	25,785	7,500	
1874	20,339	27,172	5,691	
1875	19,289	27,395	4,306	
1876	20,020	27,626	4,109	
1877	19,922	27,736	5,280	
1878	19,969	27,464	5,820	
1879	20,316	27,400	8,710	
1880	19,326	25,300	9,230	
1881	19,184	25,300	10,650	
1882	19,278	27,240	9,945	
1883	19,657	26,930	11,900	
1884	19,701	26,952	10,718	
1885	20,321	26,600	12,000	
1886	19,827	25,460	15,160	
1887	20,155	25,250	15,900	
1888	19,630	25,620	14,440	
1889	20,067	25,600	12,700	
1890[1]	20,424	24,160 (27,154)	12,770	
1891	19,480 (19,686)	24,788 (29,243)	13,250	
1892	19,736 (19,950)	25,610 (30,183)	13,810	
1893	19,715 (19,913)	25,360 (29,954)	13,470	
1894	19,707 (19,904)	25,200 (29,808)	15,200	

[1] Between 1889 and 1907 certain duties were collected for the Local Authorities by the Imperial Government and assigned to the three divisions of the United Kingdom in the manner prescribed by the Acts 51 and 52 Vict., c. 41; 51 and 52 Vict., c. 60; 52 and 53 Vict., c. 50; 53 Vict., c. 8; 53 and 54 Vict., c. 60; and 57 and 58 Vict., c. 30. They were a share of the Probate Duty and (after 1894) of the Estate Duty, additional Beer and Spirit Duties (Customs and Excise) and the yield of certain Licenses. The part of the taxes so allotted to Local Taxation Accounts was not included in Exchequer Receipts. Consequently, it is necessary to revise the figures for these years in order to render them comparable with those of other years. The revision required is indicated in brackets.

APPENDIX

THE YIELD OF THE STAPLE TAXES, 1815-1918—*contd.*

Year (ending March 31st.)	Customs. £000	Excise. £000	Income Tax. £000	Estate, etc., Duties. £000	Excess Profits Duty. £000
1895	20,115	26,050	15,600	8,754	
	(20,311)	(30,173)		(10,872)	
1896	20,756	26,800	16,100	11,600	
	(20,959)	(31,510)		(14,053)	
1897	21,254	27,640	16,650	10,830	
	(21,463)	(32,367)		(13,963)	
1898	21,798	28,300	17,250	11,100	
	(22,005)	(33,267)		(15,328)	
1899	20,850	29,200	18,000	11,400	
	(21,054)	(34,285)		(15,633)	
1900	23,800	32,100	18,750	14,020	
	(24,028)	(37,336)		(18,521)	
1901	26,262	33,100	26,920	12,980	
	(26,489)	(38,397)		(17,195)	
1902	30,993	31,600	34,800	14,200	
	(31,203)	(36,794)		(18,510)	
1903	34,443	32,100	38,800	13,850	
	(34,650)	(37,415)		(18,086)	
1904	33,850	31,550	30,800	13,000	
	(34,053)	(36,946)		(17,196)	
1905	35,730	30,750	31,250	12,350	
	(35,908)	(36,066)		(16,669)	
1906	34,475	30,230	31,350	12,970	
	(34,645)	(35,603)		(17,329)	
1907	32,930	30,350	31,600	14,400	
	(33,115)	(35,704)		(19,084)	
1908	32,490	35,720	32,380	19,070	
1909	29,200	33,650	33,930	18,370	
1910	30,348	31,032	13,295	21,766	
1911	33,140	40,020	61,946	25,452	
1912	33,649	38,380	44,804	25,392	
1913	33,485	38,000	44,806	25,248	
1914	35,450	39,590	47,249	27,359	
1915	38,662	42,313	69,399	28,382	
1916	59,606	61,210	128,320	31,035	140
1917	70,561	56,380	205,033	31,232	139,920
1918	71,261	38,772	239,509	31,674	220,214
1919	102,780	59,440	291,186	30,262	285,028

[1] Including Munitions Levy.

POPULATION.

Census Year.	England.	Wales.*	Scotland.	Ireland.	Total.
1811	9,491,333	672,923	1,805,864	5,937,856	17,907,976
1821	11,206,659	793,577	2,091,521	6,801,827	20,893,584
1831	12,991,797	905,000	2,364,386	7,767,401	24,028,584
1841	14,865,510	1,048,638	2,620,184	8,196,597	26,730,929
1851	16,757,966	1,169,643	2,888,742	6,574,278	27,390,629
1861	18,771,511	1,294,713	3,062,294	5,798,967	28,927,485
1871	21,291,858	1,420,408	3,360,018	5,412,377	31,484,661
1881	24,396,906	1,577,533	3,735,573	5,174,836	34,884,848
1891	27,226,120	1,776,405	4,025,647	4,704,750	37,732,922
1901	30,514,846	2,012,997	4,472,103	4,458,775	41,458,721
1911	33,649,534	2,420,958	4,760,904	4,390,219	45,221,615

* Including Monmouthshire.

INDEX

(* Indicates a Chancellor of the Exchequer).

H

INDEX

INDEX

W

Y